Women of Value, Men of Renown

Texas Press Sourcebooks in Anthropology
University of Texas Press, Austin

Women of Value, Men of Renown

New Perspectives in
Trobriand Exchange

Annette B. Weiner

The publication of this book was assisted by
a grant from the Andrew W. Mellon Foundation.

Library of Congress Cataloging in Publication Data

Weiner, Annette B. 1933–
    Women of value, men of renown.

    Bibliography: p.
    Includes index.
    1. Ethnology—Trobriand Islands. 2. Women—
Trobriand Islands. I. Title.
GN671.N5W44 392' .09953 76-14847
ISBN 0-292-79019-8 (pbk)

Printed in the United States of America

First Paperback Printing, 1983

To Linda & Jonathan

Contents

Illustrations

Acknowledgments

My work in the Trobriand Islands and the writing of this monograph involved the help of many people. Prior to my field research, my training as a graduate student was shaped under the guidance of Frederica de Laguna and Jane C. Goodale. I am especially grateful for the influence their own outstanding scholarly contributions had on my work. During this time the late A. Irving Hallowell gave a series of seminars at Bryn Mawr College. The importance of his work and his influence on my thinking are apparent throughout this book. My research in Kiriwina and the writing of my dissertation were supervised by Dr. Goodale. My debt to her is very large.

I appreciate conversations with William Davenport, Ward H. Goodenough, David M. Schneider, and Nancy D. Munn concerning the organization of various aspects of my data. Dr. Munn spent ten days with me in Kwaibwaga in 1972 and her own theoretical interests were very stimulating to my research. I am indebted to Harold W. Scheffler for his careful and critical reading of my dissertation and this manuscript. His extensive comments were extremely valuable to me in the preparation of this book. I also thank Marshall D. Sahlins, S. J. Tambiah, and Remo Guidieri for their suggestions concerning revisions of my dissertation. I gained much perspective on my work from my participation, in the spring of 1975, in part of a graduate seminar on the Trobriand Islands, organized by S. J. Tambiah and Terence S. Turner, Department of Anthropology, University of Chicago. I thank the students and faculty who attended the seminar for their excellent criticisms and suggestions. I also thank Jerry W. Leach for his reading of and helpful comments on my dissertation.

I have been influenced by the work of Richard N. Adams on social power and I am very grateful for his perceptive and critical observations on the theoretical chapters in this book. I also want to thank Robert Alan Fernea for his comments on sections of the manuscript.

To Holly Carver, manuscript editor at the University of Texas Press, I want to express my sincere appreciation for her excellent final editing of the manuscript. For editorial and bibliographic assistance respectively I thank Kevin David Batt and Barry Solow, graduate students, Department of Anthropology, University of Texas at Austin. I am grateful to both of them for their insightful and sensitive criticisms of parts of the manuscript. For typing various drafts of the manuscript my thanks go to Juanita McBride, Carole Smith, Betsy Parrish, and Ann Manley.

During my field work in Kiriwina, members of the Australian administration and the expatriate community were very kind to me. I especially thank Jannis and Lola Daris-Wells, Heather and Duncan Dean, and Danny and Janet Wong for their assistance. I am very grateful to Dr. Ann Chowning for the help she gave me in Port Moresby.

For my Kiriwina friends there are few words to convey my regard and admiration. Without their patience, their belief in the value of my work, and their trust in me, my insights would have been severely limited. This book is a small expression of a very large debt, but my greatest hope is that they appear to others as they did to me: sophisticated and complex human beings. My indebtedness extends especially to Bulapapa, Dabweyowa, Waibadi, Vanoi, Lepani Watson, Kulutubwa, Masawa, Bunemiga, Kilagowola, Yobwita, Bweneyeya, Ipukoya, Yaulibu, Kadesopi, Mekiyasi, Ilabova, Naseluma, Bomapota, Boiyagwa, Emory, and Becky.

Finally, my esteem of and great indebtedness to the work of Bronislaw Kasper Malinowski.

Introduction

The research forming the basis of this book was conducted in two field trips to the Trobriand Islands, Papua New Guinea, undertaken while I was a Ph.D. candidate at Bryn Mawr College. My first field trip to Kiriwina was funded by a Mary Bullock Workman Traveling Fellowship awarded by Bryn Mawr. From June until October 1971, I lived in the village of Kwaibwaga. Originally I had planned to study the styles of traditional and contemporary wood carving to see if these styles could be examined as a projection of Trobriand world view adapting to new ideas and influences. My interests widened considerably, however, following the first day in the field. In October 1971 I returned to Bryn Mawr to organize and analyze my data. By this time I had become interested in the way different objects and styles of exchange denote varying values of social relationships. The following year I spent from May to November in the same village, funded by National Institute of Mental Health Predoctoral Research Grant 1F01-M.H. 5422-01.

For those familiar with any social science, the Trobriand Islands need little introduction. Their renown is due to the voluminous and often brilliant writings of Bronislaw Malinowski, who lived in the Trobriands for two years between 1915 and 1918. Part of his field work was done in the village of Omarakana, about three-quarters of a mile from my house in Kwaibwaga. Because of Malinowski, there exists a mystique about the Trobriands, the power of which I only gradually became aware. It is not my purpose to analyze this mystique; I speak only as an informant having experienced the effects of doing field work in what must be one of the most sacred places in anthropology.

This sacred place was first visited in 1904 by C. G. Seligman, who included the Trobriands in his ethnographic survey of the Massim area. After Malinowski, several members of the Australian administration contributed descriptive accounts (e.g., Austen 1939, 1941, 1945a, 1945b; Julius 1960; Rentoul 1931, 1932) of various Trobriand activities. It was not until H. A. Powell revisited Kiriwina in 1950 that another contribution to Trobriand ethnography was made. Powell (see, e.g., 1956, 1969a, 1969b) lived in Omarakana from 1950 to 1951. Following Powell, there was another hiatus until the late 1960s. In 1968 and 1969, Peter Lauer (1970a, 1970b, 1971) visited the Trobriands as part of a study on the pottery trade in the neighboring Amphlett Islands. While I was living in Kwaibwaga two other Ph.D. candidates, Susan Montague and Jerry W. Leach, were gathering ethnographic data in the Trobriands. Montague's (1974) research on kinship and exchange was conducted on the neighboring island of Kaileuna, and Leach (1975a), working on Kiriwina, has recently produced an ethnographic film on Trobriand cricket playing.

Although Trobriand culture remains traditional in fundamental ways, some changes made part of my field situation different from Malinowski's time. Several informants who had read sections of Malinowski's books on the Trobriands told me that Malinowski did not explain some things as they were because so few people spoke English when he lived in Kiriwina. Therefore it was often difficult to explain things to him properly. My own mastery of the Kiriwina language was much less than Malinowski's. When I wanted to explore a subject in depth, I was forced to work through an interpreter. Although my handicap had its own range of limitations, my lack of fluency had a positive side. Several Kwaibwaga villagers speak English quite well, and our relationship became personal as well as professional. We interacted on many levels and my friends developed a sincere concern for the things I sought to understand. For my part, I came to respect the complexity of Trobriand culture. My lack of ability in the native language heightened my sensitivity to gestures, facial expressions, and the repeated use of Kiriwina words and expressions. In this way, I gleaned cues from disparate events and later saw that they often linked together in meaningful ways.

The tempo of traditional activity seems to have altered from Malinowski's time. Although Kiriwina remains traditional in many respects, the degree of elaboration is less intense. Motor launches instead of beautifully decorated canoes are now more often used for *kula*, the overseas exchange network first described by Malinowski (1920, 1922). The most dramatic activities, such as dancing and large feasts, are infrequently organized on a grand scale. In the appendix of *Coral Gardens and Their Magic*, volume 1, Malinowski noted at length some of the areas where his data were weak. He wrote: "I was lured by the dramatic, exceptional and sensational. . . . I have also neglected much of the everyday, inconspicuous, drab and small-scale in my study of Trobriand life" (1935a, p. 462).

Of necessity, I observed the small-scale, daily activities. While I was living in Kwaibwaga, the annual harvests were small and mortuary ceremonies were the most often organized intervillage activity. In total, I attended ten women's mortuary ceremonies, two of which were held in Kwaibwaga. In addition to the women's distributions, I participated in the burial rituals and mortuary exchanges following the deaths of two men—one from Kwaibwaga and one an important man from Tubuwada village—both of whom died in 1972. I also attended three mortuary ceremonies organized by men only, which annually commemorate relatives who have died during the past years. Aside from *kula* activities and an uneasy political situation, mortuary ceremonies were for me "dramatic . . . and sensational."

A much more fundamental observation, however, made mortuary ceremonies sensational. On my first day in the village, I saw women performing a mortuary ceremony in which they distributed thousands of bundles of strips of dried banana leaves and hundreds of beautifully decorated fibrous skirts. Bundles of banana leaves and skirts are objects of female wealth with explicit economic value. My greatest departure from Malinowski's and Powell's work was my concern to make "women's business" my business. Thus, mortuary ceremonies initially became my central concern.

Unlike Malinowski, I lived in a village that did not have a high-ranked man in residence. The former important man of Kwaibwaga had died about forty years ago. His six sons live in his hamlet in Kwaibwaga village, and some of them control the land once controlled by their father. Kwaibwaga, with a population of three hundred, is divided into six hamlets (see fig. 1). One man is in control of both hamlet and garden land for each hamlet. None of these *karewaga* (men of authority) is a man of high rank and none has been able to establish himself as leader of the entire village at the present time. Therefore, for the most part, I observed the common person.

Malinowski (1935a, p. 475) lamented that his study of harvest yam transfers was primarily focused on men of rank. He felt that, had he attended to the harvest exchanges of the common man, his analysis and descriptions would have been more complete. Yam exchanges do differ dramatically in economic and political significance for men of high rank. But a major issue concerning yams presented to men of rank is that Malinowski and Powell erroneously considered these yams to be tribute. They ignored the reciprocal return due the givers of yams because they neglected the active role that women play in exchange.

In the second part of my field work, I had access to the knowledge and activities of men of high rank. Vanoi and his heir apparent, Waibadi, at the time the most powerful and influential men in Kiriwina, became my good friends and valued informants. Va-

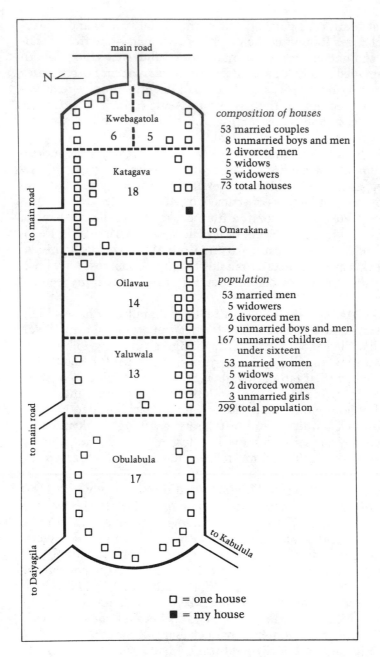

main road

N

composition of houses

Kwebagatola

6 : 5

53 married couples
 8 unmarried boys and men
 2 divorced men
 5 widows
 5 widowers
73 total houses

Katagava

18

to Omarakana

to main road

Oilavau

14

population

53 married men
 5 widowers
 2 divorced men
 9 unmarried boys and men
167 unmarried children
    under sixteen
53 married women
 5 widows
 2 divorced women
 3 unmarried girls
299 total population

Yaluwala

13

to main road

Obulabula

17

to Daiyagila

to Kabulula

□ = one house
■ = my house

Figure 1. Hamlet division within the village of Kwaibwaga, with composition of houses and total population in 1972

noi lives in the center of Omarakana in an elaborately decorated traditional house which he built in 1971, ten years after the death of his predecessor. Standing in front of Vanoi's house gave me a sense of both anthropological and Trobriand history. In the ground, ten yards in front of Vanoi's house, lies a stone marker on the grave of Touluwa, who was Malinowski's friend and the man whom Malinowski called the paramount chief of the Trobriands. Not far from this grave site, another stone marks the grave of Mitakata, successor to Touluwa and Powell's informant in 1950. Mitakata died in 1961, and Vanoi became his heir. Waibadi is very close to Vanoi in age and is often his rival. Waibadi lived in the hamlet of Kasanai, next to Omarakana, but shortly after Mitakata's death he moved his own hamlet to a vacant parcel of land close to the main vehicular road. Unlike Omarakana, Kwaibwaga, and many other villages which are accessible only via narrow paths, Waibadi's new hamlet, Omulamwaluva, is in full view of all who pass along the main road.

Beginning in July 1972 the power of Vanoi and Waibadi, not yet so strong as that of their predecessors, was seriously contested by John Kasaipwalova, a young Kiriwina man in his twenties. He had been educated in Australia and was then a student at the University of Papua New Guinea. Kasaipwalova left the university to return to Kiriwina and establish a cooperative economic association called Kabisawali. In time he confronted and usurped Waibadi's powerful position as president of the Local Government Council. The council was established in 1965. In 1973, Kasaipwalova was elected president by a one-vote margin, and the council was disbanded in favor of Kabisawali. During this period, Vanoi shifted his support between Waibadi and Kasaipwalova several times, but at present he has joined Kasaipwalova's association. Waibadi, his associate Lepani Watson, once an elected member to the House of Assembly in Port Moresby, and their followers have organized the Tonenei Kamokwita movement. By early 1975 Waibadi's group had not yet gained much momentum. The Kabisawali movement has organized village trade stores, drama groups, a carving school, daily bus transportation, and a bank and has formalized plans to build a native hotel (Leach 1975b). But, by mid-1975, Waibadi's group started to export yams and fish to Port Moresby (Damon 1975).

During the last five months of my field work, Kasaipwalova's activities precipitated many political disturbances, discussions, and public debates. To add to these complications, the loss by fire of the Trobriand Hotel, which provided weekend accommodations for thirty-five to fifty guests, on the night of September 4, 1972, brought a halt to the large-scale sale of carvings. At the same time, a drought threatened to destroy the newly planted yam and taro crops. I obtained much important information by observing the political conflicts and the anxieties created by a decrease in available cash and the lack of rain. But the growing tenseness of the situation often made my field work more difficult.

Nevertheless, my most important informants, both men and women, remained concerned about my work. Kwaibwaga women taught me to make women's wealth; they showed me how to distribute it properly in mortuary ceremonies. I learned from men some of the reasons that women are valuable to them. When a death occurred in Kwaibwaga, I received my own bundles of banana leaves as payment for being part of the mourning group. From then on I participated as a woman in mortuary ceremonies. Women taught me how to obtain additional women's wealth. I spent time talking to them and they showed me things about the care and meanings of the bundles that I would never have thought to ask. On the other hand, I learned much from the men who came to my house and who would sit for hours chatting and gossiping with each other, pausing to tell me stories and explanations of events. I found formal interviewing productive only when I took my lead from cues in observations and conversations, rather than basing inquiries on preconceived notions of what might or might not be present or relevant. As a general statement of my own interaction with men and women, men *told* me about things and women *instructed* me in things.

Throughout the book I incorporate passages from Malinowski's Trobriand writings as both a literary and a methodological device. Rather than using subheadings to divide sections of chapters, I begin each new topic within a chapter with a quotation from Malinowski. This procedure serves several important functions. First, rather than include long digressions on the differences in our analyses, the selected quotations will immediately frame the specific problems and highlight both our different and our similar points of view. Second, I believe that this method presents the reader with a sense of historical tradition in Trobriand society and Trobriand ethnography without my having to belabor the point. And, finally, the similarities in our observations will become apparent so that the reader will perceive that Malinowski

was for the most part explicitly concerned with the most significant areas of Trobriand culture. Only in this way can I economically share both the eloquent insights and the knotty problems of
Malinowski's research.

Women of Value, Men of Renown

Chapter 1
The Theoretical Framework

I

It is difficult to convey the feelings of intense interest and suspense with which an Ethnographer enters for the first time the district that is to be the future scene of his field-work. Certain salient features, characteristic of the place, at once rivet his attention, and fill him with hopes or apprehensions. The appearance of the natives, their manners, their types of behaviour, may augur well or ill for the possibilities of rapid and easy research. One is on the lookout for symptoms of deeper, sociological facts, one suspects many hidden and mysterious ethnographic phenomena behind the commonplace aspect of things. Perhaps that queer-looking, intelligent native is a renowned sorcerer; perhaps between those two groups of men there exists some important rivalry or vendetta which may throw much light on the customs and character of the people if one can only lay hands upon it! Such at least were my thoughts and feelings as on the day of my arrival in Boyowa I sat scanning a chatting group of Trobriand natives.—Malinowski 1922, p. 51

I first arrived in Kiriwina, the largest island of the Trobriand group, in June 1971.[1] After exploring the central and northern parts of the island for a few days, I went to introduce myself to Vanoi, the Tabalu chief who lives in the village of Omarakana. I explained to him that I wanted to study the wood carvings fashioned by Kiriwina men in response to the growing tourist trade, and he suggested that I live in the village of Kwaibwaga, reputed for its excellent carvers. Using a government interpreter, I spoke to the men of Kwaibwaga and told them of Vanoi's suggestion. They agreed to build me a house, and five days later it stood com-

*Plate 1. Kwaibwaga women arranging their bundles of banana
leaves prior to the beginning of a women's mortuary ceremony*

pleted in the center of the village. I moved into my quarters late
in the afternoon.

It was very quiet the next morning, with the kind of silence
that seems to hang in the air until the sun burns off the early
morning mist. I would not have been aware that anything special
was going on, if two young girls had not come to my house to tell
me that we were going to a women's mortuary ceremony in another village. I walked to another hamlet in Kwaibwaga, where
the sisters of the men on whose land I was living had taken huge
woven baskets out of their houses. The baskets were about eight
feet long and were filled with between five hundred and one thousand bundles of narrow strips of dried banana leaves. Each woman
was bent over her basket, counting and sorting the bundles. A few
women were separating bundles into smaller baskets (see plate 1).
One woman had seven fibrous skirts piled one on top of the other,
and she was tying them together with a string (see plate 2).

I watched while a girl carefully blackened her mother's back
with a charred coconut husk. Other women used mirrors to make

Plate 2. With her husband watching, a Kwaibwaga woman counts the skirts she will distribute as wealth in a women's mortuary ceremony in another village

certain that their black make-up was evenly applied. In another hamlet I saw two men having their heads reshaved. I remember thinking that, although people seem to make themselves look "dirty" when they observe mourning rituals, they don their mourning apparel with all the care and attention that young people give to themselves before a dance.

By about 8:30, people began to leave the village. A few women walked together with small baskets of bundles on their heads; men carried yams or taro and several young men supported a very large basket of bundles on a pole between them. The main road was crowded with women from other villages. Some of the older women on the road were wearing skirts made of coconut leaves. Their bodies were blackened, heads shaved; black mourning beads were draped across their chests and blackened woven fibers called *kuwa* were fastened around their necks. As the women walked, the blue gray fibers of their skirts rhythmically swayed back and forth in perfect timing with the movement of their hips. As the sunlight caught the colored fibers, making them look like strips of celluloid, these women were as lovely to watch as the young girls in their brightly colored short skirts.

It was hot on the main road and young girls walked together laughing and chattering. In addition to donning their elaborately decorated skirts, they had tucked flowers into their hair and into arm bands. Some of the girls had designs of black and white painted on their faces. Two young girls were wearing *kula* necklaces. As the girls walked along, the shells hit against each other with the sound of a wind chime.

For the most part, the women walked in single file along the side of the road to escape the full force of the sun. There was very little conversation between them; they walked quickly and quietly, intent on their destination. The patterns of color on the road seemed sharply regulated by age: the young in red and white and the older women in black, gray, and tan. Even those wearing trade-store clothing blended with this pattern: the young girls in bright printed fabrics and the older women wearing faded and dirty-looking dresses.

We passed groups of men on the side of the road, talking and chewing betel (*buwa*). At their feet were baskets of yams and bunches of taro. One group of Kwaibwaga men called out to us, "You go first, we will come later." After about two miles we left the main road and walked along the footpath which led through several deserted hamlets. Finally we approached another hamlet that was bursting with activity. Suddenly the rhythm of the walk halted. A milling crowd of several hundred people filled the hamlet and the center was filled with women.

Women were throwing fibrous skirts and bundles of dried banana leaves into the central clearing while other women waited to hurry into the center and gather up a pile for themselves. It was hot as the morning wore on, but the throwing of bundles and skirts continued for five hours. A few times a Kwaibwaga woman handed me some bundles and pulled me with her into the center. Other women laughed uproariously and I was frankly embarrassed, without a clue to what was happening. Throughout the day, however, I began to notice that the distributions often differed. At times, bundles were thrown directly on the ground; at other times, they were carried into the center in baskets. Further, the amounts of bundles presented in a single transaction changed considerably, ranging from as few as twenty bundles to as many as five hundred. Later I was to learn that it is not unusual for thirty thousand bundles to be distributed in one day and that each bundle is equivalent to one cent Australian.

Women were laughing, shouting, and swearing. Occasionally a fight broke out. Although I had little notion of what was being enacted, the great amount of time, energy, and emotion involved made me sense the importance of the event. During the distribution of skirts and bundles, men remained on the periphery of the hamlet. At the end of the proceedings, women rushed into the center, shouting for bundles for their husbands. Then long lines of women and men formed: each woman carrying a handsomely decorated fibrous skirt and each man carrying objects of his wealth. I was handed a skirt and walked in line to the house of the father of the deceased, where all the valuables—including the skirts—were piled up. A similar line of people then walked to the house of the spouse of the deceased. Meanwhile, other men had taken over the central clearing and were distributing yams and taro to the villagers who had come from other hamlets to participate in the mortuary exchanges.

When I returned to Kwaibwaga late that afternoon, I looked in Malinowski's accounts for several of the new words I had just learned. Although I found general mention of the importance of women in mortuary ritual (e.g., 1922, p. 54; 1929, pp. 36–38), I failed to find information concerning women's wealth of skirts and bundles and the particular events of the day. My original research proposal was not concerned with the study of women, but from that first day I knew that women were engaged in something of importance that apparently had escaped Malinowski's observations. The women's mortuary ceremony was a Pandora's box; it opened up the whole question of relationships between men and women. The exchanges, each differing in objects, style, color, quality, and quantity, gave as much information about the living as they did about the dead.

Mortuary rituals encompass much more than the sacred, solemn celebration of the deceased and the revitalization of society in a Durkheimian sense. Death is an antisocial event occurring sporadically and often without more than a few days' or hours' warning. At that critical moment, every person linked in some way to the deceased and to her or his spouse and father is on display. During the course of elaborate and lengthy ceremonies, the strength and parameters of each man and woman's networks of relationships undergo a dramatic public accounting. The loss of a person is a continual threat because, at that unforeseen moment, the living must gather together, disperse, recapture, and reassert all that they have in investments.

This study is an ethnography in the sense of being an interpretation of Kiriwinans' relationships to each other through a cycle of life and death. Aside from adding to Trobriand ethnography, it is also intended to contribute to the theoretical controversies generated by Malinowski's seminal work. The major focus is on the meaning attributed to the processes of social interaction. In attempting to explain a wide range of symbols and symbolic actions, I am unable to confine myself to the terms of traditional anthropological social categories. Similarly, I find the distinction between etic and emic[2] frameworks of analysis inadequate to accommodate the multiple layers of significance informing people's words and behaviors. I believe that people act out their views of the way their world is constructed, but not in a straightforward, immediately interpretable manner. In order for an outsider to read even part of that complex of actions, she or he must be willing to search widely for meaning and to withstand the confusion of apparently irrational contradictions.

Fifty-six years separate my field work from Malinowski's. In 1915 there were anthropological problems of a different nature to be solved. The dissonance that we both sustained in the field was probably greater in Malinowski's time. He had general universal issues to confront from the works of such men as Durkheim, Freud, Rivers, Hartland, Frazer, and Briffault. His views on the nature of all "primitive" life were directly formulated from the particular details of Trobriand society. He was one of the first modern anthropologists to see things with his own eyes for a long period of time. Thus he came to proclaim the cardinal importance of seeing through the eyes of one's informants.

The nature of his genius rendered Trobriand ethnography a place of prominence not only in the history of anthropology but also in the annals of theoretical debate. Others, following Malinowski, have accorded his Trobriand material a central place in the development of debates over theoretical issues concerning kinship and the family, primitive economics, law, magic and religion, myth and ritual, the study of language, and psychological phenomena. Anyone restudying the Trobriand Islands faces the plethora of previous data, ideas, theories, and reinterpretations found in the accretion of anthropological writings.

It is interesting that most theoretical arguments around Trobriand data arose from areas where Malinowski's notion of the rationality and pragmatism of the "primitive" appears in doubt. Yet one of Malinowski's greatest contributions was to disprove the then current concepts of "irrational man" and "prelogical mentality." E. R. Leach cogently attributed the Janus-like Malinowskian dilemma to his being the harbinger of original ideas, who was "nevertheless held in bondage by the intellectual conventions of his youth" (1957, p. 135).Woven into the issues that became the common currency of theoretical debate are the mystique of magical practices, the puzzle of "virgin birth," the dilemma of the benign loving father caught in the jural confines of a matrilineal society, and the drama of exchange reduced to giving for the sake of giving. For Malinowski, these were the areas that, at any attempt at creative interpretation, dissolved into a view of the savage mind conditioned and ruled by custom.

The publication of Malinowski's diary in 1967 brought forth a rash of reassessments and critiques of him as a fieldworker. (See, for example, Geertz 1967, 1975; Hogbin 1968; Panoff 1972; Powdermaker 1970; Wax 1972. See also Firth 1957 for critiques by Malinowski's students of his contributions to anthropology.) But the shock waves precipitated by the diary were produced less by Malinowski's personal failure to live up to his own myth than by our unquestioning acceptance of a naïve assumption about the meaning of rapport. As Clifford Geertz so eloquently argued, inherent in Malinowski's caution to see things from the native's point of view was "the sentimental view of rapport as depending on the enfolding of anthropologist and informant into a single moral, emotional, and intellectual universe" (1967, p. 12). If the ethnographer cannot create a single universe with his or her informants, he or she carries an enormous burden into the relationship. In the struggle for knowledge, the ethnographer forces issues, digging deeper for understanding. In the process, discomfort is generated by both parties. Informants tire of explanations that do not seem to satisfy or that seem illogical in the first place. They, much luckier than the ethnographer, dissipate their uneasiness by saying "I do not know" or "I can't remember." But the ethnographer's discomfort can be displaced only by finally ordering what seems unintelligible into something logical and coherent. The speed with which one needs to displace the confusion (either consciously or unconsciously) seems a critical element in determining how deeply and widely one explores for understanding.

A priori convictions that clan or family has structured reality are comforting to take into the field. Collecting genealogies or myths is tedious work but produces concrete information. If one ties one's data into superficial units too quickly, as I believe Malinowski did, then such distinctions as emic and etic become necessary issues. If, however, one can live with increasing dissonance and explore a wide range of symbols and actions before becoming dependent on preconceived unit parameters, then it becomes apparent that the natives do know what they are doing.

This view makes Malinowski's brilliance and failures more understandable. His Trobriand ethnographies are rich in data, and he was more often than not insightful. But there were critical issues that demanded deeper understanding. Here he fell victim to his own view of things instead of discovering the view of the native. If Malinowski's informants referred to their father as "stranger" (*tomakava*) and if fathers were not recognized as genitors, then without further search Malinowski had much to say about the nature of matrilineal societies and the psychological dimensions of the Oedipal complex, important issues of the day. Kiriwinans had very little understanding of their own behavior, so there was little reason to search further to understand *their* meaning of father. Symbolic analysis and abstract explanations were irrelevant for his purposes. The *surface structure* of what people *said* was the organizing principle for understanding the native's world.

Thus the very nature of the Trobriand ethnographic heritage dictates that a return to Kiriwina means a return to ethnographic beginnings. The Trobriand situation dramatically supports Geertz's statement that "studies do build on other studies, not in the sense that they take up where the others leave off, but in the sense that, better informed and better conceptualized, they plunge more deeply into the same things" (1973, p. 25). Hence the "plunge" of this study reaches back once again to "the same things." But, unlike the earlier Trobriand ethnographers, this ethnographer is a woman. A critical difference between myself and my male predecessors is that I took seemingly insignificant bundles of banana leaves as seriously as any kind of male wealth. I saw Kiriwina women as active participants in the exchange system, and thus I accord them an equal place beside Kiriwina men. In my return to the beginning, I move the role of women into the foreground.

II

In tribal life, the position of women is also very high. They do not as a rule join the councils of men, but in many matters they have their own way, and control several aspects of tribal life. Thus, some of the garden work is their business; and this is considered a privilege as well as a duty. They also look after certain stages in the big, ceremonial divisions of food, associated with the very complete and elaborate mortuary ritual.—Malinowski 1922, p. 54

My assumption in this book is that, regardless of the variation between the economic and political roles of men and women, the part that women play in society must be accorded equal time in any study concerned with the basic components of social organization. I argue that in Melanesia female/male symmetrical and complementary oppositions constitute elements basic to a conceptualization of the social order, as Gregory Bateson in his classic study *Naven* (1958) so brilliantly demonstrated. My perspective is that the structural significance of male/female relationships does not fit *initially* into traditional configurations of division of labor or descent principles. Nor may the interrelationships of women and men in a given society be explained solely in terms of the development of economic and political power, another starting point for much recent work concerned with women. I do not propose a universal theory of the nature of women's role in society, nor do I present a model that encompasses all levels of female/male interaction in the Trobriands. Rather I introduce the view that control and power[3] are exercised by both men and women, but they must be seen operating not merely within the "politics" of social relations. Power extends beyond the social to concepts concerning articulation with cosmic and transcendental phenomena.

Although the early work in Melanesia was very sensitive to the importance of female/male interaction (e.g., Bateson 1958; Deacon 1934; Fortune 1932; Mead 1930, 1935), much ethnography contains a male overload. Many male ethnographers freely admit that they are unable to enter into the world of women, but in many cases this may have been a self-fulfilling prophecy. I do not dismiss this problem lightly, however, because in many societies secret ritual knowledge sharply segregates the society into male/female isolates, making more difficult analyses of the complementarity between female and male roles. However, in the Trobriands, I did not receive any secret knowledge about women's activities. A primary reason that certain important dimensions of the value of women have been overlooked is not, I venture, due to a lack of willing female informants. Rather, traditional areas of investigation have too often blinded us to the complexity of female and male interaction.

Our assumptions of the social construction of reality are bound to follow a male-dominated path when we deny, for example, the significance of objects labeled women's things. The Trobriand situation presents a case in point. On my first day in the field, when I was taken to a women's mortuary ceremony, I excitedly approached a Kiriwina man whom I had met earlier (and who could speak English) and asked him what was happening. He told me, with what I mistakenly thought at the time was disdain, that it was "women's business."[4] Perhaps both Malinowski and Powell were also told by men that women's mortuary ceremonies were the business of women and thus came to believe women's exchange activities to be unworthy of careful study. Surely, strips of banana leaves do not hold the same aesthetic appeal as do elaborately decorated *kula* valuables. In *The Sexual Life of Savages in North-western Melanesia* (1929), Malinowski referred repeatedly to the general importance of women in rituals associated with death. Several of his photographs in the book show women performing mortuary distributions (see plates 1A and 12). But nowhere did he specifically describe what and why women do what they do. In 1950, Powell made an ethnographic film in the Trobriands. In one segment of the film, women are shown distributing their bunches of banana leaves. Powell (1956) also mentioned that women play a considerable role in mortuary events, but he considered the role of women inconsequential to a formal analysis of social structure.

Unfortunately, the Trobriands are not an isolated example. In *Women in Between: Female Roles in a Male World*, a study by a woman about the Melpa women of Mount Hagen in the New Guinea Highlands, Marilyn Strathern began with a beautiful description of the importance of net bags in dowry exchanges. She then went on to say that "women's things are divided among women; men are not particularly interested in the netbags" (1972, p. 15). Nevertheless, whether men say they are interested, there are many references throughout the book to the distribution of net bags across affinal, consanguineal, and intergenerational lines. But Strathern does not seem to take these transactions seriously and analyze them fully. She therefore falls into the traditional male trap, for, in the constitution of Melpa relationships in which net bags are important objects of exchange, men of necessity have an interest. Furthermore, although net bags are the symbol of wombs, there are occasions when net bags filled with male objects symbolize male *and* female concerns.

In Robert Gardner's film about the Dani, *Dead Birds* (1961), the bier which holds the corpse of the young boy is surrounded by women's net bags and, later in the film, women are shown distributing the bags to other women. Karl Heider (1970), writing on the same West Irian group, did not present any details of exchanges of net bags in his analysis. Further, he noted only briefly that men make women's fibrous skirts. This seems a highly significant division of labor. In the northern New Hebrides, mat money was at one time an important object of wealth, and these pandanus mats were manufactured by women (Codrington 1891). In a recent study that treats more seriously the structural role of women and men, Erik Schwimmer (1973) analyzed the importance, among the Orokaiva, of female/male symbolism in such objects as betel nut and coconut. Both objects are important at mortuary rituals. Schwimmer also discussed the significance of social relationships maintained by women through gifts of cooked food in opposition to men's gifts of raw food.

From these few examples, one must not infer that all female objects should be treated as wealth or that a more precise under-

standing of women's exchanges will show women to be politically equal to men. Rather, in a variety of social contexts, objects
laden with some kind of social and cultural significance are being
transferred and controlled by women. Even when these objects
are exchanged between women, they seem to be part of marriage
and/or mortuary distributions, exchanges involving male relationships. Given that women control some kinds of cultural resources defined as their own, it follows that they maintain some
degree of power that differs from male power. Therefore, if we begin to understand the social and cultural dimensions of this power in its own right, rather than focus only on power in its political
phases, we not only learn about women but we also learn about
men. Further, if we approach the problem from a larger perspective and consider, for example, the cosmic order as an integral
part of the social order, we begin to learn something significant
about the "total culturally constituted environment" (Hallowell
1955).

Thus, when a Melpa woman dances in splendid ceremonial attire at a pig feast, is she merely being granted a favor by her husband, as Andrew and Marilyn Strathern (1971) suggested? Or, regardless of what Melpa men *say* about her activities, is she acting
out an aspect of her own power which is structurally central to
the sociocosmic dimension of Melpa realities?

It is not what male informants say about women that is at issue
here. In the Trobriands, men occasionally talk in derogatory ways
about their "dirty wives" who have worked all day in the gardens
or who are in mourning attire. They say "women have no brains"
when women appear at a loss in dealing with some Australian cir-
cumstance. Yet when a woman's own kinsperson dies her husband will work for months from morning until late at night trying to accumulate as much women's wealth as possible for his
wife. Men quite openly say they are working for their wives and,
in these instances, they never speak in derogatory terms about
their wives. Behind every big-woman who distributes more wom-
en's wealth than anyone else during a mortuary ceremony stands
a man. It is not that Trobriand women are totally free agents, but
neither are men. No woman or man becomes a strong person (e.g.,
powerful, beautiful, wealthy) without investments made in her or
him by others. At issue is the way men must work through or
around or in opposition to the limitations set up by women's control in certain contexts.

Therefore, we may inquire whether the power hierarchy of men
(e.g., in ritual or in trading systems such as *kula*) differs cross-cul-

turally as a result of differing areas of control by women. This question contrasts with those posed in many recent studies concerned with correlating male/female status with degrees of male control over resources (Friedl 1975; Rosaldo 1974; Sanday 1974). Further, the Trobriands make an interesting comparison with the New Guinea Highlands societies (see, e.g., Brookfield and Brown 1963; Langness 1967; Meggitt 1964; Read 1965; Reay 1959). In the Trobriands, men are the yam growers and yams are the most strategic resource. Trobriand women, on the other hand, control their own system of wealth, whose importance is publicly acknowledged. Trobriand women are not considered polluting agents and their sexuality is not thought to deprive men of their strength. In the Highlands, women raise pigs and thus they directly control a man's most strategic resource. Yet women are polluting and in many cases the relationship between women and men appears symmetrically opposed. Thus, when men gain control over major resources (as in the Trobriand case) are they less anxious and fearful of women? Does the greater direct control of their resources by Trobriand men strengthen the complementarity between the sexes? Or are there other variables to be considered? I only pose these questions to suggest the importance of viewing a cultural system objectively from a base line that includes an appreciation of the resources and power inherent in *both* female and male domains.[5]

Further, we must ask whether in our comparisons of Melanesian societies we have depended too exclusively on such variables as descent systems, pollution beliefs, and marriage exchange patterns. A more significant comparative classification should be based on the differences in the sociocosmic distributions of power and control. For example, in some societies (e.g., Siane, Orokaiva, Maring, Trobriands) women control an aspect of the regeneration of ancestors. This is extremely significant because this control occurs in societies other than those that reckon descent through women.

Among the patrilineal Orokaiva, women carry their infants into the garden each day. By putting the child in a net bag which is hung from a stick placed in the ground, a woman allows the ancestral spirit of the previous landowner to enter the child through the stick. The transmission of ancestral substance not only precipitates the growth of the child but also imposes an obligation on the child to care for this particular plot of land in adulthood (Schwimmer 1973, pp. 92–95). What Schwimmer did not tell us is whether women "grow" only their male children in this way, what kind of relationship the woman has had with the deceased landowner, or whether net bags have any other symbolic or social value. But clearly women are involved in the transmission of land rights, ancestral transformations, and generational continuity.

In the Trobriands, matrilineality is experienced primarily as the cultural fact that women impart a significant aspect of social identity, that is, ancestral essence, to their children. But women, besides serving merely as conduits of matrilineal identity, are actively engaged in various ceremonial and economic activities which function to maintain that identity. To describe the Trobriands as matrilineal without examining the full consequences of women's actions is as uninformative as what Leach labeled "butterfly collecting" (1961*a*, p. 2).

The call for a revised approach to the study of kinship and descent is not new to analyses of Melanesian societies. Beginning in the late 1950s, anthropologists working primarily in the New Guinea Highlands were becoming increasingly aware that traditional approaches to descent and kinship did not seem adequate for a description of the so-called loose structure of Highlands social organization (e.g., Brown 1962; Glasse 1959; Reay 1959; Salisbury 1956). John Barnes's (1962) paper on the inappropriateness of imposing African models on New Guinea societies ignited the round-robin debates which had as their basis the question of the universality of certain propositions in Meyer Fortes's classic essay, "The Structure of Unilineal Descent Groups" (1953). Alternative views have been presented in an attempt to solve the analytic problems created when recruitment and affiliation do not always correspond to "rules" of descent (e.g., de Lepervanche 1967–1968; Keesing 1967; Langness 1964; Meggitt 1965; Sahlins 1965; Salisbury 1964; Scheffler 1965; A. Strathern 1972; Wagner 1967). Today the debates continue, most notably Scheffler's (1973) proposed solution to the Highlands "problem," La Fontaine's (1973) "Descent in New Guinea: An Africanist View," and Strathern's (1973) summary of the progenealogy and antigenealogy views. The arguments have revolved around the relationships of genealogy to such other assumed primary principles as residence, territoriality, the clan, and exchange.

Following the work of Schneider, Wagner (1967), Salisbury (1965), and Silverman (1971) have shown the importance of examining the relationship of shared substance to native views of descent and filiation. Recently Strathern suggested that, in the cultural domain, kinship in the Highlands "is a combination of filiative rules and ideas based on upbringing, nurturance, and consumption of food" (1973, p. 29). If this view is correct, as the Trobriand situation indicates it to be, analyses need to be restated so that the structural role that women play is given full value.

"Upbringing, nurturance, and consumption of food" and ideas concerning shared substance are critical concerns, but they must be examined from both a male and a female perspective of power domains. Thus we must ask what parts of nurturance women and men individually control and what this means in cultural terms. How is shared substance or ancestral substance further symbolized for men and women in other parts of the social and cultural systems? By bringing the domains of female and male controls into equal analytical focus, traditional anthropological categories of family, descent, and kinship automatically take on multidimensional meanings which exceed previous definitional boundaries. It is only by according women value, by refusing to see them as mere pawns exchanged by men or as reproductive objects, that we can offer an answer to the question posed in Schneider's provocative essay "What Is Kinship All About?" (1972).

This discussion is not merely polemic to bolster the feminist point of view; it comes from the ethnographic fact that the natural value of women is made culturally explicit in a variety of primary social and symbolic contexts (but see, e.g., Ortner 1974; Rosaldo 1974; Sanday 1974, all of whose arguments begin with the premise that women's roles are usually regarded as secondary to men's roles). Malinowski, by no means a feminist, clearly affirmed that motherhood "is never allowed to remain a mere biological fact. Social and cultural influences always endorse and emphasize the original individuality of the biological fact" (1930, p. 62). In the Trobriands, these social and cultural influences, however, are not a casual undercurrent but are flamboyantly dramatized and publicly acknowledged. Even the transvestism performed by a boy's mother's brother during the Naven ceremony among the Iatmul (Bateson 1958) seems on one level of meaning a public dramatization about womanness and about the structural role that women play.

A few recent studies of Melanesian societies have begun to explore the essential problem of the relationship between power and male/female interaction in a much broader framework. Lewis Langness (1974) suggested that men's secret ritual activities found, for example, among the Wogeo (Hogbin 1970), the Bena-Bena (Langness 1969), and the Gahuku-Gama (Read 1965) must be viewed in relation to the power men *cannot* exert over women's reproductive capacities. Using a structural approach,

Remo Guidieri (1975) developed a model to show the way men construct ritual hierarchies of power using such ritual to tilt the balance of social power from women to men.

What the Trobriand material suggests is that, in order to effectively establish cross-cultural comparisons in Melanesia (and in other parts of Oceania), it is necessary to focus on the structural details of exchange proceedings. Although part of the power differential between women and men seems related to reproduction, in addition to birth, women usually control other social and cultural phenomena. Thus, if women control some aspect of ancestors, then men must complement that control, or contain it, or reverse it. Richard Salisbury (1965) has demonstrated this process in an insightful analysis of Siane male/female interaction.

But Salisbury's essay was addressed to concepts of religion and was not concerned with the kind of exchange analysis that I am suggesting. If food has a symbolic significance in the society, then what are the social and symbolic differences in the styles and kinds of food that women and men exchange? If land is of importance in understanding the significance of kinship, then what kinds of controls do women and men exercise over continuity of land? What symbolic qualities are recognized in the objects men and women control, which then infuse exchange events with significance that reflects basic cultural premises? When the role of women is being publicly dramatized, what statement is a woman making about the structure of the social and cosmic order? And, if in some cases women's power is publicly acknowledged only through men, how does this kind of male power differ from that in other societies? How do the separate male/female power domains necessitate borrowing between domains, or integration, or points of articulation?

In this book I address these questions in relationship to the Trobriand situation. Therefore, the first frame of reference that I use for the basis of this study is the division of society into two separate but articulating female and male domains. Within their own domains, men and women control different kinds of resources and hence effect different degrees and kinds of power over others. A hierarchy of power develops from the structure of these two domains as men borrow from the female domain. Thus it is essential to understand the way differences in power structures, for both sexes, are culturally integrated into logical orders of events that distinguish different codes and forms of behavior. It is from this view that I consider female/male units of discourse as being of the first order.

A male/female dichotomy is fixed by genetic coding. One's position relative to it remains the same throughout one's life. Age, however, is not a fixed component. Hence the fixed sex structure incorporates the aging process and in doing so manipulates it to serve ends of power and control. The means to these ends are transacted in social exchange. Therefore the second frame of reference that I analytically superimpose over the frame of female/male domains is the developmental movement of individuals through a cycle of life and death.

III

Among the natives of Kiriwina, death is the starting point of two series of events which run almost independently of each other. Death affects the deceased individual, his soul (baloma or balom) leaves the body and goes to another world, there to lead a shadowy existence. His passing is also a matter of concern to the bereft community. Its members wail for him, mourn for him, and celebrate an endless series of feasts. These festivities consist, as a rule, in the distribution of uncooked food; while less frequently they are actual feasts in which cooked food is eaten on the spot. They center around the dead man's body, and are closely connected with the duties of mourning, wailing and sorrowing for the dead individual. But—and this is the important point for the present description—these social activities and ceremonies have no connection with the spirit. They are not performed, either to send a message of love and regret to the baloma *(spirit), or to deter him from returning; they do not influence his welfare, nor do they affect his relation to the survivors.—Malinowski 1916, p. 149*

The dynamics of Trobriand exchange give insight into the way a total social person is created through transformations which occur during specific phases in a life cycle. Of equal importance is the way this total social person is split apart at death (both physically and ideologically) and reintegrated into the world of the living. In the cycle of life and death, men and women effect transformations of persons differently. They thus basically control differing aspects of generational time. Women control the regeneration of matrilineal identity, the essence of person (the *baloma* or spirit; see chap. 2) that moves through unmarked cosmic time. Therefore, the power of women, operating in an ahistorical continuum of time and space,[6] is particularly meaningful at conception and death. Men control property, a resource contained within sociopolitical fields of action. The male domain of power and control is situated in historical time and space that, unlike unmarked time, are particularly meaningful in relating specifically named individuals over various generations. For example, because men, through their knowledge of the history of a plot of land, may control that land, the power that men effect continues through specific generations of historical time. The symmetrical and complementary integration of these two aspects of time and space produces complex patterns of interaction between women and men, enacted in exchange events throughout their lives.

Malinowski was fully aware of the importance of a life-cycle approach. In "Parenthood: The Basis of Social Structure," he described the significance of the development of an individual through a life cycle as the key to understanding the meaning of kinship. Kinship "starts with birth, it grows and modifies as the organism matures, it passes through several crises, above all that of marriage. Even with death its bonds are not completely broken, for kinship is the basis of ancestor worship" (1930, p. 75). Using the Trobriand case, he described the early development of a child within the nuclear family unit. This first developmental process was disrupted when the adolescent child separated from the close relationship with its mother and father and became more directly attached to the group relationships within its clan. I am not interested in making this methodological split in the notion of kinship as a separate institution, nor do I use the clan or the family as categories in a formal analysis.[7] What I explore in this book is the process of growth as individuals move through a developmental cycle, acquiring social and cultural artifacts from others. I use the term "artifact" to denote the broad range of such elements as food, blood, milk, land, shell valuables, women's wealth, knowledge, body decorations, magic spells, and taboos. At each important phase in the cycle (i.e., conception, birth, marriage, death, and rebirth), a transformation of person occurs as artifacts are detached from others and invested in ego.

My view of a developmental cycle comes in part from the important contribution made by Fortes et al. (in Goody 1958; also see Fortes 1949). Fortes introduced the concept of "fusion" and "fission" inherent in the formation and the fragmentation of the domestic group (1958, pp. 9–12). For Fortes marriage is the moment of fission. Marriage marks the attainment of jural adulthood and thus splits the domestic group into newly formed fusing units. My reference point for a developmental sequence is grounded in processes of fusion and fission. It is not, however, the structure of the domestic group which is at issue but rather the question of a changing pattern of social contexts relevant to the individual at different points in a total life cycle. Further, in my analysis, neither marriage (cf. Lévi-Strauss 1963) nor parenthood (cf. Malinowski 1930) is conceived as the basis of social structure.

In Trobriand mortuary ceremonies, both the spouse *and* the father of the deceased are equally on display as benefactors for the care they gave the deceased throughout his or her life. Further, mortuary rituals demonstrate the significance for the living of the regeneration through cosmic time of ancestral substance. The spouse, father, and ancestral interaction all contribute essential elements to each ego's development. In my emphasis on cyclicity in the social and cosmic ordering of the Trobriand world, I do not separate ancestor worship as a religious institution or as a genealogical construct.[8] I also accord relationships with the father as much importance in a life cycle as marriage ties. Thus marriage is only a further extension of one's network of relationships that grow out of the earlier paternal connections. In this way, the significance of historical and ahistorical cyclicity becomes manifest. In so far as these modes of time are controlled separately by women and men, the two frames of reference—sex and age—provide a deeper understanding of social structure than either concepts of marriage or parenthood.

In a small-scale, horticultural, island society, natural and cultural resources are limited. Individuals need to be provisioned with the labels and baggage necessary to social life. This is first done by others who themselves have previously received artifacts from their predecessors. At one time or another, artifacts are detached from one individual and invested in another. In other words, the artifacts are fastened onto the growing person. Thus a child receives artifacts from its mother and her kinspeople and from its father and his kinspeople, all of which contributes to the growth of the child into a total social person. This process may be likened to self-individuation. The power and strength of each person vary with his or her ability to maximize a social (and political) position through the collection of artifacts taken from both male and female domains. In time, a reverse process of separation disengages the very same kinds of artifacts from the individual. She or he must reinvest in others to further extend relationships. The original giver is investing not only in ego but also in ego's ability to develop future relationships with others which continually feed back to the original giver. Thus the network of relationships that each ego constructs remains important not only for ego but also for all others associated in a variety of ways with ego. As individuals move through a life cycle, they are creating a recycling of artifacts and social relationships.

At a death, it is essential that the accumulation of social resources (including social relationships) be preserved for the living. The tremendous upheaval of the society is symptomatic of the accumulated social value of each woman *and* man. Death momentarily short-circuits the developmental process, but the input through time has been too great to be suddenly and completely lost. The rituals of death are an attempt to evade the danger caused by the shattering of the life cycle. The process of transformation at death, the final fission of a total social person, separates the elements of body, artifacts, and spiritual essence so that each element continues to infuse the world of the living.

In mortuary rituals, men and women control different kinds of exchanges, demonstrating more sharply than at any other time the significance of male and female domains of power. Through their exchanges of women's wealth, women free the deceased from all her or his obligations beyond those acquired at conception. In these transactions, women enter the sociopolitical domain. With their wealth, women reciprocate to others who have contributed in some way to the care of the deceased. Symbolically women untie the dead person from all reciprocal claims: thus securing a *baloma* that is pure ancestral essence. Kinsmen, conversely, control the material body of the deceased by giving payments to all others whose function in the deceased's social network has been most crucial. These people now care for the grave site and for parts of the body of the deceased (i.e., fingernails, jawbones, the skull, long bones, and hair) which have been exhumed. Over a period of five to ten years (or more), those who care for the relics of the deceased receive periodic payments from the dead person's kinsmen. In this way, the social aspect of the deceased ritually continues its living existence as men, through the material effects of the deceased, regenerate the social networks so violently disturbed at the moment of death. Thus men control historical time, seeking to maintain the continuity of social relationships within and between generations.

The controls within the female and male domains, however, are more complex than I have outlined. The power that men exert on stabilizing the continuity of social relationships does not last for all time. Finally kinswomen reclaim the material effects of deceased persons by giving skirts in exchange for these relics. This act dramatizes the dilemma of male power, for the extent of the male domain is delimited by men's inability to control the ahistorical cosmic dimensions of time and space. The trauma of death exemplified in the short circuiting of social relationships mirrors the inherent danger in all social relationships when exchange is viewed as materialistic and social gain. As Lévi-Strauss and Mauss clearly state, exchange mediates relationships, but the act of giving does not change the nature of the actors. In the process of the attachment and separation of artifacts during life, individuals are attracted into relationships, but adverse individual desires and finally death disrupt the continuity. My informants said that giving makes someone "interested in you"; but exchange does not enable anyone to gain control over another person's mind or to know what that person is thinking. Thus the inherent dilemma. The willful nature of persons in the social world and the final control by women of the cosmic cycle leave men destined to borrow some of the symbols of women's power and to create, through women, artificial extensions of their own historically bounded time.

Therefore, a cycle of life and death must be analytically penetrated by viewing the elements of male and female power and controls at important moments when artifacts are attached and separated from ego. Further, the artifacts themselves carry metamessages, symbolic of the meaning of descent, kinship, and social interaction. Only from this perspective can the structural role of women take on its significant, inherent value.

My plan of presentation in this book follows the path of an individual through a cycle of life and death. I also try to sketch the larger social scenes in which the individual acts. I am concerned with a transactional analysis of exchange (see, e.g., Barth 1966), in which I explore the social and symbolic significance of each major exchange. Therefore, I focus on the symbolic qualities attributed to artifacts and show how these qualities express differential power in male and female domains.

Although I am interested in the nature of power, I am not concerned with the general dynamics of politics per se. I am primarily concerned with internal exchanges of female and male wealth at the hamlet level. I have not integrated *kula* activities into the internal exchange structure in any significant way. During my field work, I had the opportunity to observe *kula* activities only in a peripheral fashion.

Chapter 2 begins with an overview of Kiriwina today. In the second part of the chapter, I describe the significance of the levels of organization of Trobriand social life. In chapters 3 through 8, the material is organized according to one of anthropology's more common literary and analytical devices, that of a prototypical life cycle. I have chosen, however, to begin my account of a Trobriand life cycle with death rather than birth. This departure from tradition reemphasizes the cyclicity of death and life, a point that seems to have been lost in the linear convention of beginning at the beginning. If we take the metaphoric circle seriously, then the starting point of an account is arbitrary. Trobrianders seem to attend to that arc of the circle which curves into death as fully as they attend to life's emergence in the form of a new child. Therefore, in chapters 3 and 4, I present a detailed account of death rituals, including the role that women play in mortuary events. I then describe and analyze in chapter 5 the various transactions that serve to develop the growth of an infant from the moment of conception through adolescence. Chapter 6 focuses on the exchange events of men primarily in regard to the maintenance of social relationships between men and their sons. In this chapter I introduce discussion of land tenure, including both managerial and use rights to land. In chapter 7 I am concerned with the power that young men and women have at their disposal during their premarital life and the shift in power as they, now married men and women, enter the formal exchange system. Chapter 8 focuses on annual yam distributions from men to women and assesses the social and symbolic meaning of these distributions and their relationship to women's distributions of their own wealth in mortuary ceremonies. In chapter 9 I discuss theoretical implications concerning the nature of Trobriand exchange. I conclude in chapter 10 with an evaluation of female and male domains of power.

Chapter 2
A Return to the Beginning

I

---

*Perhaps as we read the account of these remote customs
there may emerge a feeling of solidarity with the endeavours
and ambitions of these natives. Perhaps man's mentality will
be revealed to us, and brought near, along some lines which we
never have followed before. Perhaps through realising human
nature in a shape very distant and foreign to us, we shall
have some light shed on our own.—Malinowski 1922, p. 25*

In *Argonauts of the Western Pacific*, Malinowski (1922, pp. 49–
80) vividly described the physical setting of Kiriwina. Many passages could be quoted today with little change. For eighty years,
foreigners have lived on Kiriwina soil; from time to time their
presence has caused disjuncture with some traditional elements
of Kiriwina life styles. But the disintegration of Trobriand culture has not come about as rapidly as Malinowski predicted (ibid.,
pp. 464–466). Many superficial elements have changed, but the
dynamics of social interaction and the ways people relate to, attract, and use each other still seem fundamentally grounded in
the traditional cultural system.

Unlike most of the other islands in the Massim (see map 1), the
Trobriands (except for Kitava) are low-lying flat coral atolls. Kiriwina, with a population of approximately ten thousand, is spatially and politically the central island, with Kitava to the east,
Kaileuna to the west, and Vakuta only a few miles off the southern tip (see map 2). Kiriwina is approximately seventy miles
square with the largest section of land and population in the
northern bulge of the island.

Beautiful beaches and coral reefs follow the northern and eastern shores, providing excellent fishing grounds. A scattering of

*Map 1. The series of is-
lands to the east and
north of mainland New
Guinea, called the Mas-
sim by C. G. Seligman.
The D'Entrecasteaux
Archipelago includes
three large islands, Goodenough, Fergusson, and
Normanby, as well as the
smaller island group of
the Amphletts and Dobu
Island. To the south, the
Louisiade Archipelago in-
cludes Rossel, Misima,
and Tagula islands, as
well as the smaller island
of Panaeati. The Trobri-
and Islands, Woodlark Is-
land, and the islands of
Iwa and Gawa, in the
Marshall Bennett group,
are located in the north-
ern part of the Massim.*

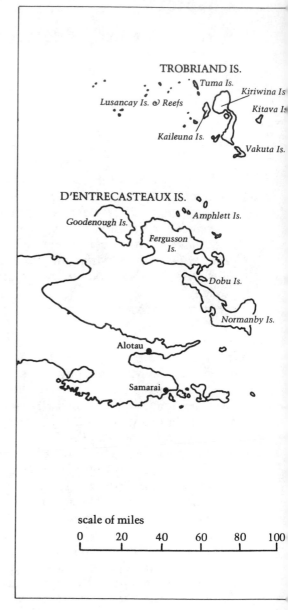

TROBRIAND IS.

Tuma Is.

Kiriwina Is

Lusancay Is. & Reefs

Kitava Is

Kaileuna Is.

Vakuta Is.

D'ENTRECASTEAUX IS.

Amphlett Is.

Goodenough Is.

*Fergusson
Is.*

Dobu Is.

Normanby Is.

Alotau

Samarai

scale of miles

| 0 | 20 | 40 | 60 | 80 | 100 |

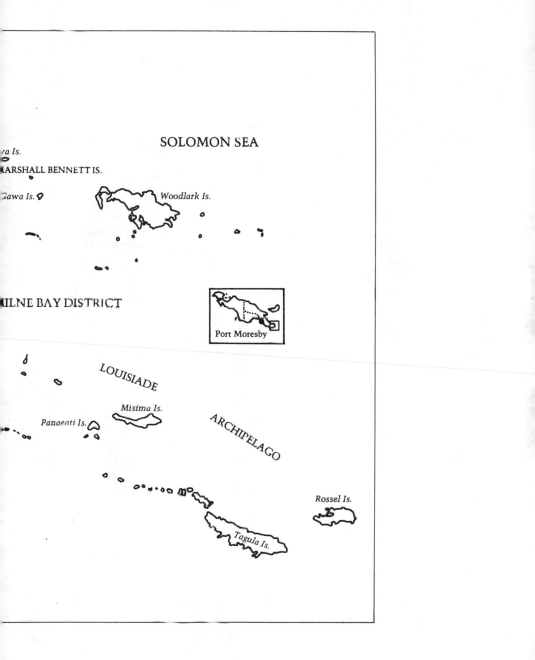

SOLOMON SEA

a Is.

MARSHALL BENNETT IS.

Gawa Is.

Woodlark Is.

MILNE BAY DISTRICT

Port Moresby

LOUISIADE

Misima Is.

Panaeati Is.

ARCHIPELAGO

Rossel Is.

Tagula Is.

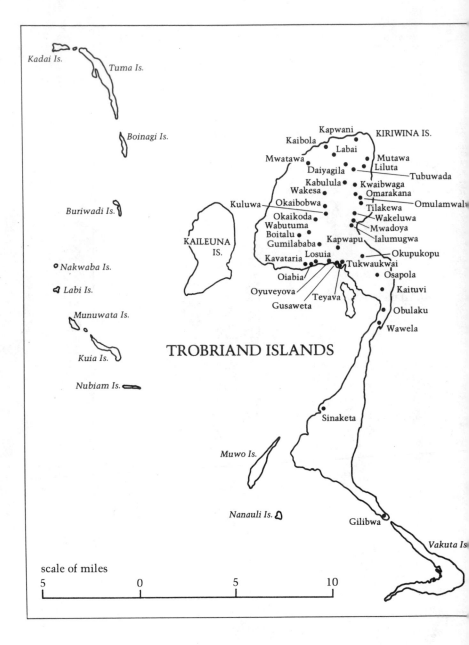

Kadai Is.

Tuma Is.

Boinagi Is.

Kapwani

KIRIWINA IS.

Kaibola

Labai

Mwatawa

Mutawa

Liluta

Daiyagila

Tubuwada

Kabulula

Kwaibwaga

Wakesa

Omarakana

Kuluwa

Okaibobwa

Omulamwal

Buriwadi Is.

Okaikoda

Tilakewa

Wabutuma

Wakeluwa

Boitalu

Mwadoya

KAILEUNA
IS.

Gumilababa

Kapwapu

Ialumugwa

Nakwaba Is.

Kavataria

Losuia

Okupukopu

Oiabia

Tukwaukwai

Labi Is.

Oyuveyova

Osapola

Munuwata Is.

Teyava

Kaituvi

Gusaweta

Obulaku

Kuia Is.

Wawela

Nubiam Is.

TROBRIAND ISLANDS

Sinaketa

Muwo Is.

Nanauli Is.

Gilibwa

Vakuta Is

scale of miles

5   0   5   10

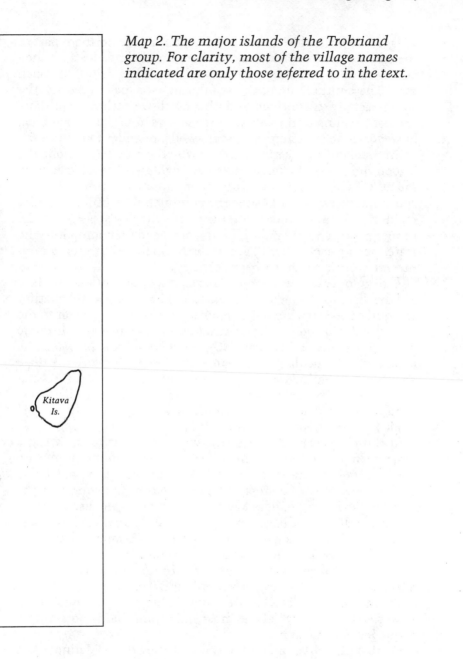

Map 2. The major islands of the Trobriand group. For clarity, most of the village names indicated are only those referred to in the text.

villages are built close to the beaches, but in the northern part of the island expanses of coastal areas are uninhabited because they belong to inland villagers. Most coastal villagers fish in the open seas. The churning up of the sea during two major seasons, the south-easterly tradewinds and the north-westerlies, interrupts open-sea fishing during most of these seasons. The lagoon area, however, protected from the great swells, provides food from the sea throughout the year. Fishermen who live in villages along the lagoon run a brisk Saturday afternoon fish-cash interchange with inland villagers. Late in the afternoon, hundreds of men line the shore and the wharf at Losuia, the administrative center, waiting for thirty or more canoes to return with the day's catch. As the canoes approach the landing, young boys and men jump into the water, racing each other to get to the boats first. Within ten minutes, the entire catch has been sold.

A ridge of coral outcroppings runs along the north-south axis, a short distance inland from the beach. Here and there, beautiful tranquil caves have formed, supplying fresh drinking water to the nearby villages and providing wonderful places to swim. In some areas along the ridge, where deep pockets of soil between the coral can be found, large *kuvi* yams are grown.[1] Between the ridge and the beach, lush jungle vegetation provides bush foods, special medicinal plants, and flowers and plants for magical spells. Wood from the trees is now used for carvings, and occasionally copra is made from the nuts of coconut palms.

In the north central part of Kiriwina and a bit to the west, a large swamp covers ten square miles. Grasses from the swamp are used for roof thatching, but the swamp cuts into the availability of land for the surrounding villages. Land on the fringes of the swamp, however, provides moist soil for taro gardens. Often in periods of drought villagers move their taro plants to these locations even though they have to walk greater distances to the gardens. Droughts occur periodically and intermittent years of famine have been recorded since the turn of the century. Heavy rains also occasionally destroy garden produce. Today, as in Malinowski's time, crop disasters caused by weather are attributed to the power and displeasure of the most important man who controls magic for rain and sun.

Garden plots look much the same as they do in Malinowski's photographs. The major difference in gardening practices is that the long cycle of garden magic organized by the men of Omarakana has not been performed for over a decade. Individual garden magic, however, remains a valuable possession. Shifting cultivation is practiced, but in some areas fallow time has decreased from the usual five to eight years to two to three years due to a shortage of land and an increase in population.[2] However, these instances seem to be the exception rather than the rule. The most fertile garden lands for yam cultivation are found in the northern part of Kiriwina, especially in the district of Kilivila where Omarakana and Kwaibwaga are situated. In the southern part of the island, the soil conditions support taro as the major crop.

Kiriwina is extremely flat; only a few inland rises offer a wide vista of the surrounding land. Coconut and areca palms seem to enclose most inland villages. From the veranda of my house, I felt totally isolated from the rest of the island. But that was only my impression. For the villagers, news and gossip travel quickly. Informants said that their communication system operates as fast as the Australian telegraph.

Travel throughout the island is much improved since Malinowski's day. During World War II, American and Australian troop camps were established on Kiriwina in preparation for Allied attacks against the Japanese.[3] Two airstrips were built; the one near Losuia remains in operation today. At the same time, a major transport road was constructed from Losuia on the lagoon to the beach at the north end of the island near Kaibola village. The villagers call this the main road because it continues to be the road on which almost everyone walks or rides north and south through the upper part of the island. In 1972, the Australian administration, with funds from the Kiriwina Local Government Council, was trying to complete construction of a road south to Sinaketa. Unfortunately there were technical and financial difficulties, and only part of the road is in use. Footpaths, the traditional mode of travel, connect all villages. Kiriwinans are able to cover the distance from one end of the island to the other without much difficulty. In 1972, there were about twelve vehicles on the island. The Local Government Council owned a tractor, a truck, and a car, and Kabisawali, the recently formed opposition group, owned two old trucks. In 1972, they both operated a Saturday transport service along the main road, charging twenty-five cents a ride.

Over four hundred indigenous people live in Losuia, most in government-style housing. Trade stores, a small hospital, schools, government headquarters, and missions are part of the "urban" Kiriwina scene. On Saturdays it seems as if the rest of northern Kiriwina has invaded the area. The villages and gardens are practically deserted as everyone walks or rides to the lagoon.

Fish is bought, yams and taro are sold, and trade-store goods are in demand. People visit each other, and some drinking takes place among married men and young bachelors. But the major Saturday activity until mid-1972 was the sale of wood carvings to tourists, missions, and the occasional dealer. Over the past ten years, the revitalization of wood carving has been in progress. Tourism had rapidly expanded with scheduled weekend charter flights from elsewhere in Papua New Guinea and Australia. Wood carvings had become the major source of Western cash for the local population until the tourist charter flights ceased following the Trobriand Hotel fire.

Foreign economic ventures have peaked and fallen, however, throughout the past century. Although British New Guinea administration policy did not come face to face with Kiriwina tradition until the turn of the century, the Massim area was the scene of much activity during the nineteenth century.

As early as 1793, the Trobriands were sighted by Bruni D'Entrecasteaux, navigating the French ship *L'Espérance*. The Trobriands were named for Denis de Trobriand, the first lieutenant of the vessel (Jansen 1961). American whalers were in the Massim during the 1840s, and "blackbirding" ships from Queensland made frequent kidnapping excursions to other islands near the Trobriands in the 1880s (Corris 1968). A. C. Haddon (1893) reported that in the early 1890s Germans from New Britain were coming to the Trobriands to purchase yams. From my observations of wood carvings collected during this time, it seems that an art renaissance, stimulated by outside influences, was already under way.[4]

During the last decade of the nineteenth century, the Methodist Overseas Mission (now the United Church Mission) established its headquarters near Losuia along the lagoon at Oiabia. New styles of carving were introduced by the missionaries. Today, the mission operates an artifact store on its station and one in Port Moresby. In the early 1900s, traders settled at Gusaweta, four miles east from the Methodist Mission along the lagoon. During the 1930s, Mrs. Hancock, one of the traders, paid the carvers of Boitalu village to produce carvings from pictures of animals. In 1937, the Roman Catholic Sacred Heart Mission built a station at Gusaweta, but its influence was never as widespread as that of the Methodist Mission. Both missions, however, established elementary schools long before the Australians did. Today there are preliminary plans to build a high school so that students need not leave the Trobriands, as they do now.

In 1905, a year before British New Guinea was officially transferred to Australian administration, a permanent government station was built in Losuia. Throughout the years, many kinds of
economic enterprises have been attempted. Except perhaps for
Assistant Resident Magistrate R. L. Bellamy's (1913) extensive
project of planting coconut groves throughout the island from
1911 to 1913, most commercial plans have not had long-lasting
results. Until the present time, the colonial affairs of the Trobriands have been administered from Port Moresby as part of the
territory of Papua New Guinea. In December 1973, Papua New
Guinea began self-government. Complete independence from
Australia became effective in September 1975.

With the advent of Europeans in the 1900s pearling and *bêche-
de-mer* fishing became the major foreign enterprises, lasting until
the late 1930s. During this time, the local population received
tobacco, rice, and ceremonial objects as payment for any services
rendered.[5] World War II halted all foreign activities, and the expatriate population was evacuated. The newly installed troop
camps became a resource for the local population. Employment,
food, metal, and other supplies were available for some people.
Except for brief encounters with a few low-flying Japanese planes,
the island was never under direct attack. Villagers still talk about
their soldier friends. They also complain that, unlike themselves,
Europeans and Americans know how to make bombs and guns.
Since the end of World War II, the sale of copra and the establishment of cooperative trade stores were major administrative efforts, but only Vakuta has carried on a successful enterprise.

Kiriwina men continue to pursue fame and fortune through
kula. The exchange of decorated armshells (*mwali*) and spondylus necklaces (*soulava*) with men living on other Massim islands
continues to be played in Kiriwina for high political stakes (see
plate 3).

Entering a Kiriwina village for the first time is a déjà vu experience. Most island villages are not as concentric as Malinowski
described, perhaps because of shifts in residence. But yam houses
(*liku*) stand prominently around the central clearing, dwarfing
the dwellings situated around the edge of the village site. Except
for the occasional use of metal roof coverings, metal doors with
locks, empty gasoline drums for catching rain water, and the
building of many houses off the ground on piles, the date could
be 1915. Young girls look as enticing as ever in their beautifully
decorated fibrous skirts, although girls and women at times wear
Western-type dresses and skirts. Old men and some young un-

Plate 3. The owner of this kula *canoe, a man from the village of Sinaketa, had just returned from an overseas* kula *voyage to Dobu in 1971*

married boys still wear the traditional white pandanus pubic covering, but most men wear shorts or colorful *lap-laps*, long pieces of cloth tied at the waist. At cricket matches and other special events, most men return to their traditional dress.

Early in the morning villagers awaken and breakfast on cold leftover food. The men sit on their verandas chewing betel; women and young girls walk to a cave to fill their water bottles. The only loud sounds come from young children playing games in the central clearing. By eight o'clock the village rapidly empties as everyone goes off to their gardens or to the bush. Some men who are carving stay behind, and women who are preparing for a forthcoming mortuary ceremony sit together at home preparing banana leaves for the manufacture of their wealth (see plate 4). Most of the children and young people go off to play in the bush or on the beach, or they follow to help their elders. Women and men work both separately and together in the gardens. Women cultivate their own sweet-potato plots. They usually only enter the yam gardens to dig out tubers for the main meal. However, a few women work their own yam gardens, a fact always pointed out with pride by Kiriwina men. Men perform the major tasks of clearing land, planting, and building fences, but women usually

Plate 4. Kwaibwaga women cutting banana leaves in preparation for making bundles and skirt fibers

help with these tasks. The growing cycle of yams demands much effort and care, and this is primarily attended to by men. During August, the major planting time, men and women often work in the gardens until seven or eight o'clock at night.

Usually by three o'clock in the afternoon the village has come back to life. Women return and begin to prepare a meal of boiled yams, taro, and sweet potatoes. Men eat separately from their wives, but close kinsmen are always invited to eat with the men. Throughout the year, the diet varies as, by December, the supply of yams begins to dwindle. Squash, corn, bananas, tapioca, bread-fruit, beans, and cassava fulfill additional subsistence needs. In addition to yams and taro, rice and fish from tins are served to special guests. But a man who does not garden and feeds his children only trade-store food is considered a "rubbish man" (*tobeso-beso*). Yams and pork remain the most prestigious foods. The pig population, however, is small, and pigs are only slaughtered for special occasions. A few chickens are owned by each household, but the major source of protein comes from the sea. Inland vil-

Plate 5. Attractively dressed, Trobriand girls gossip together at a large feast organized by the village of Okupukopu following a series of cricket matches in late summer, 1971

lagers, however, only eat fish once or twice a week. Betel chewing is a formal and necessary part of every meal.

The tempo of daytime activity is low-keyed. Except for roving bands of youngsters and teen-agers, there is little large-group interaction. People work hard in the gardens, but they pause every half-hour to sit and chew betel. (Without betel, they say they cannot work well.) The quiet of the daily routine is sharply broken when feasts or other major events occur. But, for the most part, people go about their business in very individual ways. At times, quarrels between people suddenly erupt. Everyone within earshot listens, but no one moves to interfere. Only if violence threatens is there some attempt to abort the action, and then only kin enter the situation. Other men and women stand shouting and trying to direct the conflict, but they do not enter the fray directly. Even when children fight, no one moves to comfort a crying child.

As darkness falls, fires and a few lanterns illuminate the village, casting mysterious shadows. Teen-agers busy themselves with their rites of beautification: anointing themselves with coconut oil, adorning their bodies with flowers, painting their faces white with Johnson's Baby Powder, teasing out their hair, and donning brightly colored clothing (see plate 5). Young people disappear from the village proper, going to nearby areas where they sing and dance. Some wander off to meet special friends of the moment with whom they will spend the night. Within the village, women sit gossiping over their banana-leaf projects. Men carve, talk quietly with each other and with their wives, or wander off. By midnight, most of the men have retired into their houses with their wives and young children.

But men, unlike married women, sometimes walk about at night. Night is the time when sorcery abounds. Men meet in secret places, creating alliances that have no place in daytime activities. Occasionally a shriek is heard in the village when someone has seen a *bwagau* (sorcerer) on a roof or at the back of a house. Many times, men hurried into my house, asking to borrow a lantern so they could chase away a *bwagau* they had just seen or heard. Throughout the night into the early morning hours, solitary, silent figures move about the village. Details of nighttime activity do not go unobserved. Secrecy is difficult to maintain. Unlike the day, the night is filled with danger and excitement. An ethnography of night would have its own special set of characteristics.

Today, many Kiriwinans are quite sophisticated about Western society. At an all-night dance the evening before I left Kiriwina for the first time, I noticed that the young dancers, although decorated with flowers and powder, were wearing Western clothes. As they danced to rock music played by the Kwaibwaga string band (three guitars and a xylophone), I asked why none of the girls wore traditional skirts. The answer I received was, "When we dance to European music, we dress like Europeans."

II

Every Trobriander, man or woman, believes that by birth and descent he or she is connected with a definite spot, and through this with a village community and with a territory. For everyone believes that his lineage, in the person of his first female ancestress in direct line, issued from a definite spot in the Trobriand territory. The myth of first emergence is definitely a matrilineal one. It always refers to a woman, at times accompanied by a man who is her brother not her husband. This belief, combined with the principles of matrilineal descent, furnishes the charter of citizenship and land tenure to every Trobriander. For by the act of first emergence all the descendants in direct female line of the original woman have acquired the right of citizenship in the territory surrounding the spot of her emergence.—Malinowski 1935a, pp. 341–342

Kiriwina villages (*valu*) are divided into discrete hamlets (*katuposula*). Leach (1958) and Powell (1969a, 1969b) differ regarding whether the hamlet or the village is the primary residential unit of organizational significance. Powell follows Malinowski's description of the village as the locus of organization; however, my data and analysis agree with Leach's reinterpretation. To the uninitiated eye, there are no observable markers to distinguish between one hamlet and another.

In Kwaibwaga, there are six individually named hamlets (see fig. 1). (Two contiguous hamlets share the same name, because the land was originally founded by members of one *dala*.) These founders, called *tabu*, are specifically named women and men. At some time in the distant past, they came out of the ground from a place of emergence on the island, or they came to the island by canoe. Although the stories as told today mention men and women coming together (usually identified as brothers and sisters), I never found an explicit reference to the "first female ancestress" in Malinowski's description. When land was found, it was often a man who put his house foundation in the ground and who took control of the land. Perhaps the men who told me these origin stories had become more chauvinist than men in Malinowski's time. Yet, in comparison with Malinowski's reporting, many details in the stories I collected remain the same. How could something as fundamental as a female ancestress have been forgotten?

I suggest that the problem lies in another area, thus necessitating a reevaluation of the word *dala*. *Dala* was glossed as "subclan" by Malinowski and Powell and occasionally referred to as "lineage" in Malinowski's and others' works. To return to the passage quoted above, it seems quite obvious that Malinowski is trying to equate birth, descent, women, the place of emergence, and hamlet land (i.e., "village community" and "territory") with matrilineality as a total gestalt.

From my perspective, this total gestalt must be split apart. Whereas, according to Trobriand belief, conception requires a spirit child (*waiwaia*) to enter a woman's body, this ancestor spirit is not conceptually identical to an ancestral founder of hamlet land. The former spirit is reincarnated from an ancestral being called *baloma*, while the latter is *tabu*. *Baloma* are amorphous figures of the past who through time are not remembered for activities in which they engaged as social persons. Only as *baloma* transmit *dala* substance in the form of a new child through its mother is the *dala* maintained (see Malinowski 1916, pp. 215–220). Thus, the ahistorical (i.e., cosmic) cycling of *dala* through unmarked time, that is, *dala* "as it was in the beginning, is now, and ever shall be," is created and maintained by the blood which unites the reincarnation of *baloma*, woman, and child. In this sense, a person's "blood" remains pure and uncontaminated throughout his or her lifetime. No one can take away one's *dala* blood. As the Trobrianders say, "Same *dala*, same blood." Because of the exigencies of life, however, one may want to fictively disguise, hide in shame, or wear like a symbol of royalty one's blood identity.

When property (e.g., magic spells, body decorations, taboos, and land) becomes associated with the name of a *dala*, *dala* identity is transformed into external holdings. The history of *dala* property does not remain as "pure" as *dala* blood: property circulates, it is loaned to others, it is stolen, it becomes lost forever. In other circumstances, property can also increase. Further, men control the distribution of *dala* property, but in some cases women reclaim property that has been loaned by men to others. Therefore, to understand the significance of *dala* as it refers to property, it is necessary to introduce a male frame of reference and examine the way property becomes identified with *dala*.

Tabu, the name used in the origin stories to refer to the founders (glossed as "ancestors" by Malinowski and others), is a kin term which has been the subject of much anthropological debate (see, e.g., Malinowski 1929 and the Leach 1958/Lounsbury 1965 debate on Trobriand kinship terminology). When referring to the original founders of land, *tabu* is used to designate particular individuals, ancestors whose specific names and accomplishments are remembered. Unlike *baloma*, a spirit without personal identity, the term *tabu* in the origin story refers to a discrete, named kinsperson.[6]

According to the origin stories, many founders claimed unoccupied virgin hamlet and garden lands. Some *tabu* lived for a time in a series of hamlets, often displacing other groups already in control of the land. In some cases, the original residents shared part of their land with new arrivals. For a few founders, garden land of their own was never available: "They came too late; the garden land was already taken by others." Today, in one hamlet near Omarakana, the manager can claim only the hamlet land, because his *tabu* came too late for garden land. The site of original emergence had little to do with rights to land (although Malinowski [1935a] suggests the opposite for all except *dala* of importance). According to my informants, land always had to be found and often had to be won, sometimes very far from the place of emergence.

Men and women were already members of named *dala* when they came out of the ground. They were adult persons, some of whom brought decorations, wealth, taboos, knowledge of magic spells, dances, and carving techniques, all associated with their *dala*. Land came after blood, decorations, and so on. When land was found, the *tabu* transmitted her or his own *dala* name to it. The foundation of a house, according to my informants, marked this transference. A hamlet site, "a place to sink one's foundation" (*tumila*), took precedence over garden land. Garden land was taken next, and often this became a gradual process of accumulation, a process still going on today.

Unlike blood, land attached to *dala* is subject to economic and political perils. This is important because land genealogies take on a political significance that differs from the significance of personal, individual genealogy. When genealogy has consequences for the allocation and control of resources in the present, its importance far surpasses whatever value attaches to the recitation of a personal genealogy. Origin stories of the founders are among the most coveted and valuable kinds of knowledge. Land disputes can only be settled by a recitation of the genealogy of the land from the time of the founders through current appropriations. Knowledge of the history of the land should only be known by those few men who control the land. In the course of a generation, however, the knowledge of origin stories and genealogy is sometimes learned by men who are not managers, and these men will often share this knowledge with their sons. In other cases, uterine lines die out, or men lose their land through fear, misfortune, or the power of other men.

Genealogy of land differs from personal genealogy. These latter genealogies are very shallow; usually people do not remember more than three previous generations. But land genealogies are more detailed. The genealogy must be traced back to the wanderings of the original founders. The details of the social relations established during the course of finding land are critical elements in the adjudication of land claims.

Native court cases are settled by a committee of important managers who live in the vicinity of the land in dispute. When the Local Government Council was functioning, its president was headman of this committee. The following excerpt from a native court case which I witnessed, involving a land claim, will illustrate the importance of the activities of the *tabu*. The disputing claimants were Mosakuna and Mokepwesi. The president of the council, Waibadi, not speaking aloud himself but whispering his words to his assistant who in turn spoke them aloud,[7] said, "Where do we begin—with the gardens [today] or with *tabu*?"

Mosakuna spoke first: "My founders—two sisters and their brother, Kadakumu, Bokota, and Udakapatu—came first. They found hamlet and garden lands for themselves and then they went into the bush for a rest. Mokepwesi's founders came upon them in the bush. His *tabu* had been walking around Kiriwina looking for land. [He gave the details of their route just as he had previously given the details of his own founders' arrival.] One sister said, 'Already we have our land and we sit here and rest. I am talking to my sister, because my brother does not have a mouth.' [The brother's name, Udakapatu, means 'no mouth.']

"Mokepwesi's founders said, 'We will try to make him a mouth.' So they took a sharp stone [*memetu*] and said some magic into the stone and cut Udakapatu a mouth. My founders were very happy and they gave Mokepwesi's founders some of their body and house decorations as payment. They also showed the men some land in the bush and said, 'Take this land for your gardens.' Then they took the men to their village [Okaikoda] and gave them a hamlet site for their *tumila*."

Mokepwesi, who was claiming some of Mosakuna's land, then told his story. He said Mosakuna was wrong and *his* founders had come first. He detailed somewhat different wanderings and said that when his *tabu* found Mosakuna's ancestors they were sitting in the bush without any land. Mokepwesi said his ancestors met three sisters and their brother and the third sister's name was Imwakova. As soon as Mokepwesi mistakenly said "three sisters" the tenor of the meeting changed dramatically. There were outbursts of anger; "men's eyes became red." Most men believed Mosakuna, and for the next two hours arguments over the identity of Imwakova continued.

The recitation of the history of land is not only a "mythical charter," in Malinowski's terms, but is also a means of argumentation. Claims are awarded on evaluation of the accuracy of living memory; therefore, a man's memory makes him strong. Bateson emphasized that, for Iatmul men, extensive knowledge and ability to manipulate a vast range of totemic ancestral names were highly significant to the development of the male ethos (1958, pp. 27–29). Similarly, in Kiriwina, recitation and manipulation of details of land tenure serve as a political underpinning for the male domain.

The name of a *dala* is retained only as long as men can trace their genealogy (sometimes fictively arranged) back to this specific *dala*. "Same land" is a Kiriwina expression used to designate "same *dala*," but in the course of events land undergoes splits and irregular successions as men manipulate the deeds of founders to enforce a land claim.

Every man who lives in a hamlet (whether or not it is his own *dala*'s land) must prepare a yam garden for the hamlet manager. Conversely every hamlet manager tries to gain control of workpower in order to cultivate as many yams as possible on the land he controls. In terms of residence, a hamlet is not a corporate *dala* unit (see Powell 1969a). The Trobriands are usually presented as a classic example illustrating the "rules" of avunculocal residence. In actuality, most men live in their fathers' hamlets. Avunculocal residence applies only to those few men in each generation who are heirs to the status of manager. In other words, a man moves to live in his mother's brother's hamlet only when his mother's brother is manager of *dala* land and when he himself is next in line. Most men never have the opportunity to manage their own *dala* land and do not reside on it.

Thus, through the political dogma of origin stories and through the manipulations of those few men in each generation who manage land, a hamlet is identified with the name of a particular *dala*. In the male domain, the name of a *dala* is made strong not by the work and effort of each *dala* member but by the processes which admit into the hamlet unit men identified through blood with other *dala* lines. The accomplishments of a hamlet manager make the name of a *dala* stronger, weaker, or forgotten. Thus, the regeneration of *dala* land depends both on the activities of the land manager and the people who live with him on his land. These other people are the manager's "sons" and "brothers" rather than his "sister's sons" (see chap. 6 for details of residence and land tenure).

Women also play a role in the loss of *dala* land. Without women to reproduce, the *dala* ceases to exist. This fact is recognized by Kiriwinans, who often discuss the value of women in this fundamental capacity.

No one has automatic rights to live on *dala* land, even her or his own *dala* land, without contracting an exchange relationship with the hamlet manager. *Dala* members can and are ordered to leave the hamlet by the manager. The only automatic birthright that anyone has to land is at death. Members of a *dala* have the right to insist that their dead be buried on land claimed by their founders. Death, however, often becomes the occasion for a political contest between the living, and many people are buried elsewhere. Usually, however, it is only at death rituals that all members of the same bloodline assemble to mourn for a kinsperson. After many years, the bones of the deceased are taken from their burial site at the edge of the hamlet and put to final rest in a cave designated for that *dala*. Meanwhile the *baloma* of the deceased has gone to live on the island of Tuma, northwest of Kiriwina (see Malinowski 1916). At some future time the *baloma* will cause a spirit child to enter a woman, and thus the transgenerational cycle of *dala* blood continues. But rights to land, far from being fixed by a structure of descent or by an eternal mythical charter, are continually negotiated between living members of Trobriand society.

III

Take for instance the unquestionably paramount chief of Omarakana in his relation to his military rival, the chief of the province of Tilataula, resident at Kabwaku. The paramount chief has the highest rank. He is the wielder of the rain and sunshine magic; that is, master of tribal fertility. His personal prestige, the aura of power and dignity around him, are incomparably higher and more august. At the same time, he could be

beaten and driven out of his home on occasions by his rival.
This rival again has the right to certain ornaments which
the chief would not, but also could not, use.—Malinowski
1935a, p. 38

Included in the stories of the origins of land are references to
some men and women who arrived in Kiriwina with special kinds
of decorations, taboos, and knowledge. Some men, Vanoi said,
even came with architectural knowledge for building unusual
round houses. But no one today remembers how to build these
houses. Villagers regard the above social distinctions as cause for
some *dala* to be of higher order than others. Thus, there exist
dala of eminence or rank (*guyau*), hierarchically arranged in
terms of power and status, and *dala* of lower order, or commoners
(*tokai*), whose *tabu* came to Kiriwina less well endowed. The
Tabalu of Omarakana are the highest-ranked *guyau dala*. Within
each social division, however, individuals are able to gain more or
less power depending upon the possessions and rights gained
from earlier generations in conjunction with the conditions of the
present situation.

Today women and men who from birth belong to one of the six
dala of higher order (two lines having died out) are called *guyau*.
Through the original dispersion of the founders, several of these
guyau dala have subsegments of people living in different parts of
the islands, controlling their own lands. But they continue to use
the name taken from the founders. These subsegments are also
ranked in terms of power, just as the *guyau dala* are ranked. The
segmentation of people identified with a particular *dala* continues today even among men born to low-order *dala*. There is competition over ascendancy to the position of hamlet manager.
When a hamlet manager is not a *guyau*, his hamlet is called *vilotokai*. This term is used even if the land at one time was controlled by a *guyau*. In villages where a *guyau* controls the hamlet,
his hamlet is called *viloguyau*. Although he may exercise political power over residents of all other hamlets in his village, he will
not have jural control over land other than that of his own *dala*.

The term *guyau* presents a problem of definition in a political
context. *Guyau* refers to the original *guyau* founders, to all people
identified as members of a *guyau dala*, and to those few men who

manage their own *guyau* land. Villagers, translating into English, refer to these latter men as chiefs. In translating the Bible into Kiriwina, the missionaries used *guyau* for God. In the past I have heard Vanoi or Waibadi referred to by some villagers as the "king of the Trobriands." Since the time of European contact, the Tabalu *guyau* of Omarakana (now Vanoi and Waibadi) have been the most powerful men in the Trobriands. But, even at that time, their power was constantly being challenged by other men. Malinowski (1935*a*) called the Tabalu of Omarakana "paramount chief," although Seligman (1910) introduced the term (see Firth 1975). Since then the subject of whether the Trobriands have chiefs has been debated by anthropologists (Bradfield 1964, 1973; Cunnison and Gluckman 1963; Fortune 1964; Groves 1956; Powell 1960; Uberoi 1962; Watson 1956) and by the Australian administration. In the records of the annual reports written by officials living in Kiriwina, there was always a concern over how much support to accord the Tabalu of Omarakana (see, e.g., Julius 1960). Was he really a chief? At times the administration did much to stabilize and elevate the power of the Tabalu.

Powell (1960) attempted to show that the Tabalu's power was not all-pervasive; he used the word "leader" to emphasize the difference between a formal institutionalized office of chiefdomship and the Trobriand situation. I have been faced with a similar problem. These men share all the difficulties of building and maintaining a constituency that are found among big-men in other parts of Melanesia (see Sahlins 1963 and Strathern 1971 for discussions of Melanesian big-men). And they are *not* to be considered chiefs in the Polynesian sense of chiefdomship (see, e.g., Firth's [1936] description of a Tikopia chief and Sahlins's [1963] discussion of the differences between big-men and chiefs).

There are three features, however, which tend to differentiate the Trobriand *guyau* from big-men in other parts of Melanesia. First, the Trobriand "chiefs" seem to adhere strictly to hereditary claims. Thus, when the eighth *guyau* chief died, no one claimed rights to his position since he was the last member of his *dala*. Second, the paraphernalia of decorations and social and physical taboos serves as an effective means of rank separation. Michael Allen (1972), however, pointed out that in the New Hebrides extensive use is made of this kind of paraphernalia to differentiate rank. Third, and of the utmost importance, is the fact that only the few *guyau* men who are hamlet managers are polygamous. Monogamy is the rule for all *tokai* and also for all *guyau* men who are not in control of their hamlets. According to informants, the right to be polygamous comes from the founders, who were themselves polygamous. Further, the number of wives that a chief can take is also ranked. Thus the chief of Omarakana can have as many wives as he is able to obtain. Vanoi has nine wives in residence with three more promised to him in the near future. Waibadi has four wives, but he said that he will not go beyond five. All other *guyau* chiefs each have three wives only. Again the reason for this ordering in number is always directed back to the dogma of the founders. But chiefs can lose their wives and can have trouble marrying women if the political situation undermines their power.

The system of chiefs is not to be found in any other Massim island. The style of being a Trobriand chief, however, retains much of Melanesian big-man dynamics. The fundamental difference is that, whereas other Melanesian big-men must individually establish their position of authority without the advantage of hereditary claims, only Trobrianders who have a hereditary claim to the position may become chiefs. Therefore, the dogma of hereditary right gives only a few Trobriand men potential access to more resources than anyone else. Through these beliefs, Trobrianders grant chiefs this privileged position. Therefore, Trobriand "chiefs" must be clearly distinguished both from big-men and from chiefs elsewhere.

The following excerpts taken from a very long Tabalu origin story[8] show the way segmentation between members having the same *dala* identity occurred, at least in the oral tradition. Further, these excerpts will illustrate the way the Tabalu of Omarakana gained ascendancy over all the other Tabalu. There are similar origin stories from other *guyau dala* which are much shorter but contain similar principles of exchange and rank differentiation.[9] (See appendix 1 for a list of body decorations for *guyau* and *tokai dala*.)

The entire origin story was given to me by Vanoi and Waibadi at different times (see plate 6). In some cases they added to or expanded each other's versions, and Waibadi included some additional explanations about other *dala* (not presented here). The first excerpt was told to me by Vanoi and the second by Waibadi.

> The Tabalu with members of other *dala* came out of
> the ground at a spot called Obukula near the northern vil-
> lage of Labai. When they first came out of the ground, they
> stayed for a time near Labai until one day one brother turned

Plate 6. *Vanoi as he stood at Obukula telling me part of the Tabalu origin story. Before we left Obukula, Vanoi said, "Old men always told of the Tabalu coming out of the ground, but I know there is only dirt in the ground. Maybe they came by canoe."*

to another brother and said, "I think I will leave you here and I will move on. I want to hear the gossip of Kilivila. I will walk to the middle of Kilivila and I will stay there. You stay here and I will take our things with me."

He stood up and turned to his brother and said, "Now you take our things to Kilivila because I am going to make a net for our fish. You take all the *kesawali* [decorations for the house] and also you take the *guguwa* [body decorations]. I am going to work here to catch the *kalala* [mullet].[10]

"You take *segadula* [a string of red spondylus shells that hangs from the top of the head down the back], *kesapi* [one large white cowrie shell tied to the wrist], *saveva* [a band of flat spondylus shells tied around the forehead with several strings of smaller shells], and *luluboda* [small white cowrie shells tied below the knee].

"You take these things to Kasanai, because the work for fishing is too hard. If I put the net on my shoulder, *kesapi* will get stuck in the net and *luluboda* are too heavy and I cannot run quickly to catch the fish.

"When the time for *usigola* [dancing] comes, I will come to visit you and take all the things and wear them for dancing. When I finish dancing at *lapala* [the last day of *usigola*], you will come to my hamlet and take the things back with you."

Much later in the story, when some members of the original Tabalu are finally entrenched in Kasanai, the following situation occurred:

There were two sisters who lived in the hamlet of Kasanai, and one day Giluwata, the elder sister, went to the cave for water. While she was gone, Bonumakala, the younger sister, took some of Giluwata's banana leaves which she was using to make *nununiga* [women's wealth]. When Giluwata came back from the cave she saw that her banana leaves were gone. She was very angry and she screamed at her sister.

Bonumakala was very ashamed because her sister swore at her in front of her brother. So she took her things and ran away from the hamlet. She walked to Lokwai hamlet, but she said, "Ah, Kasanai is still too close." Then she went to Kapwapu, but Kasanai was still too close.

She went to Oyuveyova village. The people living there fished for *katakeluva*. The Tabalu who lived at Kasanai were not supposed to eat that fish. When she came to the village, she saw one woman in her house. The woman saw her too and said, "Oh, *guyau*, do not come into my house. I have *katakeluva* and you cannot eat that fish. I was just saving it for my husband and children." But Bonumakala said it did not matter and she ate the fish and stayed in the house.[11]

In the meanwhile, her sister at Kasanai felt sorry for her because she was still a small girl, so she left Kasanai to try to find her. Finally she came to Oyuveyova and Bonumakala said, "I already ate that fish and that means I am *guyapoka-la*[12] for the Tabalu of Kasanai. You go back to Kasanai because I ate that fish."

Giluwata cried for her sister [the mourning crying] and went back to Kasanai. Prior to this incident the two sisters had the same decorations and were accorded the same social taboos but now no one would shout *"guyau"* for Bonumakala before she entered a village, and people did not have to bend down in front of her any more, and she could never again wear all her decorations.

The Tabalu of Kasanai [and now Omarakana and Omulamwaluva] are called *giyobubuna* because we never made any mistakes. Bonumakala was called *giyobubusi* because she made a mistake and ate that fish.

Giyobubuna is the name given today only to the Tabalu of Omarakana (now including Waibadi's hamlet, Omulamwaluva), and this is the name which distinguishes this one segment of the Tabalu *dala* from all other Tabalu living in other parts of the Trobriands. All other Tabalu are called *giyobubusi*.

Today, the members of the Tabalu *dala* who are born to a Tabalu woman from Omarakana are still called *giyobubuna* and can wear all the decorations. The major decoration for the *giyobubuna* is a very long *segadula*. But rank in decoration does not always conform to rank in political power. Although the Tabalu of Omarakana are considered to be of the highest order in both decorations and power, the Mwari *dala*, thought to be second to the Tabalu in decorations, is not second in political power.

Decorations, therefore, give one the right to be powerful, but they do not guarantee that one will achieve power. Sometimes people own decorations that they are afraid to wear. One informant, an old man of a ranked *dala*, showed me strings of cowrie shells which he said he could never publicly display because someone might poison him. Later I learned that members of his *dala* had had a serious conflict with a hamlet manager of a higher-ranked *dala* and he had lost much of his *dala*'s land. Consequently, this man had little political power; to display the cowrie shells would be read as an attempt to reassert his power.

Some people, however, often use the display of decorations in just this way. Many fights between the long-time rivals, the Tabalu and the Toliwaga,[13] began because one of the Toliwaga appeared in public wearing one of the Tabalu decorations. Most recently, in 1972, at the National Day celebration held at Losuia, a Tabalu woman who was only *giyobubusi* appeared wearing the very long *segadula* decoration. Quietly and almost immediately, a Tabalu woman from Omarakana cut off part of the *segadula*, making it much shorter. For weeks prior to National Day, rumors had been circulating that this woman had a decoration of great length, a length to which she did not have title. Waibadi just listened to all the stories, saying, "We will wait and see."[14]

Decorations are not in themselves power, but they seem to be one of the most emotionally laden symbols of power. Without the underpinning of land, workpower, extended exchange relationships, and access to important kinds of magic, decorations are nothing more than shells. Discussion over who was using which kinds of decorations often took place while I was living in Kwaibwaga. Time and again the gossip concerned the fear people have about wearing decorations and the fact that some people fight to protect and display their heritage and others fight to gain the right to wear decorations for which they do not have a legal claim.[15]

IV

The totemic organization of the natives is simple and symmetrical in its general outline. Humanity is divided into four clans (kumila). *Totemic nature is conceived to be as deeply ingrained in the substance of the individual as sex, colour, and stature. It can never be changed, and it transcends individual life, for it is carried over into the next world, and brought back unchanged into this one when the spirit returns by reincarna-*

tion. This fourfold totemic division is thought to be univer-
sal, embracing every section of mankind.—Malinowski
1929, pp. 494–495

Not only is *dala* identity transmitted to individuals at conception, but identity in a larger social category, *kumila*, is transmitted as well. In this way, all Kiriwinans become identified with
one of the four exogamous *kumila*: Malasi, Lukuba, Lukwasisiga,
and Lukulabuta. The rule of exogamy betweeen *kumila* categories is broken at times without any drastic repercussions; however, *dala* exogamy is strictly maintained.

Malinowski and Powell glossed *kumila* as "clan," confusing
the issue by assuming that a *dala* was a smaller replica of a *ku-*
mila. Leach took up the problem, left unexplained by Malinowski, and asked "why the Trobrianders should have a clan system
at all. The clans appear to play no social role as such. The effective social groupings in Trobriand society are the units which Malinowski called subclans" (1958, p. 120). Although I have explained *dala* from a different perspective than Malinowski's
subclan, Leach's query is obviously valid. Up to this point I have
described the basic divisions without referring to clans.

I defer comment on the substantive part of Leach's essay,
"Concerning Trobriand Clans and the Kinship Category *Tabu*,"
because much of his interpretation is offered from a perspective
which my experience with the Trobrianders has led me to reject.
But in concluding Leach said, "My thesis is then that the four
Trobriand clans are not really to be thought of as four unique and
separate lines of descent—Trobrianders indeed seem to have little
interest in pedigree" (1958, p. 143).

I have shown that the Trobrianders do indeed take an interest
in "pedigree" as it applies to land. The value of personal genealogy, however, is that it serves to link living people to each other
through recently deceased persons. Beyond a shallow time depth,
therefore, bloodlines do not need to be remembered in detail as
individual ancestors. But the first part of Leach's argument is correct: Trobriand *kumila* are not descent lines.

Kumila are not corporate groups, and there is never an occasion
when all *kumila* members gather as a group. Further, the origins
of *kumila* are very vague. Malinowski gave several versions of the

origin story of the Tabalu and all their friends in which a series of animals, each one identified with a particular *kumila*, came out of the ground prior to the emergence of the founders. From this point of view, Malinowski tried to show that all four *kumila* emerged from the same spot. But, in the stories collected by Malinowski himself, there are inconsistencies. In some versions, the emergence of the animal representing the Lukwasisiga *kumila* seems to have been represented sometimes by several different animals and sometimes by none. In fact, none of the details of the emergence of the Lukwasisiga seems very firmly established in Malinowski's data. "In the main emergence myth [Lukwasisiga] are either completely left out, or else their ancestral animals or person is made to play an entirely insignificant part" (1926*b*, p. 123). When Vanoi told me the origin story, he said that only a lizard, a dog, and a pig (representing Lukulabuta, Lukuba, and Malasi *kumila* respectively) came out of the Tabalu emergence hole at Obukula. Further, the founders—who later emerged through the same hole—represented only the above three *kumila*. Other informants, including Lukwasisiga people, agreed that the Lukwasisiga came from several other parts of the island, not from Obukula. Discrete clan myths are absent, as Leach (1958, p. 142) suggests.

Kumila identity is recognizable through a range of symbols, which are stable and are not valued property. Birds, animals, trees, and the lines on the palm of one's hand are all distinguishing features of *kumila* identity. People do not manipulate boundaries of *kumila* for their own personal gain, in contrast to the manipulation of *dala* boundaries. *Kumila* emphasize the distinction between "people like us" and "people different from us" in the widest sense (see Leach 1958, p. 142). *Kumila* fix certain social boundaries in the widest view of the Trobriand universe, but they are not units of descent. They are not vehicles for the transmission of jural rights to individuals nor do they act as channels for the transmission of accumulated property, even for a chosen few as in the case of *dala*. Thus, as Leach cogently asks, why clans at all?

In order to answer this question, it is necessary to examine the way clans serve to define preferable marriage partners. Malinowski was told, as was I, that it is best to marry one's father's sister's daughter. But the marriages I recorded indicated only that a man's children (both sons and daughters) should marry someone from his clan.[16] Montague (1975) reported this preference for villagers on Kaileuna Island. The term *tabu*, used to designate father's sis-

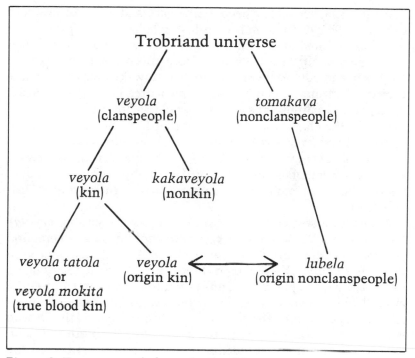

Figure 2. Taxonomy of clan relationships

ter, father's sister's daughter, and most individuals in the grand-parental generation, is also used for any person in the father's clan whom the speaker (female or male) wants to sleep with or marry. I was told this by both men and women. They all laugh-ingly said they were revealing a special Trobriand "trick" by means of which they would then marry someone from their fath-er's clan. Indeed it is a trick because these *tabu* serve as links *through another clan* back to *one's own clan*. Through *tabu* one creates significant and long-term exchange relationships with members of one's own clan.

Given that a clan relationship does not by itself entail any jural obligation, we must examine the meaning of clanspeople at two levels of semantic contrast (see fig. 2) in order to find any signifi-cance at all in clan categories. In the taxonomy of figure 2, the first level of contrast is between *veyola* (clanspeople) and *toma-*

kava (nonclanspeople): "people like us" and "people different from us." This distinction is manifest in behavior, as "people like us" share cooked food with us, but we do not share cooked food with "people different from us." From this view, *tomakava* are strangers and potential enemies in Malinowski's terms. But note that the interpretation of *veyola* as presented here differs considerably from Malinowski's gloss of *veyola* as "matrilineal kin."

Within the clan itself, there is another level of distinction: *veyola* (kin) and *kakaveyola* (nonkin). *Kakaveyola* is a term rarely used in casual conversations. Villagers say that it is always better to address a neighbor or an older villager, who is truly *kakaveyola*, by the more ambiguous superordinate term *veyola* (clanspeople/kin).

A further distinction is drawn among one's own kin (*veyola*). *Veyola tatola* (or, equivalently, *veyola mokita*) is an expression designating true kin of ego's own bloodline, a genealogy traced through *baloma*. *Veyola* (non–blood kin) trace a relationship back to the same place of origin. When founders came out of the ground, they usually came with *tabu* from other *dala* and *kumila*. All founders from *different dala* within the *same kumila* who emerged from the same place together called each other *veyola*. Through time, the descendants of the founders continued the same relationships. If founders from two different clans came from the same origin place, they called each other *lubegu* ("my friend"), thus avoiding the *tomakava* category.

In general conversation, those who are *veyola tatola* are addressed as *veyola*. The importance of blood is overtly minimized, the same mechanism used when repressing one level of meaning of *kakaveyola*. Although there are different levels of semantic contrast, recognized by all villagers under questioning, the most disaffiliative term *kakaveyola* and the most affiliative term *veyola tatola* are collapsed into the ambiguous term *veyola*. The polite use of *veyola* as an umbrella term for all one's clanspeople does not imply a specific kind of exchange relationship (other than occasional meals) between these villagers. Rather it seeks to verbally disguise the existence of differences among clanspeople.

Thus, to reverse the taxonomy and look at relationships from ego's point of view, ego is first identified through blood (i.e., birthright) with a particular *dala* premised on the regeneration of *baloma*. Second, ego has an additional set of kin from other *dala* in the same *kumila* through relationships established by her or his founders (*tabu*) at the place of emergence. All other clanspeople are viewed only in negative terms as nonkin (*kakaveyola*).

The totality of clanspeople, kin and nonkin together, stand in semantic opposition to villagers from the three other clans who are designated *tomakava* (nonclanspeople). Through the creation of specific kinds of exchange relationships, however, some of ego's own clanspeople and some *tomakava* are brought into significant relationships with ego. The term *tabu again* becomes the linking force behind the creation of these social relationships. The trick of *tabu* that my informants described in reference to sleeping with or marrying someone in ego's father's clan allows the grouping of clanspeople and nonclanspeople into a single verbal category *keyawa*.

Trobrianders, to my initial dismay and confusion, gloss *keyawa* as "others."[17] During the first mortuary distributions I attended, I tried to collect the *clan* and *dala* identity of the participants. At first, there seemed to be a lack of any pattern according to *dala* or *clan*. When I asked why people from different *dala* and *kumila* attended, I received answers that did not correlate with the lists of attendance I had made. For example, villagers say that Malasi clanspeople always help each other at mortuary ceremonies. Helping means that villagers come to the distributions with the necessary objects which will be given away by the members of the deceased's *dala*. This is one important way that the deceased's *dala* accumulates resources for distribution. I found, however, that not all Malasi clanspeople attended, nor did all villagers within any one *dala* of a Malasi clan attend.

My informants said that the mortuary exchanges are always transacted between two clans (e.g., Malasi clan always gives to Lukwasisiga clan, and later Lukwasisiga clan reciprocates to Malasi people). In other words, the *dala* of the deceased gives away their accumulated resources to members of another clan. But, again, the data I collected suggested that only certain members of another clan received payments.[18] When pressed further, however, they said that each member in attendance was *keyawa* to a kinsperson of the deceased's *dala*.

Thus, the category *keyawa* includes ego's own clanspeople and those from another clan (*tomakava*). In figure 3, I diagram the way *keyawa* relationships are established within and between clans for one man. This diagram is based on the relationships established through the observed preference that a man's children marry into his own clan. Through time, marriage and mortuary exchanges are maintained between individual members of *dala* within the same two opposite clans. Through his father's father, a man has preestablished *keyawa* relationships with his father's

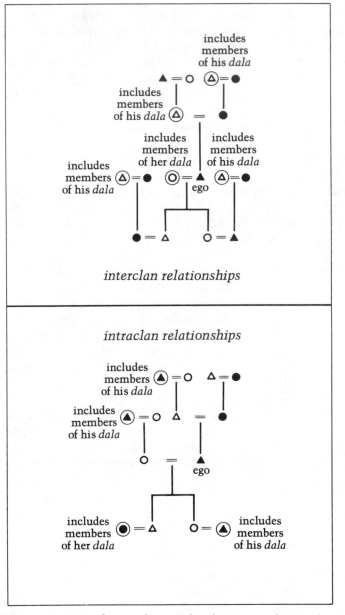

Figure 3. Interclan and intraclan keyawa *relationships. The circled kinship symbols indicate the way ego builds networks of* keyawa *relationships within his own clan and within other clans. The shaded areas refer to a member of clan A, while the clear areas refer to a member of clan B.*

father's kin and their descendants within that *dala* line. All these men and women are ego's clanspeople. When ego marries, his wife's father and his kin become *keyawa* (of the same clan) to ego. Villagers who belong to ego's wife's *dala* become *keyawa* to ego's father. In a similar fashion, ego's own sons and daughters provide him with *keyawa* when they marry. Thus the marriages of a man's children are of the utmost significance to him because, through each marriage (provided they marry someone in his own clan), he receives a set of his own clanspeople who become *keyawa* to him and are now in an obligatory exchange relationship with him. The *keyawa* that ego receives through his father's father can recede in value depending upon current social and political circumstances. But the *keyawa* relationships established through ego's marriage and his children's marriages strengthen as he reaches the peak of his career.

The categorization of people as *keyawa* constitutes an exchange system whose general properties are important to understand in order to appreciate the complexity of intraclan and interclan relationships. *Keyawa* is a means for establishing exchange relationships through nonclan relations with members of one's own clan of a different generation. For any *keyawa* linkage delineated in figure 3 (e.g., ego's wife's father, father's father, sons-in-law, daughters-in-law) ego will be concerned to maintain rapport between himself and the linking relation (e.g., wife, father, daughter, son). He will also be determined to ensure that rapport between the linking relation and his *keyawa* remains in good order. Therefore, the individual is forced to rely on others for important relationships and that reliance necessitates intergenerational and interclan linkages. In such a system, self-interest becomes the motive for social cohesion.

The *keyawa* relationships delineated above fall within ego's own clan. These people are in an exchange relationship with ego whereby they help him accumulate resources at the moment of his greatest need. He, in turn, must reciprocate when any of his *keyawa*, within his own clan, are in need of support. Ego's *keyawa* in an opposite clan are his father's, his mother's father's, and his spouse's kin and all their extended clan *keyawa*. In mortuary distributions, the transactions occur between these two *keyawa* networks in opposite clans.

Thus, in each set of mortuary distributions, particular people within a range of different *dala* come together to assist the members of the deceased's *dala*. Since these are ego-centered networks, differing in membership for each member of the *dala*,

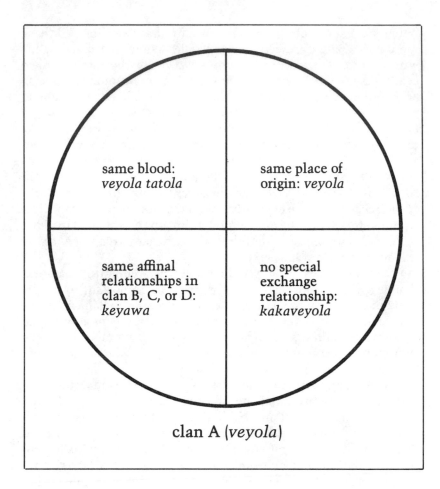

Figure 4. Relationships within a clan from ego's perspective

there is not necessarily any overriding solidarity governing all assembled *keyawa*. In fact, in other areas of social life, there could
be tension and competition among them. Informants describe
specific individuals as *keyawa* when asked, but, in general, they
refer to all present as being from the "same clan": "Malasi people
always help each other."

Keyawa is the governing principle that brings these people together, but, by superimposing the general category "clan" as an
umbrella term for all participants within one clan, any differences and personal oppositions are mediated. Absence of individuals, who should be participating but who neglect their obligations because of personal conflicts, is not publicly marked when
participation is framed by the vague category of clan. Absence is
always personally noted, but affronts are kept hidden. Cracks
should not show in the veneer of public togetherness. The clan
operates as a mechanism for fusing an array of individual oppositions among the supporting actors.

At the moment of death, a semblance of clan togetherness is
momentarily affirmed so that the larger disjuncture between the
living and the dead, between two opposite clans, between the deceased's *dala* and all other clan *keyawa* can be confronted. In
answer to the question "Why clans?" it is only at these brief moments when clan, as a social category, is necessary to disguise the
reality of intraclan divisions.

Whereas Malinowski presented a division of the social universe
into four named clans, there appears to be a deeper and more significant quadrapartite division within each clan. This division is
based on ego-centered kin terms. In figure 4, I show a logical ordering of ego's universe in terms of social relationships. Uterine
kin (*veyola tatola*) are primary. The first expansion begins with
the social relationships established at the place of origin. *Tabu*, as
founder, is the creator of these *veyola* relationships. The next
stage is affinal relationships, created and maintained through
one's father, spouse, and children. These relationships originate
through the trick of marrying a *tabu*. Thus the third category
within a clan is *keyawa*. The remaining clanspeople, *kakaveyola*,
are only negatively named, emphasizing the absence of any specific exchange obligations. Thus, blood and land origins are given
at birth through both *baloma* ancestors and *tabu* founders. But
each individual, throughout her or his life, seeks to move people
from the category of mere clanspeople to that of *keyawa*.

The fact that a fourfold universal division of Trobriand society
is replicated in the ego-centered division of a single clan is pro-

vocative, for it supports Leach's (1958, p. 141) notion that a logic of four is necessary for Trobrianders to explain the workings of their society. It must be noted, however, that this replication in no sense constitutes proof of such structural logic. Ego's four intraclan categories could just as well be sustained within a moiety system. In fact, why *four* clans, instead of two or three or even eight, remains problematic.

Chapter 3
The Rituals of Death

I

___

*For the spirit of the dead man knows nothing about all that
happens to his body and bones, and cares less, since he is already leading a happy existence in Tuma, the netherworld. . . .
The ritual performance at his twice-opened grave and over his
buried remains, and all that is done with his relics, are merely a
social game, where the various groupings into which the com
munity has re-crystallized at his death play against each other.
. . . we shall have to confine ourselves to the study of mortuary
practices in their barest outline only. A complete account of
them would easily fill a volume of the present size.—Malinowski 1929, p. 149*

___

Arnold van Gennep, in *The Rites of Passage,* originally published
in 1909, wrote that transition rites in funeral ceremonies "have a
duration and a complexity sometimes so great that they must be
granted a sort of autonomy" (1960, p. 146). In Kiriwina, mortuary
ceremonies have a "duration and a complexity" matching van
Gennep's description. In addition, the rituals of mourning visually and symbolically diagram the social categories basic to the cultural system. Throughout one's life, social interaction is mediated through the dynamics of exchange, but often it is very
difficult to observe the basic categories out of which people work
to expand their own social networks. Mortuary ceremonies are
moments of spectacular visual communication. They serve as a
vehicle for the financial and political assessment of each participant, and for an instant, through the use of such visual qualities
as style, color, and space, they frame the oppositional nature of
relationships.

The timing and rhythm of mortuary ceremonies differ throughout the length of the transitional period. The most critical and

emotional moment occurs at death and lasts until after the first mortuary distribution following the burial. There is then a relatively quiet time when only small distributions are held. People continue to observe restrictions in dress and activity. During this period of "liminality" (Turner 1964), however, enormous amounts of work are undertaken in preparation for the women's mortuary ceremony.

As Malinowski noted, there are many kinds of distributions, called *sagali*. Although each particular *sagali* has a specific term, in daily conversation villagers use the generic word *sagali* rather than a specific name. *Sagali* as a noun refers to a distribution of any kind of object of exchange, including food. As a verb, *sagali* means "to divide among everyone present." It also means "to settle accounts" or "to reclaim ownership." *Sagali* is used as a general term for all mortuary distributions.

The women's mortuary ceremony, specifically referred to as *lisaladabu*,[1] is held four to eight months after a death. The timing depends upon the hamlet manager's control over resources, the power of the uterine kin of the deceased, the status of the deceased, and the speed with which men accumulate yams and women amass bundles of banana leaves and banana-fiber skirts. The women's mortuary ceremony marks the end of the widest range of mourning activity. The huge distribution of wealth reduces many visible signs of mourning ritual. But after the women's mortuary ceremony a range of distributions (*sagali*) are given annually by men. Each *sagali* is a distribution of one major kind of production, for example, a betel nut *sagali*, a taro pudding *sagali*, a *sagali* of small *taytu* yams, a *sagali* of very large *kuvi* yams, a fish *sagali*, or a pork *sagali*.

The right to organize a mortuary distribution is incumbent on certain kin of the deceased. In this context, these uterine kin are called *toliuli*, the "owners of the dead person's things." Owners are assisted by origin kin (*veyola*) whose founders (*tabu*) came from the same place of origin as the owners' founders. The owners also depend upon individual clanspeople who are their clan *keyawa*. There is one exception to owners as uterine kin. When a dead person is buried on land other than his or her own *dala* land, the hamlet manager of the actual burial site becomes the owner. Unless otherwise noted, I use the term "owners" to designate uterine kin; "kin" to include uterine and origin kin; and "clan *keyawa*" to designate a wide range of clanspeople affinally linked through their fathers (or their mother's fathers).

The workers (*toliyouwa*) for *sagali*, those who prepare the body for burial, dig the grave, and publicly mourn for the deceased, are the blood kin of the deceased's father and spouse. Joining them are their origin kin and all their own clan *keyawa*. If the dead person's spouse and father are from the same clan, then the major distributions move between villagers who belong to two clans. In cases where marriages have taken place with villagers from other clans, the assembled workers represent more than one clan. The workers are the major recipients of most distributions; thus, the owners give away and the workers receive.

Some workers, however, play a dual role in the proceedings. They perform the tasks of workers and receive payments, but they also stand on the side of the owners and add to the owners' pool of resources. A man's married children (sons and daughters) assist the owners when their father dies or when one of their father's blood or origin kin dies. Although they stand with the owners at various distributions, they are dressed in the appropriate mourning attire for nonclanspeople of the deceased (e.g., shaved heads and blackened bodies) and thus are visually differentiated from the owners, who are not shaved and blackened. Therefore each child that "takes the place of its father" is not changing *dala* identity but, through a man, his child is temporarily on loan to another *dala* from another clan. Thus when a woman dies the married children of her brothers play this dual role.

My descriptions of the events immediately following a death and prior to burial correlate very closely with Malinowski's (1929, pp. 152–154) discussion of similar events. The major discrepancy in our two accounts occurs not so much in factual information but in feeling and emotion. Malinowski's description contains exotic comments which serve to heighten and glorify the bizarre and "primitive" quality of rituals surrounding death. From his diary (1967, p. 192) it appears that he was revolted by the proceedings prior to death. After watching these first death rituals, I was left with a sense of beauty: a feeling that to die in Kiriwina is much more humane than to die in a sterile hospital room.

II

From the moment of his death, the distinction between his

*real, that is matrilineal, kinsmen (veyola) on the one hand,
and his children, relatives-in-law and friends on the other,
takes on a sharp and even an outwardly visible form. The kinsmen of the deceased fall under a taboo; they must keep aloof
from the corpse. . . . The kindred must also not display any out-
ward signs of mourning in costume and ornamentation, though
they need not conceal their grief and may show it by weeping.
Here the underlying idea is that the maternal kinsmen (veyola) are hit in their own persons; that each one suffers because
the whole sub-clan to which they belong has been maimed
by the loss of one of its members.—Malinowski 1929, p. 150*

When death seems imminent, workers come into the house to
bathe and dress the stricken person. These particular workers are
usually sisters of the person's father or are related to the person's
father through their own mothers' fathers. They are women
whom the sick person called by the kin term *tabu*. They rub the
body of the dying person with coconut oil and apply facial painting. They dress the sick one in her or his most elaborate traditional clothes and adorn the chest, head, arms, and legs with decorations. While the person is still alive, four or five workers
remain in the house, feeding her or him, giving her or him betel to
chew, talking, sometimes laughing, and periodically breaking into loud wailing, especially each time someone new enters the
house.

Formal crying (*libu*) by women and men (the deceased's kin,
children of a male deceased, and the spouse and the father of the
deceased and their extended kin) occurs four times a day from
death until after the women's mortuary ceremony. Often the crying continues less formally and with fewer attendants for several
years. When a kinsperson of any of the above relatives returns to
Kiriwina after a long absence, he or she goes directly to the *libu*
(the house where the crying takes place) "to cry."

When death occurs, male workers related to the deceased's
father through their own fathers help prepare the body: tying the
arms and legs together and inserting pieces of coconut husks into
all body orifices. This preparation is necessary so the body will be
odorless and will remain in a straight position as it is placed over
the outstretched legs of the workers who have been caring for it.
Sad wailing accompanies the activities. The spouse of the de-

ceased sits at the head of the body, occasionally holding the head to keep it straight. In expressions of deep grief (whether real or dramatically enacted) she or he will bend over and kiss the dead person. For the rest of the day and throughout the entire night, these same people sit facing each other along the sides of the corpse with their legs straight out and "carry" the body. The women who carry the body include the deceased's father's sisters (*tabu*). Periodically, the children and the father of the deceased enter the house and throw themselves on the body with hysterical wailing, crying out "my father" or "my son" or "my daughter" (whatever the appropriate kin term is). At these moments, the weeping from everyone in the house reaches a more prolonged high-pitched tone in answer to the intense expressions of grief. Calm returns only when the bereaved withdraw from the house. The workers chew betel and talk quietly, awaiting the entrance of a new lamenter. This sorrowful process continues throughout the night. The kin of the deceased do not enter the house during this time.[2]

While all this takes place inside the house, outside the village is filled with men. Many fires glow in the night air. Male workers from other villages come to spend the night in singing (*yawali*). Men from the same village sit together around a fire. During the night some food is offered by the kinsmen of the deceased. An undercurrent of competition runs throughout the singing as each village group sings its best songs.

Singing is often used as a mechanism to avoid conflict. Many times I was in situations where some men in a small group became very hostile and angry with each other. Immediately, other men in the group began to sing very loudly until all joined in the song. In this way, confrontation is averted. The singing during the night, although competitive, has the general effect of calming a tense situation. The period immediately following death precipitates great anxiety over sorcery, since every death is thought to occur through human agency.[3]

At the moment of death, the thoughts of all the deceased's blood kin are concerned with the question, "Who killed my kin?" The living question each other: "With whom did my kin walk to Losuia?" "Who gave my kin a betel nut to chew?" "Did my kin go fishing yesterday with someone?" Those who are most suspect— father's and spouse's kin and any friend who is not *veyola*—are singing, crying, and mourning in an attempt to avert the thoughts of *bwagau* (sorcery or "poison magic," as the Trobrianders call it).[4] But, when a chief has effected the death of someone, no secret is made of his deed. In fact, his ability is publicly displayed when he walks through the mourning village, dressed in his most elaborate, brightly colored clothing. Today he might put on a colorful new shirt or tie. His style of dress, in direct contrast to the dark clothes of the mourners, is an announcement that he is a man to be reckoned with.[5]

During the night, those closest to the deceased but belonging to a different clan (that is, his children, spouse, spouse's sisters, father, father's sisters) dance a special kind of two-step called *vesali*. On the night of singing for Uwelasi (see plate 7), a Lukwasisiga chief from Tubuwada village, his sons were dressed in traditional mourning attire. They wore green unbleached pandanus pubic coverings. Each carried some object which belonged to his father, for example, bunches of black feathers from Fergusson Island or the chief's lime pot. Often they were joined in the dancing by their mothers and mothers' sisters. They would dance for a while and then stop and hold each other in their arms, wailing and crying. Traditionally, when a chief died, his burial rituals would continue for three days, but Uwelasi was buried after twenty-four hours of singing and crying. When a person not of high rank dies, he or she is buried the next morning, following one night of crying and singing.

Prior to burial, the body is wrapped in large pandanus mats. Traditionally, the body was exhumed after the first burial (cf. Malinowski 1929, pp. 155–157) and blood kin examined it for signs of sorcery. Today, the mats are carefully opened before the first burial. My informants told me about this procedure, but I did not actually see it occur. They said a hair of a pig or a leaf from a yam plant indicates that the deceased had defaulted on a proper exchange. After the death of one man I knew, some gravel was found in his burial mat. Everyone in his *dala* recognized this as a sign that the year before he had a large *kuvi* yam which he should have given in exchange, but instead he hid it in his house and cooked it for himself. A fiber from a woman's skirt or the skin of a betel nut indicates that a person had committed adultery. It must be remembered that members of the opposite clan stay with the body, and there is an entire night in which they could surreptitiously place such a sign. But I have no direct evidence that this occurs.

When a man dies, his death may not only be attributed to his own wrongdoing, it may also indicate that someone was retaliating for a wrongdoing by another man in his own *dala* or by his father. "Mistakes" that people make are thought to be remem-

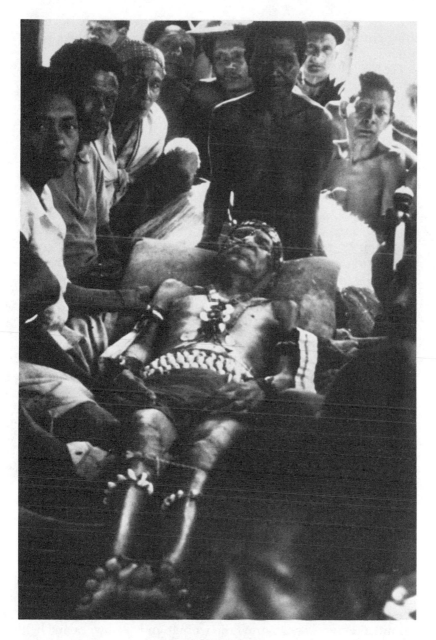

Plate 7. The sons of Uwelasi, the chief living in Tubuwada village, asked me to photograph their father while he was dressed in the shell decorations indicative of his rank, prior to his burial

bered from generation to generation. People are not only fearful of things they themselves have done, but also fear the "mistakes" of other living men and those already dead.

Although the death of a man can stand for the "mistakes" of other men, it never stands for the wrongdoing of a woman. A woman's death, however, can be read as retaliation against any other kinswoman or kinsman or her father. The death of a young woman is especially traumatic because the continuity of the *dala* is threatened by the loss of child-bearing women. An informant told me that, if a man wants to destroy an entire *dala*, he poisons the women first; then he can take his time with the men. Death gives people much room for accusations and hostility, all of which can be used to political advantage. The members of each *dala* must try to solve the mystery of a death and then quietly plan their revenge.

Situations occur in which a burial provokes confrontation between the members of the *dala* of the deceased and the manager of the hamlet where the deceased was last living. If a person dies while she or he is living on her or his own *dala* land, a problem will not usually arise over the place of burial. Everyone can be buried on their own *dala* land. But, when a villager dies who is living on other *dala* land, the place of burial must be resolved. If a person is living with his or her father on the father's own *dala* land, he or she can be buried on that land.[6] The following examples will illustrate the political implications of burial.

In one hamlet in Kwaibwaga, the land is controlled by men whose father, a chief, had been the former hamlet manager. The chief was the last member of his *dala*, and when he died his eldest son remained in control of the hamlet. One of the sons' sisters was married and lived in the same hamlet with her brothers. She died in the spring of 1971. At the same time, her mother's brother was the hamlet manager of her *dala*'s land in Wakeluwa. He and his people came to Kwaibwaga to take her body back for burial in Wakeluwa. Her eldest brother in Kwaibwaga said, "No, this is my land and I am taking the place of my father. I want to bury my sister here." His sister's son, who lived in the next hamlet, and his other brothers collected A$4 and two clay pots, and they gave these valuables to the hamlet manager (their blood kinsman) from Wakeluwa. They buried the woman in Kwaibwaga and held the women's mortuary ceremony there.

In 1972, a woman who lived with her husband at Tilakewa died. Her father and mother were both dead, but her father's *dala* land was in a hamlet in Omarakana. When she died, the Tabalu of

Omarakana went to Tilakewa and brought her back to be buried at Omarakana. The Tabalu were the people who then performed the women's mortuary ceremony for her at Omarakana. The Tabalu said they wanted her buried at Omarakana because the founders of her father's *dala* came out of the same place of origin as did the Tabalu. Thus she was their *veyola* (origin kinsperson).

No other moment I witnessed throughout my stay in Kiriwina reached the emotional tenor of a burial. After wrapping the body in large pandanus mats, many of the workers throw themselves on top of the deceased. Crying and wailing fill the air. A grave has already been dug on the side of the hamlet and men carry the body to the grave. Some men jump into the hole with the body and cover the top of the grave with one large mat. Shielded from everyone's view, the men cut the strings holding the limbs together and remove the coconut husks so that the fluid can leave the body. They then remove all the decorations and valuables from the deceased.[7] Everyone, including uterine kin of the deceased, gathers around the grave site. Men and women sob so hard that their bodies shake and tears continually stream down their faces. I myself was very moved by this sadness and felt a great sense of loss. I have no way of ascertaining how much of this enormous public outburst of grief is histrionics and how much is actual grief. However, I saw much sadness displayed privately by the wife and sons of Kulumwelova, a seventy-year-old man who died in Kwaibwaga in 1972. Malinowski (1929, p. 162) records similar situations.

If the deceased is thought to have owned *bwagau*, his body is placed face down in the grave so that his spirit (*kosi*) will not be able to free itself to walk around the village. *Kosi* is an undifferentiated spirit that has nothing to do with *baloma*.[8] Rather, it seems to represent the most dangerous magic forces that during life reside inside the body. At death, these forces are freed and if uncontrolled are capable of harming other villagers. Some men know magic spells that prevent the *kosi* from disturbing the living. After Kulumwelova was buried, a man who knew this spell remained at the grave site during the night. Immediately following the burial of Uwelasi, the chief from Tubuwada village, the ground rumbled—there are often slight earth tremors—and villagers murmured that the shaking earth was a sign of Uwelasi's powerful *bwagau* magic.

Graves are elaborately decorated, often with fresh flowers provided daily and with feathers and other decorations belonging to the deceased. The top of Kulumwelova's grave in Kwaibwaga was covered with the round poles from his yam house. When Uwelasi was buried, his long *kuvi* yams were buried with him. These three yams were the only objects placed in his grave.

An exchange called *wayala kaybila* takes place either before or immediately after the burial. It transpires rather privately either at the side of the hamlet or inside a house. In this exchange, the kinsmen of the spouse of the deceased, sometimes helped by *ke-yawa*, give such valuables as *beku* (stone ax blades), money, clay pots, *mwali*, *soulava*, or strings of cowrie shells indirectly to the uterine kinsmen of the deceased. Each man presents one valuable to the spouse of the deceased which is then taken by the men of the deceased's *dala*. This is, however, a short-term exchange. My informants told me that the exchange was not "true": they called it *sasopa* (lying).[9] Although each man gives a valuable, the next day he receives the same valuable back from the men of the deceased's *dala* with an additional valuable attached. My informants said that men give these valuables to the deceased's relatives to show respect and to make the deceased's spouse happy. But this rather confusing set of circumstances is one of the most important exchanges that occur. When both the additional "new" and the original valuables are returned by the kinsmen of the deceased, the kinsmen of the spouse are obligated to bring raw yams and other produce to a future mortuary *sagali*. Thus, raw yams are being exchanged across clan boundaries and those who are normally the principal receivers of mortuary exchanges are in this instance obligated to give.

When a man is renowned for his magic, his death precipitates a game (*mwasawa*) in which other men competitively display the range of magic spells each possesses. The game is played the night after the burial of the deceased, for his *baloma* remains with his relatives for several days before departing for Tuma. Men congregate around the deceased's house and recite magic spells to each other. At night, when the magic recital (*okayvata*) takes place, it is thought that the *baloma* will listen to the magic. When the performance of magic spells is finished, the *baloma* then departs for Tuma. Every kind of magic spell may be recited except *bwa-gau* and magic spells for curing all illnesses (*vivisa*). The men who say the magic do not have to be kinsmen of the deceased, and the recitations are politically charged.

On the night following the burial of Kulumwelova, his eldest son announced publicly that the *baloma* of Kulumwelova had come and told him he wanted to hear the magic. The *baloma* of his father cried because he had not said good-bye to his eldest son before he died. Kulumwelova's second-eldest son, Taipukwa, began to chant magic spells (vitoula, "to open the magic") because he had much more magic from his father than had his other brothers. At the end of the first recitation, Taipukwa called his father's name, indicating that he had received this magic from his father. Each recitation of part of a spell concludes with the name of the previous owner of the magic. Taipukwa then said "kata-yela" and called another man's name. This is "giving someone else the magic." The person named should then begin to chant his own knowledge of magic spells, called muvewoulo, "paying back for the magic." If the person does not answer with any magic spells, then the first person—in this case Taipukwa—is the winner of that round. Taipukwa would begin to chant again and would call someone else's name.

Only a portion of each spell is chanted, but the name of the previous owner of the spell is always given. The object is to publicly demonstrate the range of one's control over magic inherited from one's father and others. Magic spells that one acquires from uterine kin are paid for in valuables. These spells are dala property. But a man also receives magic from his father. Thus, he can expand his resources beyond the limitations of his own dala. A man gives magic spells to one son over another based on the extent of his relationship, demonstrated by the raw yams that a son annually produces for his father. (See chapter 6 for descriptions of these exchanges.)

In the course of the evening of magic-spell recitations, some of the younger married men were called upon, but they remained silent. Later they told me that they knew some spells but that the presence of older men, who knew many more, frightened them. In any public event, younger men are always being encouraged by their elders to speak out, but usually most of them are afraid. A young man who dares to speak publicly is announcing his entrance into the game of politics.

The chanting of spells continued between four men (others were called but did not answer) for about an hour. Then Bunemiga, the local government counselor, who was known to have much magic and who was trying very hard to become a big-man, began to chant his magic spells. Bunemiga stood alone beyond the houses in the center of a path. It was an exceptionally dark night and the wind was very strong. He said that he would move farther along the path so that the wind would carry his voice away. He spoke loudly, with great authority and very rapidly, pausing now and then to catch his breath. First he said magic for yams, then magic for the wind, magic for the day to dawn quickly, love magic, and magic to become pregnant. All his magic was written in a thick notebook that his son read to him for part of the time as he chanted.[10] One verse after another he shouted out, always leaving some parts of the magic spell unspoken. When he finished, no one answered him: he had won the game.

Bunemiga's father had been the chief in Kwaibwaga who was the last of his *dala*. After his death, although Bunemiga's eldest brother took control of the land, his control today is tenuous. Bunemiga, the third-eldest son, was trying to build up his own authority in the hamlet. Thus he demonstrated his vast knowledge of spells in an effort to assert a stronger position with the only weapon uniquely his own: his magic.

III

The master of ceremonies must be assisted by all those who have kinship obligations to him, but who have not carried out the mortuary duties towards the deceased. On the other hand, he has to give to all those who have in some way or other been discharging duties during the dead man's illness and after his death. Very often it happens that a man will be seen on one day contributing to the distribution because he is a relative-in-law of the master of ceremonies, and after the distribution will be seen returning home with practically the same amount of food, because he was related to the deceased as a classificatory son.—Malinowski 1935a, p. 28

Sigiliyawali, the first *sagali*, is held on the day following burial. The owners and their clan *keyawa* work quickly to collect yams, taro, and valuables for the distribution. Men and their wealth predominate in this *sagali*, but women participate first. The major purpose of *sigiliyawali* is to repay all workers for their help with the mourning and burial. When the distributions of *sigiliyawali* are finished, land claims are then made in cases where the deceased was using other people's land. If the deceased was an important man or was a woman from a strong high-ranked *dala*, then *sigiliyawali* becomes a highly political ritual. I observed only two of these ceremonies. The following is an outline of the events which take place during *sigiliyawali*.

Selubulabu. Kinswomen of the deceased and the daughters of men of the deceased's *dala* stand in the center of the hamlet. Women workers are waiting around the periphery of the center circle. The women in the center throw bundles of banana leaves to all the female workers. Bundles (usually between twenty to fifty) go to all women who in some way helped with the deceased's death and burial. Bundles also go to women who cooked food when the deceased was ill. This is only a first payment because all these women will be more handsomely repaid during the women's mortuary ceremony.

Ligabwa. Kinsmen of the deceased's *dala* and the sons of the men of that *dala* enter the center of the hamlet and divide taro and yams into piles. Each pile goes to members of a hamlet who came to mourn for the deceased.

Lumi. Individual gifts of yams, taro, large *kuvi* yams, bunches of bananas, and betel nuts are distributed by name to each male worker who spent the night in singing. The size of the transaction varies with the political status of the worker. Thus hamlet managers, men with large yam houses, and chiefs receive larger payments.

Yolova. These distributions are made at the same time that *lumi* is taking place. Money, clay pots, stone ax blades, and shell valuables are given individually to each person who actually carried the body: those who bathed and dressed the deceased, those who sat all night with the body on their legs, those who carried the body to the grave, those who carried the body from one village to another for burial, and those who dug the grave. Valuables are also given to men who collected firewood when the deceased was ill or who brought him or her fish and pork to eat.

Sagali veguwa.[11] This exchange is the return of *wayala kaybila*, the giving of valuables to the spouse of the deceased by her or his own kinsmen, which are then given to the blood kinsmen of the deceased. Now the blood kinsmen of the deceased return the exact valuable to each man who presented it the day before. The original valuable is accompanied by an additional valuable. The exchange is called *mapula*. The return of a valuable obligates the kinsmen (sometimes helped by their own *keyawa*) of the spouse of the deceased to bring raw yams and taro, supplemented sometimes with betel, fish, or pork, to another mortuary distribution held on the day following *sigiliyawali*. The bringing of such items as raw yams is called *matili*, another variation of the word *mapula*. At the women's mortuary ceremony, all men from other clans who brought raw yams are repaid with bundles of banana leaves.

Kulututu. In this exchange all kinsmen of the spouse of the deceased (or spouses if the deceased is a chief) take valuables (clay pots, stone ax blades, money, armshells, and necklaces) and present them to the blood kinsmen of the deceased. The spouse and her or his kinspeople are obligated to take care of the person she or he married throughout their lives together. At his or her death, the kinsmen of the spouse repay the deceased's kinsmen with valuables to denote their improper care and to compensate for the loss of a person. If the deceased has been killed, not through the hidden use of magic but by overt means, then the distribution assumes enormous proportions as the kinsmen of the spouse are filled with great anxiety over subsequent reprisals.

Pokala for land. When a man who has been using land from another *dala* dies, a separate set of transactions occurs after the *sagali* is formally finished. Rights to hamlet control are never part of any mortuary ceremony (see chap. 6 on land tenure).

Tadabali, the second *sagali*, is held the day following *sigiliyawali*. This *sagali* differs completely from the first. *Tadabali* centers on women's wealth distributions and the focus is on the widow or widower (see plate 8). The following exchanges occur for either a male or a female spouse, but to simplify discussion I use a female spouse as ego. At the close of *sigiliyawali*, the spouse of the deceased is secluded in a house and placed upon a very high bed called a *libu*.[12] Pandanus mats and pieces of calico are placed around the bed so that no one may see the spouse. Talking is not allowed in the house; when the widow wants something she must tap on the wall or bed. She must not come down from the bed, not even to go into the bush.

Tadabali releases the spouse from some of the most extreme rituals by the presentation of skirts and bundles to her. The blood kinswomen of the deceased, helped by female clan *keyawa* and daughters of the deceased's kinsmen, present women's wealth to the spouse. Then bundles of banana leaves are given by name to all kinsmen of the spouse who gave valuables in the anxiety-filled *kulututu* exchange at *sigiliyawali* and to the children of these men. Having received bundles, these men and their married and unmarried children (all of whom are nonclanspeople of the deceased) now shave their heads, and they continue to mourn pub-

Plate 8. Kwaibwaga widower on the veranda of his house, after the second mortuary sagali

licly for the deceased until the women's mortuary ceremony. The following exchanges take place at *tadabali*. Kinswomen, female clan *keyawa*, and the daughters of the deceased's kinsmen make the following payments.[13]

Vabusi. Bundles and one skirt are given to the widow so that she can sit on the floor instead of always sitting on the high bed.

Wolela kaladibukula. Bundles and a skirt are given to the widow so that she can now go to the bush to defecate and urinate.

Katupwela kalumweyoga. The widow is given a large rain mat (*mweyoga*), and she must cover herself completely when she goes into the bush.

Kalakatusunapula. This is the first of three payments of skirts and bundles made so the widow can walk outside. If the spouse is young, this payment is not completed until the women's mortuary ceremony, which means that the spouse cannot walk outside until then. At the *tadabali* for Kulumwelova, his widow received five skirts and two hundred bundles. However, the usual payment is three hundred to four hundred bundles, but Kulumwelova had very few relatives still alive and his own children were the major owners in that they produced most of the bundles and yams for all the *sagali*.

Kalitadabali. Ten bundles are given to each person who will shave his or her head in mourning for the deceased. All people who shave their heads must be from a clan other than that of the deceased.

Kaweluwa. Raw food brought by the widow's kinsmen is distributed. This food is for the people who are living with the widow during the period of mourning until the women's mortuary ceremony. All mourners (including sons and daughters of the deceased) stop eating "good food" (*kaula*: yams, sweet potatoes, and taro). Sometimes the closest relatives of the deceased also stop chewing betel.

IV

This intricate series of distributions stretches out into years, and it entails a veritable tangle of obligations and duties; for the members of the deceased's sub-clan must provide food and give it to the chief organizer, the headman of the sub-clan, who collects it and then distributes it to the proper beneficiaries. These, in their turn, partially at least, re-distribute it. And each gift in this enormous complex trails its own wake of counter-gifts and obligations to be fulfilled at a future date.—Malinowski 1929, p. 160

After *tadabali*, the hamlet settles into its mourning schedule, which continues until the women's mortuary ceremony. The *dala* of the deceased as well as the kin of the spouse and father of the deceased must not eat *kaula*. They may only eat *kaweluwa* (e.g., squash, cassava, breadfruit, rice). All activity, such as dancing, singing, *kula*, cricket playing, or walking to Losuia, is taboo. Women of the deceased's *dala* are not supposed to go to their gardens or to cook food, but other women workers from other hamlets daily bring food for the mourning people. Everywhere one looks, women are weaving skirts or preparing bundles. Sometimes a small *sagali* (only for the burial hamlet) is held. The men of the deceased's *dala* cook taro pudding and give it to other kin so that they can now eat "good food," although the deceased's father, spouse, and children still continue the taboo on eating "good food." This *sagali* is called *ulusilawodila*. Another kind of small *sagali*, which usually includes all the people of the village where the deceased is buried, is given by the kin of the deceased. Called *katuyuvisavalu*, this is a food distribution of betel nuts, raw yams, and sometimes pork. This distribution opens the way for dancing, singing, or such games as cricket to begin.

When my fifteen-year-old daughter Linda, who lived with me for three months in 1972, left Kiriwina to return to school, Waibadi gave a feast for her in his hamlet. Mayolu, a "cousin" of Waibadi's from Omarakana, had recently died, and Waibadi's brother-in-law, Obwelela, from Kwaibwaga, had died in April 1972. Despite the mourning taboo Waibadi decided to have a feast. About 12:30 A.M., after much guitar playing and dancing, two men carried a fat squealing pig, securely fastened onto a long pole, into the center of the hamlet. Waibadi stood up and made a speech:

> People in the other villages will scream at me because
> they think I did not respect the people who died. My brother-
> in-law died in Kwaibwaga and one woman from Omarakana
> died. Yesterday, I went to Kwaibwaga and I invited you people

to come for dancing. I kill this pig now for Obwelela and for Mayolu and also I kill this pig because Linda is leaving Kiriwina. I also kill this pig for *katuyuvisa* because I made a mistake about dancing when someone has died.

Everyone applauded and shouted. People said to each other, "Ah, Waibadi is a good man. He made a mistake but he killed a pig." This is a brief illustration of the way in which the chiefs operate; they break a rule, knowing how to make their "mistake" work in their favor.

During the liminal period and under the guise of communal mourning, the tempo of work becomes dramatically heightened. Division of labor is sharply defined. Men of the *dala* of the deceased are accumulating yams, taro, and betel nuts and trying to find pigs. They also must find cash or valuables to distribute at the women's mortuary ceremony. The deceased's kinswomen are making and accumulating skirts and bundles. Kin of the father and the spouse of the deceased are observing mourning rituals in dress, food, and activity. Husbands of the kinswomen of the deceased are obligated to help their wives accumulate *doba* (women's wealth). Thus, at this time all women owners are extremely busy gathering as much money and other objects as they can for exchange into bundles.

Exchanges of objects for bundles are called *valova*, the most important method for accumulating large amounts of bundles. My women informants told me that it is as important to know how to *valova* as it is to know how to make bundles. The knowledge of *valova* came with the founders (*tabu*). In *valova* exchanges, the market value of bundles is easily discernible, because all sorts of objects are "sold" to other villagers for payment in bundles. For example, a ten-cent stick of trade-store tobacco is purchased with cash. Then it is "sold" to someone for a return payment of ten bundles. These are casual exchanges made between any villagers. Return payment is immediate and equal. *Valova*, however, can also signify a major transaction in which a pig is exchanged for about seventeen hundred bundles.

Any item in demand can be used in *valova* exchanges, except for stone ax blades and the shell valuables used in *kula* exchange. In addition to bundles, banana leaves and all the various kinds of fibers used to make skirts are also acquired through *valova* exchange. Prior to the increase in the availability of Western cash, traffic in bundles was primarily carried out using objects of craft specialization found in different districts throughout Kiriwina.

One of the most important means for the circulation of such objects as baskets, water vessels, earrings, mats, and wooden bowls was *valova* exchange. Craft objects could be directly exchanged for bundles. Men also used raw yams to obtain craft objects which were then further exchanged for bundles.

My informants told me that, before they had access to cash, it was much more difficult to *valova*. Baskets, mats, and shell earrings, for example, do not wear out quickly, and therefore there was little demand for craft objects. Betel nuts, lime for chewing, and fish were always (and still are) objects for which the demand is unending. Such small objects as "imported" mats, baskets, black paint, and carved wooden objects, all of which men obtain through *kula* exchange, were traditionally very important in *valova* exchanges. Craft articles, which Malinowski (1922, p. 268) described as the "opening gifts" (*pari*) for *kula* transactions, are exchanged between *kula* partners when one man goes to visit another man for *kula*. *Pari* for large *kula* valuables, however, consists of exchanges of a pig or a *beku*. Many of these *pari* would at a later time be exchanged for bundles through *valova*.

Today, food stuffs purchased in the trade stores provide the most popular kinds of objects for *valova* exchanges. Because such things as biscuits, bread, fish from tins, candy, and tobacco are immediately consumed, *valova* exchanges have undergone a new stimulus. As a result, some inflation has occurred in the numbers of bundles exchanged in the women's mortuary ceremony.

One day, when women were assembling a large pile of bundles prior to the women's mortuary ceremony, my friend Kadesopi, watching the preparations and shaking her head, said, "Before one or two hundred bundles used to be enough [for one particular kind of exchange], but now everybody wants to have three or four hundred bundles in their baskets."

The primary source of cash for villagers now comes from the sale of carvings to tourists and from earnings sent home to relatives by Kiriwina women and men who are working in other parts of Papua New Guinea. Of course, not every man is a carver, nor does everyone receive money from "abroad," but through *valova* exchanges some villagers who are without cash can "find" tobacco and trade-store goods for themselves. A husband will ask his wife for some bundles so that he can "find" some betel nut or tobacco. On a minor level the functioning of *valova* exchanges allows for the proliferation of Western goods to those villagers who do not have cash at their disposal.

Variety and innovation are part of *valova* exchange. When I wanted to *valova* so I could accumulate my own bundles, my women friends told me not to buy tobacco because "too many women have tobacco to *valova*." They suggested instead that I buy candies and some large tins of fish in the trade store. Many villagers do not have enough cash to buy the fish, they said, and children are always eager for candy. On another occasion, one of my neighbors invited me to his house about 11 o'clock at night. Three fires were blazing in front of the house. Several men were relaxing around the fires with their wives, who were weaving skirts. The men were engaged in cooking scones in metal pans over the fires. The next morning, they would take the scones to neighboring villages and *valova* them for bundles—one bundle for one scone. Baking scones with self-rising flour and a tin of drippings purchased in the trade store is another new idea (and a very successful one) for *valova* exchanges.

Men who carve try to increase their output in order to obtain cash from tourists. They take yams, taro, or other garden produce to sell to the local people or to the Europeans living in Losuia, and they buy fish weekly from the coastal villagers and exchange the fish with inland villagers for bundles. Men from Fergusson Island now come by boat to Kiriwina to sell betel nuts, and large quantities of nuts are often purchased by men and divided up for *valova* exchanges. A husband's financial help to his wife, primarily through *valova* exchanges, gives her the wherewithal to make an impressive contribution to a women's mortuary ceremony. Not only are women working during the interim between the burial and the women's mortuary ceremony, but their husbands also have a great burden placed upon them.

V

The body is not allowed to remain long in peace—if the weird, noisy, and discordant din of singing, wailing, and haranguing can be so described. On the following evening, the body is exhumed, and inspected for signs of sorcery. . . . the body is taken out of the grave, and some of the bones are removed from it. This anatomical operation is done by the man's sons, who keep some of the bones as relics and distribute the others to certain of their relatives. This practice has been strictly forbidden by the Government . . . Yet the Trobrianders are so deeply attached to this custom that it is still clandestinely performed, and I have seen the jaw-bone of a man with whom I had spoken a few days before dangling from the neck of his widow.—Malinowski 1929, p. 155

Today the custom of removing bones from the body is not supposed to be practiced, because of government and mission influences, but I suspect (as Malinowski did) that in some circumstances parts of the custom continue. In addition to removal of bones, fingernails of the deceased are still worn by some people. The nails are inserted into small white cowrie shells, and women wear them as necklaces. Sometimes, in place of nails, the hair of the deceased is inserted into the shells.

Traditionally, human hair was woven into neck bands (*kuwa*), which were worn by workers. Two neck bands were worn by the deceased's spouse. Today, natural fibers are woven into mourning *kuwa* in place of human hair. During the women's mortuary ceremony, the neck bands worn by most workers are removed by the owners and colorful new skirts are given in payment. The spouse, father, and children of a male deceased continue to wear the mourning neck band after the women's mortuary ceremony. These people are the recipients of annual distributions of foodstuffs presented by the men of the deceased's *dala*.

Finally, when a spouse's mourning neck band is cut off, the spouse is completely released from further mourning ritual. The cutting occurs in a *sagali* called *winelawoulo*, in which women give skirts to the spouse and remove the neck band. The spouse may then wash the black from her or his body and wear bright clothing again. A new marriage can now be contracted. A spouse's mourning usually lasts for two years. When a spouse is old and does not remarry, he or she wears the *kuwa* until death. As long as the mourning neck band is worn, the spouse remains attached through exchange to the deceased's kin.

Workers care for the grave of the deceased, and this care falls into the same category as "carrying" the deceased's body. The wearing of part of the deceased's body or the care of the deceased after burial is also done by workers. These particular workers, however, are usually those who stand in the closest relationship to the deceased: for example, spouse, father, a man's children, and the deceased's father's sisters.

In addition to the bones, hair, and fingernails, parts of the personal possessions of the deceased are "carried" by the living. A dead man's personal basket (*sewega*) is encrusted with his living mementos: his arm bands, feathers, white cowrie shells, and rows of large betel nuts. Once I saw a man's basket to which a silver medal given him by the Australian administration after World War II had been attached (see plate 9). When the deceased is a woman, one her most beautiful red skirts (also called *sewega*), decorated with her earrings, white cowrie shells, arm bands, nosepiece, and special leaves used in love magic, is displayed.

As soon as a man dies, a woman worker, usually his daughter or his father's sister, prepares and carries his basket around her neck every day until the women's mortuary ceremony. In the same way, a dead woman's skirt is carried over the shoulder or hip of a woman (usually a daughter of the deceased's brother or her father's sister) until the women's mortuary ceremony.

The woman who carries the basket or skirt is paid in skirts by the deceased's kinswomen. When I asked women why they carried the dead person's things, they told me they carried them so that the "shadow" of the deceased's possessions would follow her or him to Tuma. In some cases, women carry a basket or a skirt for several years because their relationship with the deceased was very close. With a male deceased, this always indicates that the dead man had once been in a yam exchange relationship with the woman carrying his basket.[14]

Traditionally, the skull was the most important part of the deceased to be carried and the range of payments differs from that for the other relics. The deceased's father's sisters (called *tabu*) or a man's children attend to this ritual. Usually the head is removed only for those of Tabalu rank, for any other chief, or for married men and women who died while they were still young and handsome. Male workers exhume the body and remove the head, but women workers take the head to the beach. Through an extensive smoking process, they remove the flesh and dry out the skull bones.

When the women finish the process at the beach, they carry the skull to the hamlet manager of the *dala* of the deceased. The deceased's kinsmen and clan *keyawa* gather together yams, betel nuts, and pigs to be presented in a *sagali* to the workers. At the time of the *sagali*, the skull is decorated with red-and-black face

Plate 9. This woman, in mourning attire, is carrying the personal basket of her brother's deceased son, Kasai, from the village of Liluta. The basket is covered with betel nuts and decorated with woven arm bands, shell bands, a red kuwa necklace, and other ornaments belonging to the deceased. Kasai had been presented with the two crosses in the center of the basket during World War II, when the Allied forces stationed in Kiriwina gave medals to some important Kiriwina men for their help. Today these medals are still very highly prized.

painting, betel nuts are placed in the mouth, and shell decorations are attached.

After the *sagali*, the skull is returned to the caretaker, usually the father or sons of the deceased. Often the skull is guarded in this way for ten or twenty years. Finally the skull is again decorated. Workers now carry the skull to the beach, placing it on a cliff overlooking the sea. Upon returning from the beach, a very large *sagali*, called *sigilivalaguva*, is held in which food, male valuables, and women's wealth are distributed to the full range of kin of the spouse and the father of the deceased as well as to all the *keyawa* who participated in any of the mortuary events.

When old people die, their skulls are not removed. But, after many years, the bones of all Kiriwinans are exhumed. Each *dala* has its own special cave where bones of the deceased are placed. When the bones are dug out of the ground, they are carried to the cave of the *dala* of the deceased, regardless of where a person is buried originally. When the bones are finally restored to a *dala* place (*kabobalaguva* is the term for a cave with bones), a large *sagali* is held. This marks the last and final rite for the deceased. All workers who carried the bones receive male and female valuables from the deceased's kin. Thus finally even the bones of the deceased are returned to *dala* base.

Throughout the time that workers carry part of the body or care for the grave of the deceased, they are continually paid for their efforts in annual commemorative *sagali*, organized only by men. Each year one kind of object (e.g., yams, pork, betel nuts, taro pudding, or fish) is distributed. Each hamlet manager of a deceased's *dala* is responsible for holding one *sagali* each year. Other hamlet managers from neighboring villages who are mourning a deceased kinsperson belonging to the same clan join in the distribution. Payments are made from the deceased's *dala* to the spouse of the deceased (provided she or he has not remarried), to the father of the deceased, to the children of a male deceased, and to the sisters of the father of the deceased.

Thus the body of the deceased ritually continues its material existence. When the deceased's kinsmen lend these physical parts of the deceased, they begin to reconstitute the social network that the deceased created and maintained throughout his or her life.[15] Thus the social network remains in balance through extended distributions to those whose presence in the ego-centered network of the deceased has marked each stage of growth: father, spouse, father's sisters, and a man's children.

VI

[These views that natives live without any exchange of goods]
. . . ignore the fundamental human impulse to display, to share,
to bestow. They ignore the deep tendency to create social ties
through exchange of gifts. Apart from any consideration as to
whether the gifts are necessary or even useful, giving for the sake
of giving is one of the most important features of Trobriand soci-
ology, and, from its very general and fundamental nature, I sub-
mit that it is a universal feature of all primitive societies.—
Malinowski 1922, p. 175

Throughout the life cycle of a person, the process of Trobriand
exchange enables men and women to maintain complex networks of interdependent relationships. Regardless of the status of
each participant, each person is dependent upon the other. The
cyclical patterns of formal reciprocity aid in neutralizing the dis-
continuities of "other as opposition" (Lévi-Strauss 1971, p. 539)
by reducing the hierarchical categories of giver and receiver to a
state of mutual dependency.

But the danger inherent in all social relationships remains only
mollified and disguised. Death finally makes apparent the reality
that all social relationships are at best tenuous. Exchange can
never completely control individual desire. The extraordinary
attempt to avert the entropy of death reaffirms the mam-
moth achievement that each living person creates and sustains
throughout a lifetime of social interaction.

A death always constitutes an at least momentary short cir-
cuit of such achievement. Thus this constant danger creates the
need for equally constant attention and maintenance of social
ties. The failure to reaffirm the reciprocity within the social network as symbolized in the rituals of death would leave the basic
contradiction between personal gain and social cohesion unmodi-
fied, placing too great a stress on the system.

The emphasis on social relationships in the mortuary ceremonies compensates for dissonance within the system caused by

the antisocial event which death must always be. Death's capacity to destroy social function is symbolically negated by the ritualization of the diligent care of the deceased's body and grave. The role of sorcery as the cause of death further denies a natural end of the life cycle and reaffirms social responsibility for even the most antisocial event. Thus, the regeneration and strengthening of the social system neutralize the structurally disruptive force of death.

The emotional intensity surrounding death is heightened by the need to prove one's strength throughout the transition period and for many years following a death. Although power plays are made in the name of *dala*, they are primarily ego-centered. The need to control all property reveals itself during the mourning period: yams, taro, valuables, bundles of banana leaves, skirts, knowledge of magic, and social relationships all come together to be reevaluated, recycled, and thus reconstituted. The competition manifested in mortuary ceremonies, however, does not lie only within the sphere of politics. Mortuary ceremonies express the seeming contradiction of the oppositions between people and their continual dependence on each other.

The expression of these oppositions gives to mortuary ceremonies their momentum and force. The excessively circular exchanges and the ritualization of behavior serve to maintain oppositions while at the same time containing their potential disruptiveness. The high drama of mortuary ceremonies, however, is not an isolated event, for the dynamics of daily social interaction suggest that each individual is continually aware of others as opposition.

Face-to-face interaction is highly ritualized. A person's words and facial expressions should mask inner feelings and thoughts.[16] An angry demeanor threatens others and quickly weakens social bonds. As a person becomes more politically powerful, the code for social interaction is more explicitly defined. High-rank villagers and chiefs follow formal hereditary taboos that keep them socially and spatially isolated from others.

Whether commoner or chief, a person's generosity in giving things away allows others to move into her or his social space. Consistent beneficence serves as the means by which people bridge the disjuncture created by opposition. A composed face, however, prevents others from moving into ego's personal space. Repressed affect in exchange interactions saves each participant from total dependence on another, for such dependence would mean being under the control of someone else. Kiriwinans believe that no one can ever be certain of or have control over what someone else may do. Opposition is always part of social interaction not merely because people are in competition with each other, or because they are rivals or strangers, but because each individual is accorded the privilege of not revealing her or his thoughts.

Trobrianders recognize this discontinuity between private intent and public behavior. Therefore, Kiriwina people tend to read each other's thoughts by the way in which objects are exchanged. One day, I asked a man who had been sitting sorting yams for several hours what he was doing, and he told me he was sending yams to his married sister. He said he was sorting the largest yams and the ones free of any bruises, because if he sent poorquality yams his sister and her husband would say that he did not really want to give them yams (see plate 10).

Only through the giving of objects can the needs and interests of one person vis-à-vis another be communicated. The set of exchange objects is a nonverbal medium through which oppositions arc negotiated. While giving draws people together, the ritualization of exchange emphasizes their separateness. Bateson (1958, 1972) views opposition not as a fixed property of mind but as a dynamic communicative process. Cumulative experiences of individuals vis-à-vis each other lead to their mutual differentiation. Bateson (1958) coined the term "schismogenesis" to define this process. In the processual events of Trobriand exchange, the schismogenesis in social relations is reinforced at the same time that it is momentarily overcome.

Lévi-Strauss has taken up the philosophical problem of self in opposition to other by shifting the traditional emphasis from self and other *in opposition* to the other conceived *as opposition*.

> The problem of how myth arises is intimately connected with the problem of thought itself, the constitutive experience which is not that of an opposition between the ego and the other, but which is constituted by the experience of the other as opposition. Lacking this intrinsic property [of opposition] no moment of consciousness constituting the ego would be possible. If it were not comprehended as relationship, being would be the same as nothing. (1971, pp. 539–540; translation by Edward O'Flaherty S.J.)

My concern is not with the cognitive processes of thought and the universality and origin of such processes. I am suggesting that the mutual differentiation between individuals leads to a

*Plate 10. Kwaibwaga man carefully sorting the yams he will
send to his married sister and her husband*

definition of their relationship so that each ego views each other as opposition.

Therefore, I suggest that exchange does not mediate fixed opposed categories but continues to enforce opposition at the same time that opposition is momentarily overcome. Complete autonomy and total dependence are both anathema, for every villager feels that he or she has a degree of independence in any relationship. Death is a subversion of the balance between autonomy and control, for death is an invasion of individual power.

Thus, in order to restore balance and reduce trauma, death is surrounded by the most extravagant exchange situations, transacted over the longest period of time. Disguise becomes social practice as all others (nonclanspeople) paint their faces and bodies black and shave their heads. The statement "we hide who we are" can perhaps best be explained as a masking of personal power, for identity is in actual fact only symbolically disguised. The core of the side-taking is based on true *dala* identity, but the expansion of that nucleus to include others is accomplished through previous yam exchange relationships. This time the disguise is visually marked by the above means of body blackening and shaven heads. But it is shameful to say to any parties concerned that they need the help of others, thus intimating that members of the true *dala* are not strong enough. Further, splits within the *dala*, when men fight over the control of the body of the deceased and place of burial, are programed through reciprocal exchange channels. Even the public declaration of knowledge of magic spells is framed within the boundaries of an exchange game.

Death then calls into play the need for the greatest expression of resource control. Because individual resources are limited, mortuary exchanges display the energetic effectiveness of power relations between villagers. But, while mortuary distributions on one level display power, they also expose the inherent danger and tenuousness of relationships. The process of exchange creates a balance between control and autonomy, mediating the opposition between people yet giving full recognition to the fact that subjective desire and individual will are active components in any social relationship. At the moment that death occurs, more dramatically than any other, the balance between autonomy and each person's vulnerability is shattered. The fear generated at death, however, is only a magnification of the fear that underlies all relationships. In the context of fear, self-interest and self-preservation demand an exhibit of power as each individual at-tempts to restore her or his own weakened position. The largess of exchange distributions, in terms of quantity, energy, and kind, is testimony to the renewed integration and balance between fear and power, autonomy and control.

Chapter 4
Women's Mortuary Ceremonies

I

All the Melanesian women in New Guinea wear a petticoat made of fibre. Among the Southern Massim, this fibre skirt is long, reaching to the knees or below, whereas in the Trobriands it is much shorter and fuller, consisting of several layers standing out round the body like a ruff. . . . The highly ornamental effect of that dress is enhanced by the elaborate decorations made in three colours on the several layers forming the top skirt. On the whole, it is very becoming to fine young women, and gives to small slender girls a graceful, elfish appearance.—Malinowski 1922, p. 53

Vanoi once told me that women's mortuary ceremonies, which he called *sagali pela baloma* ("a distribution for the spirit of the deceased"), were very much like *sagali pela kula*, a highly competitive *kula* race in which men contest for shell valuables. Vanoi also said a women's mortuary ceremony was similar to *kayasa*, the competitive harvest where each man in a village attempts to outdo the others in the quality and size of his yam production. Thus, women's mortuary ceremonies constitute a game (*mwasawa*) of sorts in which women strive to be first. To be first, a woman must be affluent enough to give away more than five thousand bundles of banana leaves and twenty or thirty skirts in one day. But bundles and skirts are not women's wealth only at mortuary ceremonies. When large baskets of bundles and piles of skirts are stored in the recesses of houses, women have reputations for being "strong women."[1] Women constantly deal in bundles and skirts just as men traffic in yams and male valuables. In all competitive activities that men undertake (e.g., *kula*, cricket, warfare, *kayasa*), villagers say that men play games. In the women's mortuary ceremony, women have the opportunity to play similar games, as Vanoi described. During all the day's events, women go first; men follow behind. The male center stage is given over to women for their own performance, a performance of "total social phenomena" (Mauss 1954). With the sun as the spotlight on the central clearing, women at that moment are a composite of female and male behavior.

The objects of exchange which denote the wealth of women are classified under the general term *doba*. *Doba* refers to two specific categories of objects: colorful fiber skirts—traditionally dyed red and purple, made from banana leaves and trimmed with pieces of white bleached pandanus—and *nununiga*, bundles made from individual strips of dried banana leaves. I was unable to find any origin stories relating to the creation of women's wealth. The women I questioned said that Kilivila women always knew how to make bundles and skirts. The founders (*tabu*) emerged from the place of origin with the knowledge of making bundles, just as they emerged with their *dala* identity intact.

The term *nunu* means "breast, nipple, mother's milk." It is a term of endearment used after a mother's death. As a verb, *nunu* means "to suck." *Nunu* also means "same *dala*." The suffix of *nununiga* is possibly from the word *naga*, "to share." The duplicate form of *naga*, to emphasize the sharing, is *niganaga*.[2]

Nununiga have no use value, only exchange value. They are made from the same banana-leaf material as are the skirts; the difference is in the preparation. When bundles are too old to use as separate objects of wealth, the individual strips can be fringed and used as fibers in the weaving of women's skirts.

The value of sexuality appears clearly encapsulated in the red skirts designated as women's wealth. Young girls wear these skirts when they parade about engaged in adolescent ventures, each girl using her own self to attract and entice. When women marry, their beauty and attractiveness gradually diminish (in the eyes of Trobrianders). These same skirts become objects with exchange value in their own right. Married women never wear these skirts unless they join younger women in intervillage dances, reversing their marital status to once again appear young and beautiful. Thus, at marriage, women's inherent sexuality is symbolically masked but culturally transformed into an object of wealth.

Bits of ethnographic data from other areas of Melanesia seem to indicate that women's skirts denote similar symbolic qualities. On Goodenough Island in the Massim, according to Michael

Young, men develop an illness called *doke* ("skirt"). When a wife commits adultery, her husband's stomach swells because a woman's skirt is thought to be growing in his belly. "Symbolically, the cuckolded husband is feminized by the growth of a 'skirt' within him" (Young 1971, p. 212).

Among the Iatmul, Gregory Bateson reported that women traditionally removed their skirts and stood naked during the burial of their husband, brother, or son (1958, p. 154). Ian Hogbin described initiation rites for young Wogeo girls. At their first menstruation, women don mourning attire, and a girl's skirt, tattered and dirty, is ritually buried (1970, p. 130). According to the Wogeo, the skirt represents a corpse and thus there seems to be some connection between skirts, female fertility, and death. The Melpa women of Mount Hagen use their net bags and aprons as "small gifts" which play a role in marriage and mortuary exchanges (M. Strathern 1972, pp. 14–15, 116, 242). Further, a bride's most important net bag "symbolizes the whole dowry" (p. 117).

There also appears to be some exchange and symbolic significance attached to women's skirts and net bags (or a "woman's carrying net," as Heider called it) among the Dugum Dani. Women wear a skirt made of braided cord, and the braids are woven by a man for his daughter or his wife (Heider 1970, p. 248). Net bags are exchanged among women in mortuary ceremonies, but Karl Heider reported that this is "a woman's affair, and the men ignore it" (p. 156). Yet, in a later stage of the funeral rites, women bring their carrying nets, which are spread out in the courtyard, and men's exchange stones and shell bands—knit bands two meters in length with cowrie shells and feathers and furs attached—are placed on top of the rows of net bags (p. 161). Further, men carry sacred objects in net bags and at certain times, to conceal themselves from ghosts, they cover their heads with net bags (p. 249).

From these data, however, it seems that only in the Trobriands are skirts and the value of women given the dimensions of significant social and cultural roles. A question for future research is whether the Trobriand case is in fact distinctive or whether the importance of women in other Melanesian societies, at least in a structural sense, is disguised by the men in these societies. Have the ethnographers been deceived by male comments and the seemingly trivial economic and symbolic value placed upon skirts and net bags?

The importance of women in Trobriand society does not appear to be an isolated case, however, in the Massim area. In a recent Ph.D. dissertation on exchange and marriage on Panaeati Island in the Louisiade Archipelago, Stuart Berde described women's *hagali* distributions performed following a death. On Panaeati, women engage in yam presentations rather than exchanges of manufactured objects of wealth, and the sociopolitical significance of women's control over yam exchanges is explicitly defined in terms of land rights for men. Further, a ritual of beautification is undertaken by these women prior to the distribution. In this ritual three brightly colored, new fibrous skirts are put on over the mourning skirt, and all the skirts are trimmed in an event called "cutting the mourning skirt" (1974, p. 174).

In Kiriwina, the leaves of only one variety of banana tree (*wakeya*) are used for making both skirts and bundles.[3] Women own these banana trees. They inherit the trees when their mothers or sisters die, and men plant new trees for their wives. The leaves of the *wakeya* tree are quite large, measuring approximately ten to twelve feet in length by two feet in width. One leaf makes one bundle—one *nununiga*. (See appendix 2 for the technology of manufacturing bundles.)

Women divide bundles into categories of new, clean, old, or dirty. In all exchanges of bundles, whether for distribution or for accumulation, each category has special significance. New bundles (*yawovau*) must be made prior to each women's mortuary ceremony for a specific distribution which occurs at the beginning of the *sagali*. When freshly made, these bundles are very light tan, almost white.

Old bundles (*yabwabogwa*) are those which through time and use have become flattened out and have lost the fullness of newly made bundles. They are also bundles in which individual strips have become torn and creased. Old bundles can be—and often are—taken apart and remade into clean bundles. Torn strips are discarded, creased strips are flattened out with the blade of a knife, and the entire process of tying the strips together is undertaken so that the strips are once again stiffened and the bundle appears to have most of its original fullness. When bundles are finally too dirty (*yapagatu*) to be used, they are taken apart and the strips are dyed and fringed for use in the weaving of skirts. For exchanges to repay villagers for shaving their heads, dirty bundles may be used.

Clean bundles (*migileu*) are bundles which have either been remade or which have been used so little that they still look fresh and full. The color of dirty and clean bundles seems less significant than the shape. Clean bundles are sorted and carefully selected prior to a mortuary distribution. I discovered the im-

portance of clean bundles when Yaulibu, a woman who had a
reputation for knowing how to make very fine skirts, came to
help me sort my basket of bundles. She wanted to make certain
that I had some clean bundles for a mortuary distribution a few
days hence. Because most of my bundles were in fact dirty and
old, Yaulibu and several other women spent the morning trans-
forming some of my bundles into clean ones. They told me that,
in the women's mortuary ceremony, if a woman put dirty and old
bundles in the piles intended for exchanges made to men who
had given the owners raw yams for distribution, "women would
scream at her and call her dirty. But when you see clean bundles
you know they came from yams."

There are two major categories of skirts: *sepwana* and *doba*.
Sepwana, mourning skirts, are used as appropriate wearing apparel for mourning observances. These skirts are made of natural-
colored banana fibers. Other styles of skirts in this category are
made of coconut fibers dyed blue or black, but knowledge of the
manufacture of these latter styles has been imported from other
islands in the Massim. *Doba* are colorful skirts elaborate in decoration and styling. Although traditionally the skirts were red and
purple, today commercial dyes offer more variety. The wearing of
these skirts symbolizes the attributes of beauty, attraction, and
youth. As objects of exchange, these skirts are used in a variety of
ways. (See appendix 3 for details of skirt manufacture.)

All women weave skirts, but to weave a *sepwana* is a special
distinction. Young girls from about the age of seven are encouraged to experiment and weave skirts from natural fibers. Girls of
marriageable age are watched by their elders to see if they know
how to make skirts properly and if they work hard with their
mothers to prepare for mortuary distributions. A boy's parents
will often object to his wanting to marry a particular girl, if they
think that she is lazy and does not know how to work well in
the garden or if she does not know how to make mats and skirts.
A girl's reputation is usually founded on her physical beauty, as
well as whether or not she is a strong worker, just as a boy's reputation centers around his physical attractiveness and his ability
to be a productive gardener.

By the same token, a married woman is often judged by her
ability to make fine skirts. One of the sharpest insults is to accuse
a woman of having dirty skirts. A situation which arose in the village one day will illustrate this point. Two young unmarried girls
began to fight with each other. Bomiroru told Inatuma that she
had an ugly face and that her mother had dirty skirts. Bunemiga,

the local government counselor, called a meeting in which he began to chastise the girls:

> Bomiroru, if you call other people dirty, that is very bad.
> It is very hard [i.e., bad, wrong] to use those words and it is
> very hard for other village people to hear those words. People
> will be angry with you because they are all making good
> skirts. Listen while I tell you something: we should not say
> dirty skirts to anyone. You never hear people say other
> people have dirty skirts. Those are very hard words for you to
> use. If one girl says those words to another girl, that girl will
> get very angry with her, because all of you know that your
> work is for skirts. Some women and girls work well for skirts
> and some do not work so well, but nobody says those words.
> When your mothers did a *sagali*, did you help them with *do-
> ba* or not? It is not good for you to say those things. We
> should not say that other people have dirty skirts.

Bomiroru's mother was worried because she thought that Inatuma's mother would be angry with her. She said to Inatuma's
mother:

> I never said those words about you, because you and I work
> for *doba*. But you are better than I and you always beat me.
> Maybe Bomiroru told a lie, because you always work well.
> Nobody in Kwaibwaga can say that about you. If we say you
> are dirty people, that is very hard for us and we would not say
> those things. You must forget it, because that was only Bo-
> miroru telling a lie.

   In other situations, however, women will often refer to themselves as being dirty. When women are observing mourning ritual
by wearing mourning skirts, painting their bodies black, and/or
shaving their heads, they talk about how dirty they look. One
day I was talking with about a dozen women, who along with
most of the other women in the village were going to take yams
to a coastal village and exchange (*wasi*) them for fish. Earlier that
morning some of the men had instructed the women to take
baths and put on clean clothes before they went on the trip, and
the women were complaining to me about this. They said, "How
can we look clean when we are wearing black for those people
who have died? We always look dirty because we have to work so
hard for bundles." The majority of adult women in a village are
usually in some kind of mourning attire, whether or not they are
directly related to the primary mourners of the deceased, because

shaving one's head or wearing black is one way in which bundles can be accumulated for one's own use. But men told me later that they only wanted the women to wash the dust from their bodies from working in the gardens. Because the women were taking the yams to another village, they should look clean.

There are two kinds of *sepwana*: a long, full skirt woven every time a women's mortuary ceremony is held and a shorter, less voluminous skirt which is worn daily as an ordinary mourning skirt. Women often wear old faded dresses instead of the mourning skirts, and men who traditionally wore black body paint and unbleached pandanus pubic coverings may now wear dark blue or black shirts and shorts. Some of the women and men tie a dark blue ribbon around their upper arms to signify that they are in mourning for someone. The use of the ribbon and dark clothing is, I was told, a new idea which gained popularity as more people could afford to buy trade-store clothing. There are, however, many who still dress traditionally.

Both visually and ritually the long *sepwana* skirt stands in a category by itself.[4] One or two women wear a long skirt at each women's mortuary ceremony, and these women are the most active contributors to the distributions which take place throughout the day. There is no way to confuse the identity of these women because the long skirt is unlike any other style of skirt.

The skirt reaches almost to the ground. As the woman wearing the *sepwana* skirt strides haughtily into the center of the hamlet to throw her bundles, the natural-colored fibers (also called *sepwana*) barely skim the ground. Moreover, the skirt is not just long, it is extremely full, and the fibers are cut in various lengths so that the bottom half of the skirt appears tapered. When the *sepwana* skirt is worn, it gracefully mushrooms out from the body of the woman.

A few weeks prior to the women's mortuary ceremony two nearly identical *sepwana* are woven. The weaving event is called *vituvatu sepwana*. Each skirt is woven on a different day, usually by different people. One skirt is made by the kinswomen of the deceased's father. Female owners are helped by female *keyawa* from their own clan and their father's clan. Often neighbors and friends of these women join in the weaving in order to receive payments of bundles at the women's mortuary ceremony and increase their own wealth. The other skirt is made by the kinswomen, *keyawa*, and friends of the spouse of the deceased (see plate 11). If a person's father is dead, then only one long mourning skirt is made for the spouse and, conversely, if the spouse is dead or if

Plate 11. Part of the group of women assembled in Kabulula village for the weaving of a long sepwana *skirt, organized by the women who are members of the same* dala *as Obwelela's widow*

the dead person had no spouse, then only one long mourning skirt is made by the father's kinswomen.

The weaving of the long mourning skirt is finished in one day. On that day, forty to seventy women congregate around one house to make the skirt. The weaving is done by one woman, but those who come to the weaving each bring from five to twenty dried banana fibers, ready to be woven, for the skirt. The number of fibers contributed by each woman depends upon her relationship to the father or the spouse.

The day decided upon for weaving is usually about a week or two before the women's mortuary ceremony. When the message travels around the villages that the *sepwana* is being woven, everyone knows that the women's mortuary ceremony will take place shortly. The decision about the appropriate day for the weaving is reached by the owners. When men have gathered enough of their own yams and yams contributed from other men and when women have amassed large amounts of bundles and skirts, it is time to weave the mourning skirt. Women's mortuary ceremonies can only take place, however, from the end of April to December, when there are enough good yams available.[5]

When one long skirt is finished it is put away until both skirts are completed. Then all women who assisted in the making of both skirts reassemble together for the cutting of *sepwana* (*lituti-la sepwana*). Both skirts are cut on the same day in the deceased's burial hamlet. No special name is given to distinguish one skirt from the other.

A few women sit on the ground with the skirts spread out in front of them. The women begin to cut some of the fibers from the underneath part of the skirt; this gives the skirt its tapered and layered appearance. When the tapering is finished, the women trim the bottom or hem of the skirt. All the fibers removed are presented to the women, to be used again in the weaving of all other kinds of skirts. Each fiber is also a formal invitation sent out to the principals who will attend the mortuary ceremony, which usually takes place a day or two following the cutting of the *sepwana*.

As the women begin to cut the long *sepwana* skirt, other women sit close to them on the ground within easy reach of the skirts. As soon as the bottom of the last skirt is trimmed, the women sitting close by grab for the skirts, literally pouncing upon them. The first woman to take a skirt for herself is the one who will wear the skirt. But the skirts are so long and heavy—and usually several women are competing for each one—that to be able to grab the skirt away is quite a feat. There are crying, screaming, shouting, and fighting in what ultimately becomes a tug of war. It is at this point that men come into the melee. Usually the men settle the quarrel over who is to wear the *sepwana*.

My informants explained quarreling over *sepwana* to me in the following way:

> When a man dies, both his daughter and his sister
> want to wear the long mourning skirt. The sister's kin come
> and support her and, similarly, the daughter's kin come and
> support her. So two groups are quarreling. The dead man
> made yam gardens for his sister and his daughter. Because he
> made those gardens, they must both work hard for *sagali*.
> Who wins depends upon who is the strongest one: the one
> who will pull the skirt away and the one who has the stron-
> gest relatives. If these girls do not quarrel, people will say to
> them, "Why didn't you quarrel, that man already has made
> yams for you."
>
> If a woman dies, there is no quarreling over who will wear
> the long mourning skirt. Her daughter will wear it and, if she
> has no daughter, then her sister will wear it or her sister's

daughter. If a woman does not have a daughter or a sister,
then any woman for whom the dead woman's kinsmen
made a yam garden will wear the long mourning skirt.

Theoretically, this is the way that the wearer of the long
mourning skirt is chosen. As one would suspect, there is a bit
more involved in the quarrel over the long mourning skirt and the
subsequent victors. Women who wear the skirts must make the
largest contribution of bundles on the day of the women's mortuary ceremony. They must contribute at least one hundred (usually more) new bundles and also must contribute dirty and clean
bundles to every transaction. If a woman manages her accumulation and distribution of bundles properly, she is then the big-
woman (*napweyaveka*) of the day.

Women working alone cannot manufacture the huge quantities
of bundles that a *sepwana* wearer needs. Although all women's
husbands help them accumulate additional bundles through *valova* exchanges, *sepwana* wearers must be able to depend on
wealthy men. Not only do men help their wives, but men also
help their married daughters in the early stages of the daughter's
marriage. When someone in a man's *dala* dies, that man will
handsomely support his daughter in accumulating great amounts
of wealth if it is to his political advantage to "make his name
big."

In 1971, a woman died in Kwaibwaga. Four women fought over
the cutting of the *sepwana* skirt. In figure 5, I have indicated the
four women and their relationship to the dead woman. One skirt
was taken by one of the sisters of the dead woman, and all the
other sisters agreed that she should wear it. The other three wom-
en fought very hard over the remaining skirt, until finally the
daughter of the third-eldest brother pulled the skirt away, sat
down upon it, and began to cry. Bunemiga, her father, then said
she should wear the skirt, but the others objected because they
said she was too young. Bunemiga's daughter had only been married for four years, but finally her father succeeded in giving her
the skirt.

This incident has a political twist. Although the eldest brother
of the *dala* was a very respected man, his younger brother Bunemiga was more strategically aggressive. This was apparent in the
dynamics of the mortuary ceremony, and in other political activities (such as *kula*) Bunemiga was always trying to gain an advantage over his elder brothers.

Several months earlier Bunemiga had killed one of his pigs and

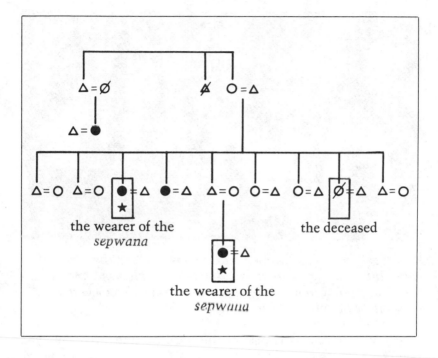

Figure 5. Wearing the sepwana

had taken it to a manager in another village hamlet who had no connection with the mortuary exchanges. Pork exchanges for repayment in bundles constitute the most significant *valova* exchanges. When a hamlet manager receives pork for *valova*, he then divides the pieces of pork among the hamlet residents, each of whom chooses one part of the pig. Each person is then obligated to return an appropriate number of new bundles of banana leaves at a later time. Men choose the pork, but their wives must sit and make new bundles to pay for the pork that they, their husbands, and their children have eaten. I have heard women complain to men publicly in a village meeting, "You men like to eat pork, but you do not have to work hard for bundles."

Each part of the pig brings the return of a specified number of bundles. For example, one strip of pork as wide as two fingers and the length of a hand is worth 10 bundles; a hind leg of the pig is

Plate 12. Kwaibwaga women and men inspecting the presentation of approximately 1,700 new bundles of banana leaves and a few valuables, which constitute a valova return from an earlier presentation of a pig

worth 40 bundles, as is part of the head portion from the eyes up. The entrails are worth 50 bundles, and the entrails cooked with the blood of the pig must be repaid with 120 bundles. This latter portion usually goes to the man to whom the pork was given, but he has a further responsibility in this exchange beyond making certain that the correct number of new bundles is returned.

A pig is killed for *valova* shortly after a person dies, so that the women who make new bundles for payment have several months to do so. New bundles, however, are not the only things returned for payment. The man to whom the pork was given must return valuables (*katupumapula*) to the man who gave him the pork. Bunemiga received 1,750 new bundles, 1 clay pot, 5 pieces of calico, 2 fibrous skirts, and A$4.60 from his pork *valova*. The valuables signify that the *valova* exchange operates as a permanent exchange relationship between two men. At any time, the man to whom the pork was given has the right to bring pork to the first man for his own *valova*. A reciprocal exchange of pork for *valova* is called *kulamapu* (see plate 12).

Therefore, the conversion of a pig into bundles through *valova* exchange is much more than a casual exchange. Not only must a man have a pig to kill, he must also be able and willing to reciprocate at a later time with bundles and valuables. Thus only men of substance (i.e., land managers or wealthy men) usually participate in *valova* exchanges for pork. A large pile of new bundles prominently displayed at a women's mortuary ceremony is evidence of this kind of male transaction and relationship. Bunemiga was trying to supersede his elder brothers. He was the only brother who had a pig to *valova*. Thus, no one was in a position to rigorously oppose his daughter's right to the mourning skirt. If there exists rivalry between *dala* members when a woman dies, the ritual ceremonies following her death are usually excellent opportunities to play the Melanesian game of one-upmanship between blood kinsmen. When a man dies, however, the stakes can be much higher because men are forced to demonstrate the range of their control. Therefore, the fighting over the wearing of the long mourning skirts is more serious and intense. Tension begins to peak with the announcement of the weaving and cutting of the long *sepwana* skirts. But the culmination of months of hard work for all connected in any way to the deceased is realized in the women's mortuary ceremony.

II

In the mortuary distributions of food and wealth, based on the idea that the members of the deceased's sub-clan give payment to the other relatives for their share in the mourning, women play a conspicuous rôle, and conduct some parts of the ceremonial distributions themselves.—Malinowski 1929, p. 37

At daybreak on the morning of the women's mortuary ceremony for Obwelela, a young married man in his early thirties who died suddenly in April 1972, several residents in his hamlet began to carefully clean the central area (*baku*).[6] Every bit of space is cleared of dirt and debris. The centers of many hamlets are usually kept free of grass, but for several hours a few villagers carefully remove any clump of grass that has begun to grow. Women are busy counting their bundles and skirts. On the day before the *sagali*, men of the *dala* of the deceased spend all their time chopping firewood and grating coconut in preparation for making taro pudding. Now they are busy starting the cooking fires. The sound of pigs being killed pierces the early morning haze. Slowly, excitement begins to mount, invading every corner of the hamlet. By nine o'clock women, children, and a few men from other villages begin to arrive. The women immediately arrange themselves and their baskets of wealth around the central place.[7] Within the next hour, the hamlet is bursting with sounds, colors, and activities of several hundred villagers.

The sun is hot, and some of the women are sitting under awnings made of palm leaves or pieces of calico—more to protect their wealth than themselves. The women closest to the center form sets of clusters. Their relationships to the deceased are apparent from the spatial arrangement. These are the women (owners and daughters of male owners) who will give all their bundles and skirts away. At the beginning of the *sagali*, each group of women is completely surrounded by baskets and individual piles of bundles. For a moment, the scene reminded me of a marketplace with women sitting at their canopied stalls calling to and joking with each other. The sounds of their conversations and directives contained elements of both camaraderie and competition.

Two women in the center of the *sagali* are wearing long *sepwana* skirts. At the beginning of the *sagali* these women are surrounded with more baskets of bundles than any other women. Interspaced between the principal givers, the owners, are other women—clan *keyawa* and the kin of fathers of the owners who came to help. These women contribute to some distributions but not to all of them. Behind these women sit all the women (workers and their *keyawa* and wives of male owners) who receive bundles and skirts throughout the day.

Men are lounging around the periphery of the hamlet, sitting with young children. Nonparticipating women who have come just to watch or to *valova* things for bundles also sit away from the center. Some men help their wives or sisters with large baskets. Once I overheard a man admonishing his wife because she was not putting her bundles and skirts into the center quickly and often enough. If a woman does not contribute very much, it looks as if her husband did not financially support her. Single boys and girls dressed in their colorful clothes stroll together in the background near the houses. Large clay pots of taro pudding cook, and occasionally a man steps down from his veranda to stir the pudding.[8] Baskets of yams and bunches of taro are piled together in several places around the hamlet. Of all the houses in the hamlet, two are most important: the house of the spouse and the house where the father of the deceased is staying. If both the spouse and the father of the deceased are alive, they each sit in a separate house during the women's mortuary ceremony. If either one has already died, then another blood kinsman takes her or his place. In one *sagali*, a son took his mother's place as the spouse of the deceased. In another *sagali*, the father's brother of the deceased took the place of the father.

Although black is used predominantly for mourning, the overall impression around the hamlet is of a palette of brilliant colors. Even the black body paint appears as intense as the red fibers of skirts. The piles of bundles, their whiteness heightened by the sun, make a strong backdrop against which the women stand. Some women in the center are in black. These women are from other clans: daughters of the deceased's kinsmen and the sisters of the father of the deceased. The deceased's own kinswomen wear natural-colored mourning skirts, but their bodies remain unpainted and their heads unshaven. Prior to the beginning of the *sagali*, other women come to the owners with additional bundles or skirts. These women are "friends"; whenever they need to do a *sagali*, the bundles will be reciprocated by the women who just received them.

Just before the *sagali* is about to begin, lines of women queue up. Each line marches single file across the central open place to a specified woman sitting among the primary circle of women; the transactions are called *kabiyamila*. Each marching woman carries a colorful skirt, or a stick with bundles of banana leaves attached, or a piece of trade-store calico or clothing.

All women who receive annual gifts of baskets of yams and bunches of taro from their brothers line up in single file and walk across the central area to their brothers' wives. In this exchange, each woman who is an owner is on display as she receives these additional objects of wealth to supplement her own stores. Her husband is also on display in that his kinswomen make the contribution (see fig. 6).

Following this parade of colors and women, the *sagali* begins with the presentation of a huge pile of new bundles, carefully tied together and symmetrically arranged on a flat woven basket. They are presented by the two women who are wearing the long mourning skirts, each of whom has contributed at least one hundred new bundles. The two piles, one for the father's kinswomen

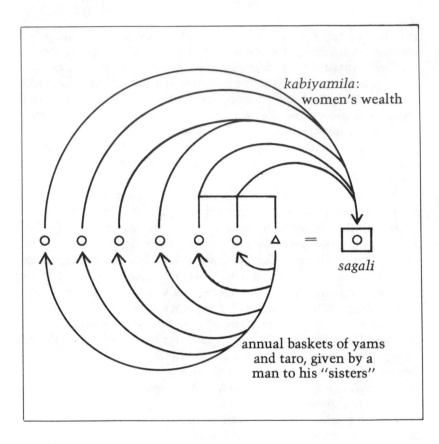

Figure 6. Exchanges between a man, his "sisters," and his wife prior to the women's mortuary ceremony

and the other for the spouse's kinswomen, who made the long skirts, remain intact throughout the day's activities. Later, the bundles are divided among all the women who contributed fibers toward the making of the long mourning skirts. On top of each pile is placed one or two beautifully decorated skirts, payment to the woman who actually wove the long *sepwana* skirt.

This exchange is called *doba pela sepwana* ("women's wealth for the *sepwana* skirt"). When the piles are divided, kinswomen of the spouse and father each take twenty bundles; other women who helped because they needed bundles, but are not directly related, receive ten bundles. Figure 7 is a replication of the direction of the major payments: the workers now receive bundles and skirts from the owners.

The routine which is to continue for most of the day then begins. One woman, wearing the long mourning skirt, walks into the center and drops five or ten bundles on the ground, calling out a word to define why the bundles are given and the recipient's name. Then other women (owners of the *sagali*, daughters of the men of the deceased's *dala*, *keyawa*, and friends) hurry into the center and add bundles. Bundles are arranged in stacks of five, and women usually contribute five or ten bundles to each distribution. One woman then comes into the center, gathers all the bundles, and carries them back to her own baskets.

The same kind of exchange goes on and on for hours, although each individual exchange does not usually take more than three or four minutes. However, during the day there are differences in the styles and amounts of distributions. Some bundles are thrown directly on the ground, while other bundles are carried into the center on flat woven baskets and placed on the ground. In some distributions, skirts and pieces of calico are added to the pile of bundles. Some individual exchanges are quite large, with as many as one thousand bundles and ten skirts; other exchanges only have twenty or thirty bundles thrown. In some exchanges the names of married men and young boys are called, but only women go into the center to give or receive bundles.

During the course of the day, women often shout and even fight with each other: "You already called that woman's name!" "You forgot that woman!" "Put more *doba* on that pile!" There are also much laughter and joking: women making fun of each other and calling swear words to each other. As the day wears on, more men arrive, but they remain in the background. One woman shouts to the others, "Hurry up and finish, we want to eat!"

Fourteen separate sets of exchanges, in addition to the two des-

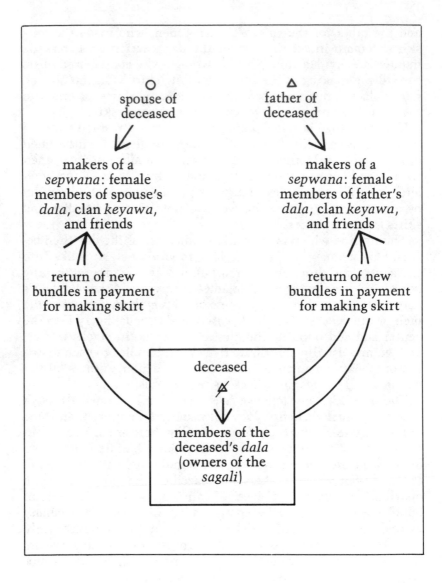

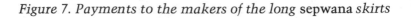

Figure 7. Payments to the makers of the long **sepwana** *skirts*

cribed above, comprise the distribution. Each set of exchanges is briefly outlined below.

Iwoulasi sepwana. At the time of death, women workers bring mourning skirts of regular length (*veyola sepwana*) to the deceased's kinswomen. These skirts are worn until after the women's mortuary ceremony. The owners rush into the center of the *sagali*, shouting "Who brought *sepwana*?" while they hold up bundles in their hands. The numbers of bundles distributed to each woman depend upon the kind of mourning skirts that women brought. Coconut-fiber skirts are worth only twenty bundles per skirt—the knowledge of the manufacture of these skirts is imported—while traditional banana-fiber skirts are worth fifty bundles each.

Uvisalawaga. When a *kula* man dies, the owners give bundles to each *kula* canoe owner who lives in another hamlet in Kilivila. The name of each canoe is called, and the canoe owner's wife claims the bundles. About sixty bundles are given to each canoe owner.

Bubu. One of the women weaving the long *sepwana* skirt calls out the names of friends of the deceased and the specific activity which they shared. For example, at Obwelela's *sagali*, the woman called "Yobwita, for playing the guitar," "Monobogwa, for going to Losuia." When a woman dies, women's names are called. About one hundred bundles are given to each friend. Sometimes a skirt is added to the pile of bundles. Old bundles are thrown on the ground for these exchanges.

Kalimapuyoyu. Names of those who have recently died in other villages who belonged to the same clan as the deceased are called by the owners. These deceased are clan *keyawa* to the owners. About thirty bundles per name are given. Old bundles are thrown on the ground.

Lisaladabu nakakau and *lisaladabu tomakapu*. The term *lisaladabu* means payment for shaving one's head. The first exchange is made to the spouse (called *nakakau* when in mourning) and the second is made to the father (called *tomakapu* when in mourning). This is a large payment (about two hundred bundles and several skirts each) for observing the mourning ritual of remaining secluded, shaving the head, and wearing black.

Lisaladabu. Those workers who shaved their heads and painted their bodies black receive old (or even dirty) bundles from the owners. All these people originally each received a first payment of ten bundles at *tadabali*, the second *sagali*. Between twenty to sixty bundles per person are given.

Kaweluwa (for uncooked food). Payment is made by the owners to those workers who brought uncooked food at *tadabali* and also throughout the major mourning period. The amount of bundles returned depends upon the kind of food brought, but all bundles given in these exchanges must be clean ones. Payment for uncooked food is a most important part of the day's distribution. All bundles are given in baskets, rather than being thrown directly on the ground. If a woman gives old or dirty bundles other women scream at her and call her *natokamu*, which means "you are only eating." In my informant's words, this means "all you do is eat, you do not know how to make *doba*." The following distinctions are made according to types of food brought—yams: fifty bundles; pumpkin, cassava, and *bisiya* (aerial yams): twenty to thirty bundles; trade-store food mixed with other produce: fifty bundles. In addition to the smaller payments, one large basket of three hundred bundles is usually given to both a spouse and a father.

Kaweluwa (cooked food). People who brought cooked food during the time of mourning receive payment. Old bundles are thrown on the ground, and twenty bundles per person is the usual amount given. The names for payments for cooked food are now often read out of a notebook because there are so many people to repay. (Once I attended a political meeting about *kula*, where Waibadi said, "Today, we run *kula* with pencil and paper like a trade store.")

Kaymelu. This is the most important exchange involving bundles. In this exchange women give bundles by name to their own kinsmen. If a woman does not have enough bundles to distribute for all exchanges, she will always save clean bundles for *kaymelu*. In the previous exchanges women are not usually selective about contributing bundles for a particular name, but in this exchange everyone waits with their bundles (except the women wearing the *sepwana*, who still try to contribute to every distribution) and adds them for specific men. This exchange is given for all men who brought raw yams and taro plants to any of the previous and the present *sagali* (see plate 13). Men's wives claim the *doba*.

Only clean bundles can be used and all bundles are placed in baskets. Skirts are also added to the bundles. The amount varies widely. For example, one thousand bundles, eight skirts, and four pieces of calico were given to one man, while only twenty to thirty bundles were given to another man. The discrepancy centers around relationships to the deceased: brothers and other blood

Plate 13. Women, one of whom is wearing the long sepwana *skirt, carrying baskets of bundles of banana leaves into the center of the women's mortuary ceremony, for the important series of presentations of women's wealth to men who contributed yams to all the mortuary ceremonies for the deceased*

kinsmen of the deceased receive the most wealth because they have contributed the most yams. Sons of the deceased (if the deceased is male) also can receive large amounts of wealth, if they have brought many yams for the owners to use. All women who have ever received raw yams from a man must contribute when that man's name is called.

An older man will usually come into the center to help the women call the names for these payments. Women have difficulty remembering the names of all men who have contributed yams, for the giving of yams is the domain of men. This is the only time that a man comes into the center to help the women.

Kalipewalela kabeyamila. This is the last exchange of bundles. All women owners go into the center of the *sagali* together, each carrying a small basket. Each woman shouts "Give some bundles for my husband," because her husband helped her perform the *sagali.* Other women throw clean bundles into her basket. About fifty bundles are given to each woman.

Kalilakuvili. The owners (who are not painted black) now take brightly colored skirts and tie them around the waists and over the mourning skirts of women who belong in the worker category (i.e., women from other clans). But these women have played a dual role by standing in the center of the *sagali* and distributing bundles and skirts with the owners. These women are daughters of a male deceased; daughters of the deceased's kinsmen; daughters "following their mothers," who stand in the above two categories to the deceased; women who lived as an adopted child with a man and do *sagali* either for him or for anyone in his *dala*—each of these women has at some time received raw yams from a man in the deceased's *dala;* and sisters of the father of the deceased. After the skirts are given, the owners then cut off the mourning neck bands and remove the black mourning beads. Often the women fight to keep their beads and neck bands. Women should fight if they have received many yams from a man in the deceased's *dala.* Removal releases them from further mortuary ritual. Now each woman can wash her body. She has been publicly changed from mourner to nonmourner, from dirty to clean.

Kalakeyala kakau (*kakau* is also a term for *nakakau*, "widow"). Villagers form long lines at the side of the hamlet. Each person in line carries a valuable. Men carry clay pots, ax blades, shell decorations, pieces of calico tied to long poles, which look like large flags, or dollar bills tied to little sticks, resembling a small souvenir-type flag. Women walk first, each woman carrying a brightly colored, beautifully decorated skirt. Some women (who

Plate 14. Women marching with their skirts as valuables to the house of the deceased's spouse, in a women's mortuary ceremony held in Kwaibwaga in 1971

have been too busy or too lazy) carry pieces of calico. Each line of women and men proceeds first to the house of the deceased's spouse (see plate 14). The hamlet manager of the spouse's *dala* stands beside the house and grabs all the valuables except the women's skirts. These skirts are piled up high on the veranda and distributed to all the spouse's kinswomen. Male valuables are not so freely distributed. This exchange, my informants said, is to bring valuables to the spouse for having taken care of the deceased when he or she was alive. The villagers who present the valuables include those of the same blood and also those from the same place of origin; men and women who at some time received raw yams from the deceased or from a male relative of the deceased; and women and men who are clan *keyawa* to the deceased's kin.

This distribution and a similar one made to the father of the deceased are among the most important exchanges, ranking with the distributions of bundles for men who contributed yams (see fig. 8). Between one hundred and two hundred villagers participate. Men and women walk together: lines of men in back of lines of women. This is the only exchange in which both sexes participate together. In this exchange women's skirts are called *veguwa*, the same term used to designate male valuables. In the more democratic redistribution of skirts to all kinswomen of the father

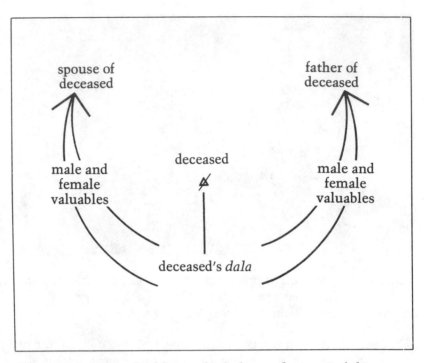

Figure 8. Giving valuables to the father and spouse of the deceased at the end of the women's mortuary distribution. The deceased's dala *includes owners of the* sagali *plus all those related to the deceased through previous yam exchanges.*

and the spouse of the deceased, women make the presentations of their wealth a *dala* affair. In the quick control of male valuables by one or two men, the difference in the power structure between female and male domains is significantly demonstrated.

Kalakeyala kapu (kapu is an abbreviation for *tomakapu).* Similar lines march to the house of the father of the deceased. Men and women who present valuables to the father stand in the same relationships to him as outlined for people who give valuables to the spouse. My informants said that the distribution presented at the father's house is to honor one's father, who gave his child everything that his child needed. (A man is not jurally obligated to give food and other things to his children because he is not a uterine kinsman [*veyola tatola*].)

Ligabwa. This is a distribution of raw yams and taro plants brought by male owners, the sons of male owners, and male clan *keyawa*. These yams and taro plants were already repaid with bundles and skirts in the *kaymelu* exchange. Men now, for the first time, occupy the center of the hamlet, and they divide one pile of ten to fifteen yams and approximately six taro plants for each hamlet represented at the *sagali*. The names of each hamlet are shouted out, this time by men, and the women from that hamlet come into the center to take the yams and taro plants. These are then individually divided among all the women from each hamlet who participated during the day.

This was the end of the *sagali*, I thought, as I watched the women pack up their baskets and skirts in preparation for their return home. The huge baskets in the central clearing were empty, and the owners of these baskets—the women of the *dala* of the deceased and the children of the men of the *dala*—had all finished their *doba*. Other people slowly left the hamlet, but the women, who had given all their wealth away, would now receive a feast of food (including pork, taro pudding, and betel nuts) prepared for them *by men*: the deceased's kinsmen and the sons of these kinsmen. Such a feast is called a gift (*bobwelila*); it is a man's way of saying to his kinswomen:

Agutoki kweverka besa yokwami pela sagali.
I thank all of you very much for the *sagali*.

By the end of Obwelela's *sagali*, 30,000 bundles had changed hands, in addition to 212 colorful skirts, 139 pieces of trade-store cloth, $A25, and 13 clay pots. A total of 1,035 individual transactions had occurred, although some of these transfers went to the same individuals. This was the largest *sagali* I attended. The above figures should be somewhat larger because there were a few distributions that I was unable to count in full. Obwelela was not a person of high rank, although one of his sisters was married to Waibadi, one of the Tabalu chiefs. What made Obwelela's *sagali* so large was that he was a young man in his early thirties.[9] He had many strong brothers-in-law, some of whom used this *sagali* to affluently support their wives in order to display their own strength. Two of Obwelela's sisters wore the *sepwana* skirts. They participated in every exchange of the day; they were "wealthy girls."

Once, near the end of the *sagali*, Obwelela's sisters were challenged by women who came from a village near Losuia. One of these women came into the center and threw down some bundles, calling out a woman's name from her own village. Each time this happened the two girls wearing long skirts had to contribute to the piles. This is one of the reasons that women prefer older women to wear the long skirts, because an older woman will be more aggressive and will shout at other women, keeping them in line. Later, Kadesopi, Obwelela's mother, told me that she almost won the *sagali*. But she ran out of bundles before her daughters' stocks were depleted. In a sad voice she said, "I am getting too old to work hard for the *sagali*."

But Kadesopi's husband, Mekiyasi, still works hard for yams. He is also well known for his extensive knowledge of love magic, affording him a steady income from those who seek his services. For months prior to Obwelela's *sagali*, I watched both Kadesopi and her husband constantly work for her accumulation of wealth. Even though Kadesopi is an old woman, she almost surpassed her daughters.

III

To the sociologist, therefore, who studies a particular type of society, those of its customs, ideas, and institutions which centre round the erotic life of the individual should be of primary importance. . . . But the erotic phase, although the most important, is only one among many in which the sexes meet and enter into relations with each other. It cannot be studied outside its proper context, without, that is, being linked up with the legal status of man and woman; with their domestic relations; and with the distribution of their economic functions.—Malinowski 1929, pp. 1–2

Women strong in a *sagali* are thought by female and male villagers to be the most knowledgeable and important women. Single girls help their mothers, but they do not own their own wealth. Widows only participate minimally because "they do not receive yams from a man." But a widow who has a talent for fine weaving will often be given the honor of weaving the long mourning skirt. When women cut pandanus strips to weave into *doba* skirts or scratch the banana leaves while making bundles, they usually introduce new designs. A woman's cutting tool (*kaniku*) plays a significant part in all her *doba* activities. The fame of individual women comes through a talent for making *doba*. Women and men compliment other women on their ability to create especially fine skirts with intricate pandanus designs.

Kiriwina women play a productive role that is given full public recognition. In their performance during the mortuary rituals, through wealth distributions, women account for the strength of men as well as for their own economic power. Unlike the Melpa women of Mount Hagen, who are described by Melpa men as "mere producers" rather than "transactors," a term used to define male roles (M. Strathern 1972, p. 133), Kiriwina women engage in both production and transaction. In their efforts, women are supported by their brothers, fathers, and husbands. Most significantly, the economic amount of male support is publicly documented and measured through a woman's own wealth activities. Thus Kiriwina women play a valuable economic role concerned with production and distribution of wealth, and in this role they remain decision makers in their own right. If a woman cannot be wealthy without a man standing behind her, Kiriwina men cannot become powerful without a woman who in yams and *doba* exchanges comes first (see chap. 8 for details of female/male yam exchanges).

In New Guinea Highlands societies, women play an important role in exchange, both as pig raisers and as integral links between their own kin and their husbands' kin (see, e.g., Langness 1967; Meggitt 1965; Rappaport 1968; Reay 1959; Strathern 1971; M. Strathern 1972). But a public role directed by women in which they communicate their own part in these exchanges does not seem to occur. Perhaps this is one of the reasons for female/male anxiety in the Highlands. Women's roles between affines and own kin are not usually accorded public documentation, yet women work continually to accommodate, mediate, and expand these relationships.

As Ann Chowning (1973, p. 32) pointed out, however, Melanesian women often do perform in dances and other ceremonies (see, e.g., Codrington 1891; Deacon 1934; Salisbury 1965; Strathern 1970; Strathern and Strathern 1971; Williams 1930). In Mount Hagen, there are big-women whose prestigious economic value is given testimony by their performance in dances celebrating *pig-moka* (M. Strathern 1972, p. 138). But Marilyn Strathern stressed that being called a big-woman is only a compliment that men are paying women (p. 139). One could argue that Trobriand women are performing as representatives of their own *dala* whereas, in societies where descent is reckoned through males, women tend to be in an ambiguous position. But, in the Trobriands, women also document publicly the importance of their fathers' and husbands' *dala*. I do not deny the fundamental importance of matrilineality vis-à-vis women's power, but the nature of descent in the Highlands and the importance (in many cases) of shared substance make me wary of founding a solution fully on descent principles. Perhaps, in the Highlands, a man's role vis-à-vis other social relationships is just as ambiguous as a woman's (maybe even more so). Therefore, male uncertainty might generate the need for stronger separation of the sexes and greater male dominance.

In sharp contrast to many other Melanesian areas, Kiriwina women do not transmit any polluting qualities. Men are not afraid to have sexual intercourse with menstruating women. If a man appears sluggish at work, other men will tease him about sleeping with a menstruating woman, but such sexual contact is not considered dangerously debilitating. (See, for example, Allen 1967; Goodale and Chowning 1971; Hogbin 1970; Langness 1967, 1974; Meggitt 1964; and Read 1952 for descriptions and analyses of New Guinea societies where women are polluting agents.) Further, the Trobrianders do not have any male secret societies or initiation rites for girls or boys. Some Kiriwina women practice witchcraft, but a few men are known as witches (*mulukwausi*) too.[10]

Fear of sexuality, which permeates so many other Melanesian societies, seems lacking in the Trobriands. Men acknowledge the fact that women and girls are the ones to choose a partner, and women have great autonomy in this direction. Men recognize the danger in competition and in the freedom accorded women, but sex itself leaves no traumatizing effect. In fact, women's sexuality is accorded even greater value, for it is transformed into an external object of exchange.

Thus, nothing quite compares with the way women (often with men watching) count out their bundles and skirts before a *sagali*. Nothing is so dramatic as a woman standing at a *sagali* surrounded by thousands of bundles. Nor can anything be more impressive than watching the deportment of women as they attend to the distribution. When women walk into the center to throw down their wealth, they carry themselves with a pride as characteristic as that of any Melanesian big-man. On the day of the mortuary ceremony, women perform with an arrogance and a self-assuredness that can only be matched by young girls in their short red skirts aggressively seducing a potential lover. Pride for both women and men is a quality to be controlled. "He [or she] is 'too proud'" is a remark playfully used among adolescents, but seriously used for adult behavior. There is danger in boastfulness. Braggarts are scorned and sometimes become victims of sorcery and illness inflicted by others. But on the day of the women's mortuary ceremony strong women have the right to act with pride.

Only women have the power to transform dirty into clean. Dirty bundles are cut (i.e., fringed) and then rewoven into skirts, thus recycling nurturance and fertility into skirts and changing that which has become dirty into an object of beauty. A similar process takes place during the women's mortuary ceremony when female owners cut off the mourning neck bands and beads and tie a red skirt around the blackened women who stand with the owners. Women also release the widower and the father of the deceased from their "dirty" appearances by cutting their mourning neck bands and presenting them with skirts.

Even when women are not directly mourning for someone, they shave their heads or help other women with mourning rituals to benefit their own coffers. A comment often heard in reference to a mourning woman is, "That woman always comes to help. She loves *doba* very much." Women are preoccupied with mourning ritual, but not because Trobriand society accords them a lowly role. A male spouse and other men look as "dirty" in their mourning as women. Women, however, remain "dirty" longer because they are basically responsible for their own wealth. Women also stay "dirty" out of respect for a man who has given them yams.

During the women's mortuary ceremonies, women give away that which is essential to *dala* and the regeneration of *dala*: skirts, symbolizing the power of being female, and bundles, the symbol of milk and nurturance. As bundles are rewoven into skirts, the skirt itself can be analyzed as an embodiment of all that is "womanness": sexuality, reproduction, and nurture. Further, the transformation of elements of the female self into an object of economic value allows women to play a public role with political implications for themselves and for men.

When a kinsperson dies, women say that through their distributions they "cut" the deceased away from all relationships established throughout his or her social career. Payments are made which on one level have significant economic value. But I suggest that economic value is transcended by the fact that at death rituals women must restore that which is *dala* to their *dala*. Women cut away social relationships developed through exchange and, in so doing, secure the regeneration of pure *dala*. The trauma of death is averted as women once again, as at conception, reproduce a being now disconnected from the widest range of social networks.

The cosmic statement of regeneration of pure *dala* substance—*baloma*—comes at the end of the most extensive public mourning, thus clearing the way for the resumption of normal activity. Earlier, men through the process of lending begin to bind the shattered social networks through the distribution of the physical parts of the deceased's body. Men reconstitute social relationships in the name of *dala*, but they do not restore any substance or property to *dala* other than the return of leased land. In their distributions of male wealth at the end of the women's mortuary ceremony, men walk behind women in what seems to be a symbolic attempt to enter the domain of women. But men are stopped short physically at the entrance to the house of the father, and the house of the spouse of the deceased, by a controlling man who forcefully snatches male wealth for himself.

Male valuables are significantly more politically charged than female valuables, thus necessitating immediate individual control. Women's wealth exceeds explicit individual control because women control a cosmic sphere (ahistorical time) to which men are denied access. Thus, on this level, women's wealth can be seen as collective wealth, in that skirts and bundles symbolically represent *dala* and the value of women. As we shall see, male valuables seem to come closest to a representation of man's attempt to effect and control some form of his own generational continuity. But the inherent quality of male valuables remains ego-centered rather than *dala*-centered, thus imposing limitations on the male field of action. If we collapse traditional distinctions between social, political, and religious institutions into what Hallowell (1954) has called a "total culturally constituted environment," we must then pose the question of whether men have *more* power than women or only *different* power.

Chapter 5
To Be Young and Beautiful

I

These natives have a well-established institution of marriage, and yet are quite ignorant of the man's share in the begetting of children. At the same time, the term "father" has, for the Trobriander, a clear, though exclusively social, definition: it signifies the man married to the mother, who lives in the same house with her, and forms part of the household. The father, in all discussions about relationship, was pointedly described to me as tomakava, *a "stranger," or, even more correctly, an "outsider." This expression would also frequently be used by natives in conversation, when they were arguing some point of inheritance or trying to justify some line of behaviour, or again when the position of the father was to be belittled in some quarrel.—Malinowski 1929, p. 5*

In the Trobriand belief system, a woman conceives when a *wai waia* (spirit child), brought by a *baloma* (an unnamed matrilineal ancestor spirit), enters her body. Men are not thought to play any part in conception. Malinowski's description of the absence of the knowledge of physical paternity in the Trobriands generated enormous controversy, and debates have continued until the present.[1]

Today, it is difficult to reaffirm the kinds of statements made to Malinowski. Some villagers say that old men and women who died long ago believed that women could conceive without men. But now, they continue, they know the biological facts as taught by Europeans. However, I found that there are times when Trobrianders, publicly at least, rely on the facts of reproduction as remembered from old people.

For example, an unmarried Kwaibwaga woman who had a child told me that she became pregnant because she refused to sleep with a married chief. In retaliation he then used pregnancy magic—calling the *baloma* to come to a woman—to make her pregnant. In another case, a woman was being taken to the government court at Losuia because her husband, who had been away from Kiriwina for almost a year, accused her of adultery when she became pregnant in his absence. The woman's grandmother testified that her magic, not another man, had made the woman pregnant. In both cases, informants privately verified that the women became pregnant because they had been sleeping with their respective lovers. But to each other as well as to Europeans, Trobrianders accept the power of magic, rather than sexual intercourse, to direct a spirit to enter a particular woman as a fact in the public domain. Adultery in Kiriwina is a common occurrence, but discovery is dangerous. Therefore, the concept of "virgin birth" operates functionally to disguise inappropriate behavior. In other words, when circumstances precipitate a public statement, the role of the genitor is publicly denied. "Virgin birth" is an ideology for public consumption which protects all the parties concerned. In this context, it must be understood as a strategy for preventing shame and open conflict and as a mechanism for protecting the woman and her child.

Nevertheless, underlying this contextual use of "virgin birth" is the belief that women and men contribute differently to conception and to the growth of the fetus. In myths, in old people's beliefs which came from the original founders (*tabu*), and in informants' statements told to me and to others (Austen 1934; Malinowski 1916, 1929; Powell 1968; Rentoul 1931, 1932) who have discussed these matters with Trobriand informants, there is the notion that women can conceive alone without men. Yet accompanying this notion is the understanding that men contribute to the physical development of the fetus. In the Trobriand case, as in other cases where ignorance of physical paternity was presumed (see Leach 1967; Scheffler 1973), there exists the knowledge of female/male complementarity in reference to the relationship between genitor, genetrix, and offspring (see also Scheffler 1973, p. 751, who suggested the recognition of the complementarity of these relationships as a cultural universal).

In the Trobriands, the inner substance of a child is *dala* blood, conceived through the union of a woman and a spirit child who has itself been reincarnated from an old *baloma* (see Malinowski

1916). Thus, Trobriand women provide the fertility for the regeneration of that which is pure *dala*, and in this view only women recapitulate *dala* through time. Conversely, the growth of a child (i.e., its external form) is shaped by a man from another *dala*. A man develops and maintains the growth of the fetus and contributes to the shaping of the fetus through repeated sexual intercourse with his wife (see Austen 1934; Malinowski 1929, pp. 207–208; Powell 1968, p. 603, for similar statements).

To Malinowski, a seemingly curious facet of the ethnographer's problem of understanding Trobriand ideas of conception and birth is that a child is expected to resemble its father's physiognomy. But this "artificial physical link" (Malinowski 1929, pp. 204–209) is not an aberrant phenomenon. It fits into the Trobriand scheme with ease. Malinowski's informants told him that, in addition to the shaping effects of copulation, men give food to their children, thus molding them in their own image (ibid., p. 208). My informants gave me similar information. Today it is still extremely shameful to attribute the resemblance of someone's facial features to anyone other than her or his "true" father (*kalitonai*). Men contribute directly to the growth of their children prior to birth and throughout their children's early years. In this way, each child receives nurturance from another *dala* and this fact is publicly documented in a variety of ways.

For women, *dala* blood is not the only element of *dala* identity transmitted. *Nunu* ("mother's milk") designates "same *dala*." A woman provides this first internalized nurturance to her child. Under circumstances involving the death or illness of an infant's mother, the new baby can be given to a woman from a different *dala* to nurse. In this situation the wet nurse is given a valuable (usually a stone ax blade) by the infant's mother's brother.[2] The giving of a valuable is said to be repayment for the milk, thereby establishing the infant's identity within the *dala* of its true mother. In other words, the valuable given reclaims the child for its natal *dala*.

As long as a mother is able to nurse her child, it is not transferred to live with someone else until after weaning. The transfer of children who have already been weaned from true parents to other parents is a frequent occurrence in Kiriwina and takes place among the kin of either parent.[3] Once a child is weaned and transferred, there is never any exchange of valuables between the adopted parents and the true parents.

Children are taken by members of their father's *dala* (including father's sister) and by members of their mother's *dala*. A child calls the woman and man with whom it now lives "mother" and "father," but everyone knows the child's true genealogy.

As long as a child's true parents are still alive, residence with another set of parents adds to the possibilities for attracting a larger network of relationships. This suggests that adoption does not effect a severance between the child and its true parents. If a child is unhappy, its true parents take it back. While some children remain with adopted parents into adulthood, many children return to live with their true parents. Without exchange of a valuable, jural rights to the child are not transferred.

A woman nurses her child until some time between a year and a year and a half. Weaning is extremely abrupt; one day the mother nurses her child in the morning, and at nightfall she leaves it and stays with a kinsperson for a few days. The baby, however, has been receiving a diet of mashed yams, begun a few days following birth. Now, after weaning, yams continue as the major source of food. On the night that a woman leaves her nursing child, the baby begins to sleep with its father and continues to sleep in its father's bed until about the age of ten or until a younger child is weaned. Husbands and wives have separate beds; a woman always sleeps with her nursing child or alone, and her husband always sleeps with a child who is a bit older. Many times, late in the evening, I would hear a child crying; when I would go to inquire about it, the mother would tell me that it was crying for its father who had not yet gone to bed.

Malinowski (1927, pp. 50–51; 1929, pp. 5–7, 161) placed great emphasis on the classification of father as *tomakava*, glossed as "stranger" rather than as own kinsman (*veyola tatola*). My informants said that no one would ever call their father *tomakava*. They said that he was the most important kinsman (*veyola*) they had. It was only in conversations or debates concerning jural rights of a *dala* where a man as father would be referred to as *tomakava*. As Peter explained, "We call our father's brother's children 'brother' and 'sister,' but we know that they are all really *tomakava* to us. Even if other people call our father *tomakava*, we know that he is not *tomakava* to us."

The gloss "nonclansperson" for *tomakava* seems more appropriate for understanding the role a father plays. Only in certain contexts is the term *tomakava* applied to a man as father. In any situation (e.g., fights, mortuary rituals) stressing *dala* alignment over individual alliances, a man will be designated *tomakava* by members of his children's *dala*. With the death of a man's son or daughter the *veyola* relationship between them is ruptured. Therefore, at the mortuary ceremonies his role as *tomakava* is formally reasserted.

The relationship between a man and his young child is very strong. Men carry their children about; they sit and fondle them; they massage the head of an infant to shape it; they feed their infants yams and betel. Unlike fathers in our own society, Trobriand fathers make intense physical and emotional contact with their children from the time an infant is a few months old.[4]

Once the child is weaned, its father provides succor and protection throughout the night. A man is also the major supplier of most of his child's food: yams and other produce from his own gardens, fish, betel nuts, pork, rice, and all trade-store foods. The way informants described their fathers' care was nearly identical:

> My father always worked hard for me; he always gave
> me everything for nothing. When I was a small girl [or
> boy], he cut firewood for me, he bought fish for me to eat,
> he gave me betel nuts to chew, and he always gave me
> yams to eat. Because he gave me all these things for
> nothing, I love that man very much.

Men told me that the reason they now make yam exchange gardens for their fathers is because their fathers gave so much to them when they were young; women gave me the same reason when I asked why they helped their fathers' *dala* kin in mortuary ceremonies.

A father thus gives many artifacts to his children when they are young. But these are not "pure gifts," in Malinowski's terms. What appears to be one-way giving is reciprocated at a later date by sons and daughters. The care and artifacts that a man gives freely to his children when they are young are the means by which future cyclical exchanges between father and son and father and daughter are established. What is privately given is publicly returned fifteen or twenty years later.[5]

Marshall Sahlins's (1972, pp. 191–194) model of primitive exchange follows Malinowski's (1922, pp. 177–180) notion of free gifts between close kin to demonstrate that reciprocity between kin is generalized. Thus a gift given by a kinsperson (in the generalized sector of exchange) elicits no obligation for repayment. My data illustrate the error in the simplistic assumption of free or pure gifts as a basic building block in any model of primitive exchange. (Malinowski's ambiguous use of free gift was pointed out by Mauss [1954, pp. 69–76] and later reevaluated by Malinowski

[1926a, pp. 40–41].) My analysis also demonstrates the danger in the use of the word "gift" as a generalized term. In the Trobriand case, the most critical relationships (i.e., a man and his children, a man and his sister's son, a woman and her brother, a wife and her husband) become active *kinship* relationships with all the prerogatives accorded kin only when formal exchange acts are operative. An analysis of only the gift and countergift obscures the significance of exchange as a cyclical process reversing the direction of giving through time.

At birth every child is given a name by its mother. This name denotes the child's *dala* identity because the chosen name is that of a deceased member of the child's *dala*. A few weeks after birth, an infant receives a name from its father. This name is taken from an ancestor in the father's *dala*.[6]

Either name may be used to address and refer to the child. The Kiriwina term for a name given by one's father is *laduba tamala*, and the name given by one's mother is *yagada tatola*. The preference for the use of one name over the other seems to turn on the issue of residence and rank. For example, one boy told me that while he lived with his father he would always use his father's name. When his father died, however, he might return to live on his own *dala* land, and then he would begin to use the name which his mother gave him at birth. However, when a person's *dala* is of rank and distinction, then the name from that *dala* is used. One of the Tabalu chiefs from Omarakana took great care to tell me the part of the Tabalu origin story which included the story of the *tabu* for whom he was named and other *tabu* whose names he had chosen for his children. When a man is of high rank, his own children will usually use the name from his *dala*.

The major distinction between the two kinds of names is ownership of a name as opposed to loan of a name. Names given by women are always the property of women, but names given by men can never be used beyond their children's generation. Similarly, the name that a woman gives her son (his true *dala* name) cannot be used beyond his child's lifetime. Names given by a man to his children are reclaimed by a man's sisters, who are *tabu* to his children.[7] When that name is to be reused, a man's sisters present elaborately decorated red skirts (women's wealth) to his child. In this ritual (*setabula*), women return the detached name back to *dala* property. The *dala* name continues to be used by a man's son, but, once skirts are given, the name cannot be transferred to his son's children. In the ritual exchange of names and skirts, women wear their gray brown mourning skirts and carry the red skirts in their hands. The performance resembles women's roles in mortuary distributions. Although women also receive and personally use a name from their father's *dala*, they only transmit their own *dala* names to their children.

One exception to the exchange of a name involves an extension of its use for one additional generation. When a man is old and sick, someone has to care for him. Firewood must be chopped and stored so that a fire can be kept going near an old man's bed. A man who is sick also needs assistance in bathing himself, and often he must be carried into the bush to defecate. These tasks are usually performed by a son who is living in his father's hamlet. A father can repay his son by giving him a name from his *dala* which becomes the son's own property to pass on to his own children.[8] The son's children, however, do not have any claim to this name other than its use. The women of his father's *dala* (a man's sisters) again give skirts and reclaim the name.

Trobrianders, especially young people, enhance their attractiveness by wearing decorations (see plate 15). In combination with the attractive quality of decorations is the fact that, when children wear earrings and other small ornaments on their bodies, they are making visual statements about their own parental identity. By providing a child with these symbols of social, and often political, status, a father adds dimension to his child's social identity.

When a child is only a few months old, tiny rings (*paya*) of tortoise shell are inserted through its earlobes. As the child grows, more and more rings are inserted so that a child of two years of age might have ten or twelve rings in each earlobe. Both boys and girls wear the tortoise-shell rings, but red, flat shell disks (*kaloma*) are added to the bottom part of the rings for girls. Today, the missionaries have tried to stop parents from having earrings inserted into their children's ears, but for some the tradition is still strongly followed. My informants said that earrings were very important for Kiriwina people.

Traditionally, if a child did not have holes pierced in its ears, it was called *gudukubukwabuya*, a bastard child. Such children, when addressed as *gudukubukwabuya*, are shamed to such an extent that they remain inside their houses for several days. The shame of not having a father and the fear that this fact will be publicly voiced often lead a bastard child's own kin to pierce its ears. In the case of the unmarried woman who denied sleeping with a chief and claimed "virgin birth," her child not only had holes pierced at the age of four months, but it wore more tortoise-

Plate 15. Although Bokelolu is living with her mother's married sister in Kwaibwaga, she wears earrings, a kuwa neck band, and a kula necklace from her father, who lives in another village

shell rings and red *kaloma* shells than any other child in the village.

If the holes are pierced but the earrings are absent, children are called "poor" (*namakava*). A man provides his children with "expensive things" (e.g., body decorations). Earrings denote the presence and the concern of a man vis-à-vis his children. A child is "poor" because its father is an improper father.

Kula provides an opportunity for men to give their children a special decoration—a shell necklace (*kuwa*), which specifically symbolizes youthfulness, attractiveness, and beauty. When a man does *kula*, he not only receives *kula* objects which belong to his *kula* road, he also tries to find additional *kula* objects which are not part of any established road. These additional valuables are called *kitoma*. Access to these valuables, unmarked for a specific *kula* road, provides the basis for competition in *kula*. When a man is successful and attracts a *kula* necklace, he can either put the necklace into a new *kula* road, use it as an object of exchange in the internal exchange system in Kiriwina (in lieu of a stone ax blade or money), or cut it into small parts and make short *kuwa* necklaces for his children.[9]

Today, in Kiriwina, short *kuwa* made of red shells are seldom worn by young people because they are profitable objects for sale on the tourist market (shell *kuwa* sell for A$20 to A$35). Most young people now wear red plastic beads which are strung together in the same design as shell *kuwa*. Chiefs, however, occasionally still divide a shell necklace into smaller ones for their children to wear.

To wear a red *kuwa* means that one is trying to attract someone. In this case, the attraction is directed toward the other sex. According to custom, once a man or woman marries he or she should not wear the red *kuwa* necklaces, but chiefs often do wear them. I have seen both Vanoi and Waibadi wear *kuwa* necklaces. Inherent in their role of chief, however, and especially as chiefs in the process of becoming more powerful, are the continued ability and daring to attract and be attractive to women.

The use of *kuwa* to denote attractiveness and beauty is reversed in mourning ritual. A black mourning *kuwa*, traditionally made from the deceased's hair, is worn by the dead person's children if the deceased is male, father, and spouse. Female kinswomen of the deceased exchange skirts for the removal of the *kuwa* in a ritual called *winelawoulo*.

Sometimes old people never remove the mourning *kuwa* because they have little chance to remarry. The *sagali* for removal of the mourning *kuwa* occurs prior to the remarriage of the spouse. The cutting of the black *kuwa* is the final public ritual which releases the spouse from the affinal connection which began with rituals of youth.

To summarize, Malinowski's distinction between biological and social fatherhood seems a moot point (but see Fortes 1949; Goodenough 1970; Radcliffe-Brown 1950; and Scheffler 1973 on the general problem of social fatherhood). In the Trobriands, children are created and nurtured by their own *dala and* by their father and his *dala*. Children benefit from their place within their own *dala* and from their father's position in another *dala*. Therefore, as a child represents an amalgamation of inner *dala* substance and other *dala* features, female essence and male provisioning, both a woman's *dala* and her husband's *dala* are infused with new life and new potential.

II

Who makes the beauty magic?—
To heighten the beauty, to make it come out.
Who makes it on the slopes of Obukula?—
I, Tabalu, and my mate Kwaywaya.
We make the beauty magic.
I smooth out, I improve, I whiten!
Thy head I smooth out, I improve, I whiten!
Thy cheeks I smooth out, I improve, I whiten!
Thy nose I smooth out, I improve, I whiten!
Thy throat I smooth out, I improve, I whiten!
Thy neck I smooth out, I improve, I whiten!
Thy shoulders I smooth out, I improve, I whiten!
Thy breast I smooth out, I improve, I whiten!
Bright skin, bright; glowing skin, glowing.

—Malinowski 1929, pp. 354–355

In an informal village court case the mother's brother of two young girls was severely critical of their behavior with boys. He said to them:

> You girls are both handsome girls and you should only
> sleep with handsome boys. When ugly boys come and want
> to sleep with you, you should tell them, "No, go away, you
> are ugly." But you girls are like dogs—you do not know the
> difference between handsome and ugly; you choose anyone.
> You are just like dogs who eat everything; good food and
> rotten food. When you sleep with ugly boys, you make
> our name in Kwaibwaga very bad.

Becoming handsome is the theme of many passages of love magic. This theme also fills the words of beauty magic. Beauty magic is conferred on the young by the old. Love magic is also performed by older villagers for younger people. To be the most beautiful and therefore to attract the best lover is the game in which the young engage.

The game is not merely a youthful endeavor. The growth and development of a child into a beautiful strong young man or woman are fundamental Trobriand concerns. Natural attributes and cultural artifacts are synthesized into a particular kind of power that only the young possess. A straight nose, thick hair, smooth, unwrinkled light skin, firm breasts, flashing eyes, delicately painted facial designs, red and white shell decorations, coconut oil, and flowers filled with love magic are elements that induce desire. Young people not only attract and are attracted to each other, but the power of beauty is of such a nature that older people have a direct interest in its expression.

A special period of dancing, called *usigola*, is held after the annual yam harvest (see Malinowski 1929, p. 351). My informants told me that in 1952, just before his death, the chief of Kwaibwaga organized an *usigola* which lasted for three months. During these months, according to the reminiscences of my informants, enormous amounts of food were cooked and distributed, lavish quantities of beauty magic and objects of personal adornment were heaped upon the dancers, and all the young people of Kwaibwaga looked beautiful (see plate 16). Not all the dancers, however, were young in age. Some of the older men and women, well known for their dancing ability—and with the help of magic and decorations —had momentarily reversed their old age and once again appeared young. One man told me that when he saw his mother, Ilabova, elaborately dressed for dancing, he said to her, "To my

Plate 16. *Men being decorated by their father's sister in preparation for a dance*

eyes you always looked like an old woman, but today you have changed, and now you look young and beautiful."[10]

At the beginning of the time for dancing, when everyone is practicing for the final day (*lapala*), all young people have beauty magic performed over them by their fathers' sisters (*tabu*). These women stand in a special yam exchange relationship with ego's father.

A man must give yams annually to a married woman, whom he calls "sister." If there is no one to perform beauty magic for a man's child, the yams have not been given. Since a man's children cannot receive *talilisa* (beauty magic) from any woman in their own *dala*, a child without a *tabu* (father's sister) hides in the bush in shame. *Talilisa* magic is chanted while a pearl shell is moved over the face of ego (see the magic spell quoted from Malinowski on p. 130). Although many kinds of beauty magic are known and used by women and men, *talilisa* and the accompanying pearl shell are the sole property of women. When women perform *talilisa*, they themselves are muted as objects of beauty— women wear mourning skirts in the performance of beauty magic for the young. Although men provide for the growth and development of their children, a man's sisters take over his role at the time when beauty is most desired. I once asked Bunemiga and Peter why they called their father's sister *tabu*. They thought for a moment, and then Peter answered, "Because she is the one who does beauty magic for me."

Only women who are *tabu* (father's sister) to a person give artifacts and reclaim control of *dala* property lent to others by men. Women are entering into social relationships created in the male domain. They perform within the frame of intergenerational time, cycles of time associated with specific social space and specific social persons. The muting of their sexuality suggests that women are taking the place of men, exhibiting male power. But, at the same time, they demonstrate female power, the power to control transgenerational continuity, an unmarked time that maintains *dala* identity.

At *usigola*, a village presents its wealth not only in terms of large food distributions but also in terms of its youth. Such an elaborate display is accomplished through extensive work and extensive exchange relationships, all of which culminate in the dramatic moment of *lapala*. Most dances are performed by men, although there is one dance—*karibom*—in which both sexes participate. The performers form two lines, one in back of another, the lines uniformly arranged according to the size of the participants. The lines move in circles and the dancers make careful decisive steps, walking slowly to the beat of the drums.

Malinowski (1929, pp. 249–251) describes the way sexual advances occur as the dancers easily reach out and touch each other. The sexual interplay between the dancers is not the only kind of seduction going on, however. At the same time, dancers perform for spectators. Visitors from other villages gather around the dancers, commenting on which is the most beautiful.

This kind of dance was performed, among others, during the celebration of National Day in 1972, when most of the villagers assembled at the government station. I, along with hundreds of Kiriwinans, pressed in close to the circling dancers. I observed and participated in the following series of exchanges—*tilewai*.

Malinowski (1929, p. 215) called *tilewai* a "flattery gift." When someone looks beautiful and is on display (i.e., dancing or singing), a spectator removes some part of the performer's body decoration. If the performer, however, is a high-rank (*guyau*) person, a string is tied around his or her arm, emphasizing the differentiation in rank, since it would be taboo to remove something from the body of any *guyau* person. As a result of the contact between performer and spectator, the performer is obligated to return another kind of object to the spectator in order to redeem the decoration or to remove the arm string.

According to my informants, *tilewai* are very important kinds of exchanges. Between individuals who are not of high rank, the return *tilewai* by the performer to her or his admirer consists of small valuables such as mats, betel nuts, woven baskets, or shell earrings. When a young person is the performer, this return is presented by the youth's relatives. When small valuables are reciprocated, there are no further formal exchanges. But, because these two people exchanged something, the transaction opens the possibility for other exchanges of a different nature. In other words, to take a *tilewai* is to remove for oneself part of a person's beauty props; the wordless communication implies "you look beautiful." Taking *tilewai* demands an immediate *tilewai* return to the admirer who made his or her attention public. The public statement "you look beautiful" must be reciprocated by the beautiful one. In the Trobriands, even this kind of small exchange is highly programed through nonverbal interaction. A public compliment must be reciprocated.

The exchange of *tilewai* between a chief (or his children) and other villagers involves a more heavy expenditure, a greater future obligation. A person who ties a string around the arm of a *guyau* (or the children of a *guyau*) receives a pig from the chief as *tilewai* return. Thus person A admires *guyau* B and receives a pig as payment for this admiration. At a later time, however, when *guyau* B attends a ceremony and person A (or her or his children) is dancing or singing, *guyau* B takes *tilewai* from person A, returning the compliment. Now person A must give a pig to *guyau* B as her or his return. This second pig, however, is not called *tilewai*, but *tilamapu* (the word *mapula* denotes an even exchange). When the *guyau* has a return on his original pig, the score is even.

After the National Day celebration, I received a chicken as return *tilewai* because I took *tilewai* (a feather) from Abraham, who works in Losuia. The schoolteacher who had arranged the children's performance of traditional songs took *tilewai* from one of Waibadi's children. After the festivities were finished, people gossiped for hours about the size of the pig Waibadi would send to the schoolteacher, as well as about what everyone else had received for *tilewai*.

During *usigola*, and in other similar feasts, a person has the opportunity to seek out relationships with other people directly through her or his children. At the same time, her or his children have the opportunity to seek out sexual liaisons with others. I was told several stories of how chiefs from other villages often came to watch the dancers, seeking the most beautiful girls for themselves. Often these attractions led to marriage. The older men and women who are dancers and who have for the moment reversed their age by becoming beautiful also become objects of attraction and find themselves directly involved in *tilewai* exchanges.

In Kiriwina, initiation rituals are not held. There is nothing to mark the transition from youth to adulthood in a sharp dramatic way. The ritual which comes closest to a *rite de passage* might be *usigola*, the time of dancing. On the final day of dancing, beauty, sexual attractions, music, decorations, yams, pigs, and betel nuts are dramatically presented to people from other villages after months of preparation. But all the intensity of that moment underscores the reality of the situation. Young people (especially young girls) know their own minds. They are created in part by others but they remain their own persons. Even when a chief wants to marry a beautiful young girl, there is no way she can be forced to go and live with him. A woman defies a chief in the same way that she has the option to reject any man.

In sexual affairs and marriage, women have a great degree of autonomy. Men have independence in their exchange relationships with other men. Residence changes occur easily; a man's house can be carried to another village, where he can rapidly establish (through yam exchanges) a new place of residence.

Women and men are aware of the dangers inherent in rejection and loss. Children growing up are given enormous freedom. Initiation rituals would be anathema to the way people regard each other and deal with others. Growing up is a gradual process and controls cannot be directly exercised. Older men must wait and watch, using their generosity to attract the young. In village public meetings, an older man always says something similar to "We older men sit on the top branches of the tree. We wait to hear the voices of you young men rising up to reach our ears. We are old, it is time for you young men to speak." Usually there is silence.

Chapter 6
Fathers, Sons, and Land

I

Taytu, the staple food, is to the natives kaulo, *vegetable food* par excellence, *and it comes into prominence at harvest and after. This is the sheet-anchor of prosperity, the symbol of plenty,* malia, *and the main source of native wealth.—Malinowski 1935a, p. 81*

At some point in his maturation, a young boy must effect an entry into the formal exchange system. Only when power is transformed into material control of resources does a boy dare let his words reach the ears of his elders, who sit metaphorically in the upper branches of a tree. As Malinowski described above, prosperity, plenty, and wealth are found through yams, the road of exchange that all Kiriwina men must travel.

Thus, in Kiriwina, the production of yams is firmly grounded in the male domain. The small *taytu* yam is both the basic subsistence food and the principal object of exchange. Yams in the latter category open the way to all other avenues of resource control. Kiriwina informants say, "If a man has yams, he can find anything else he needs." Occasionally a woman will plant and harvest her own yam garden, but her own produce never plays any role in the formal exchange cycles.

Yams are differentiated into categories of raw and cooked. This dichotomy can be observed in the types of gardens men work—subsistence (*gubakayeki*) or exchange gardens—and by the kinds of exchanges in which people engage—raw or cooked yam transactions. I make this distinction by referring to cooked yams as "food" and raw yams as "yams." Although I am primarily concerned with exchanges of raw yams, the distinctions between raw and cooked have important contextual implications. For example, raw yams can be stored for as long as six months. There-fore, yams can be exchanged for many purposes over an extended period of time. Unlike food, a pile of yams presents a range of recycling possibilities. But, once yams have been reduced to food, their regenerative energy is diminished. Cooked yams cannot be reinvested in other avenues of exchange, nor can they be re-planted and converted into another harvest. Thus yams, not food, are the basic commodities in formal exchange cycles.

Distinctions between the kinds of yam gardens a man plants depend upon whether the harvest is immediately converted into food for his own subsistence or whether the harvest remains in the raw state as long as possible and is therefore used for ex-change. I refer to the latter category as "yam exchange gardens" and the former category as "food gardens." A man who plants and tends an exchange garden does not own any of the yams. From the time of planting, the yams belong to the person to whom the harvest will be presented.

A third important difference between food gardens and yam exchange gardens is the absence of a formal harvest for food gar-dens. Yams are used as they are needed; no one displays a garden harvest from a food garden, nor are these yams stored in yam houses where they would be on display. Food yams are kept in-side the house or in the roof section of a small yam house where no one will see them.

The nature of the yam as a physical organic object is in part the basis for its specialized properties as a cultural object. Yams can be grown; therefore all Kiriwina men have access to some amount of yams. This is in contrast to the range of valuables made by specialists and imported from other areas. Andrew Strathern (1971) made a similar distinction between home-grown and foreign objects in his study of trade networks in the New Guinea Highlands.

Yams can be stored for about six months, and during that time each man must balance his input and output of yams carefully. He must also balance his obligations, the possibilities for new avenues of exchange, and the necessity for conversions into food.

Yams are self-propagating plants; the entire tuber of the *taytu* is used for seed.[1] Most small tubers are separated at the beginning of the harvest, and in this way seeds are stored for the next plant-ing. In addition to the categories of raw and cooked yams, a third division—seed yams—may be defined. The use of the entire tuber for seed often presents a problem. Occasionally a woman will cook all the seed yams, leaving nothing for the next season's planting. Seed yams can be purchased, but only with a valuable or with cash. People who "eat their seeds" are commonly gossiped about in derogatory terms. Fortune (1932) described similar situations on Dobu, with even more hazardous consequences because yams cannot be purchased. On Dobu yams must always stay within each matrilineal line (*susu*).

The problem of seeds introduces an interesting botanical and culturally significant distinction between yams and the other major root crop, taro. Unlike yams, the taro tuber is cooked without destroying the regeneration of another plant. A taro plant is harvested with the leafy stalk still attached to the tuber. The stalk is removed from the top of the tuber and replanted. Therefore, taro is propagated through the use of the nonedible stalk. An exchange of raw taro with the stalk intact is a presentation of *both* food and a new plant.

In Schwimmer's (1973) analysis of taro exchanges among the Orokaiva, he noted that women are responsible for intravillage transactions of cooked taro. Conversely, Orokaiva men arrange large taro exchanges for men from outside villages. In these exchanges, raw taro plants are elaborately displayed with the stalks intact. Although Schwimmer did not make this point explicit, it seems, in the case of the Orokaiva, that women are involved with exchanges of food that have no further potential for energy conversion, whereas men exchange objects that remain physically reproductive.

· Taro, however, cannot be stored, and the tuber must be eaten a few days after it is taken from the ground.[2] It is the quality of storability which places yams in a distinctive category. Yams, unlike taro, are accumulated, and accumulations can be displayed. Yams, therefore, are much more public than taro, because taro when given in exchange is given in small quantities (perhaps six plants at a time), and these plants must be converted into food and a new plant within a few days.[3]

Because great quantitites of yams can be amassed and stored, yams can be given and used for various purposes at divers times. Unlike a shell valuable, which is one object and can be exchanged only with one person at a time, a single harvest presentation of yams is subdivided and channeled through many redistributions. With yams, a man is able to establish relationships with more people than he can with any other object of exchange. Taro has the same potential, but taro is limited by the rapidity of decay. Therefore, taro cannot be culturally elaborated into the vast scheme of display and exchange in the way that yams are elaborated in Kiriwina. However, yam exchanges are in many ways like playing with poker chips; they have to be cashed in (i.e., converted into something else) before one benefits materially from them. Whereas poker chips are made from a hard substance, impersonal and imperishable, yams by their very nature are destructible. They must be converted into food or seeds within a period of time or they will rot. Figure 9 is a diagram of a yam house, representing a hypothetical situation in which the major possibilities for the conversion of yams into other objects, comestibles, and relationships are outlined.

Malinowski called yam exchange gardens *urigubu*, but in *Coral Gardens and Their Magic* (1935a, p. 196) he discussed variants and extensions of the word *urigubu*. All my informants told me specifically that *urigubu* refers to pork, areca palms, coconut palms, and betel pepper plants. Presentations of yams are not called *urigubu*. If, however, a man is questioned about his yams and the questioner uses the word *urigubu*, as I did, then the man responds as if the word were being correctly used. My error in the beginning of my field work was in talking about *urigubu* and assuming it concerned yam exchanges. It was only later, when I heard villagers using a variety of words to refer to exchange yams, that I questioned my own use of the word. The source of confusion probably lies in the fact that often a man gives *urigubu*—pork, areca palms, coconut palms, and betel pepper plants—to the same person for whom he makes a yam exchange garden.[4]

The proper terminology for yam exchange gardens includes a variety of words, each of which denotes a different stage of planting and harvesting. *Kaymata* and *kaymwila* refer to the actual yam exchange garden. *Kaymata* is a large garden, a man's main exchange garden, while *kaymwila* designates a man's second garden, which is smaller in size. The word *kubula* indicates ownership of the produce from these gardens. For example, a man might ask, "Whose yams are growing here?" And someone would answer, "It is Naseluma's *kubula*." *Kubula* is also used to refer to the display of yams in the garden prior to the filling of the yam house. When, however, the yams are brought into the village and presented to their owner, they are then referred to as *taytumwedona*. Before the yams are put into the owner's yam house (see plate 17), small baskets are filled which are presented to other villagers. These baskets of yams are called *kovisi*. When similar baskets of yams are given at other times of the year, they are called *taytupeta*.

In figure 10, I have followed the format of Malinowski's chart (see 1935a, p. 197), in which he illustrated *urigubu* exchanges, and I show the terms used for the various stages of yam growing and yam presentation.[5]

II

The father, in actual fact, always tries to give as much as he can to his own sons at the expense of those of his sister, who are his legal heirs. His natural inclinations are seconded by customary usage which almost defies and certainly circumvents the rigid matrilineal law, by giving the father a number of opportunities to favour his sons and to curtail the rights of his matrilineal nephews.—Malinowski 1935a, p. 205

Between the ages of twelve and fifteen, young boys move out of their parents' houses and into their own private sleeping quarters. The actual age when boys stop living with adults varies because younger brothers will often move in with their elder brothers. Therefore the number of brothers and the ages of each play some part in determining precisely how old a boy will be when he leaves his mother's cooking fire and the bed made for him by his father.

Bachelor houses (*bukumatula*) are quite small; sometimes boys use the roof sections of small yam houses for sleeping houses.[6] The wooden frame for the bachelor house is woven with swamp grasses which reach to the ground, and the sides of the house are formed by the sloping walls of the roof. Only the front and rear portions of the house are woven separately of coconut-frond mats. This type of house is also the kind most frequently used by old men or old women who are widowers or widows.

Spatially, bachelor houses are interspersed between, in front of, or to the side of the houses of men with whom the boy resides. The organization of work and the payment of cooked food to people who helped with the house building are carried out by a

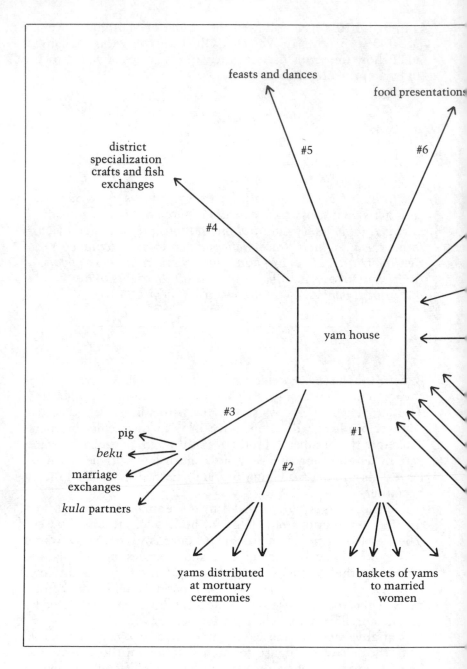

Figure 9. Yams coming in and going out of a yam house

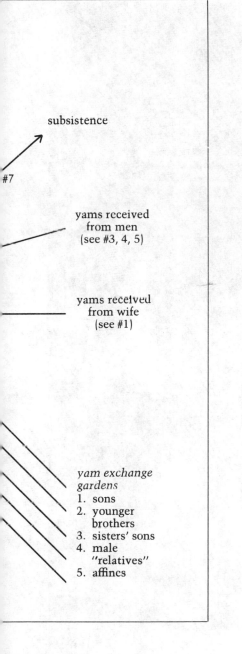

subsistence

#7

yams received
from men
(see #3, 4, 5)

yams received
from wife
(see #1)

*yam exchange
gardens*
1. sons
2. younger
   brothers
3. sisters' sons
4. male
   "relatives"
5. affines

*Plate 17. Filling a yam house in the hamlet of Obulabula,
Kwaibwaga village, 1972*

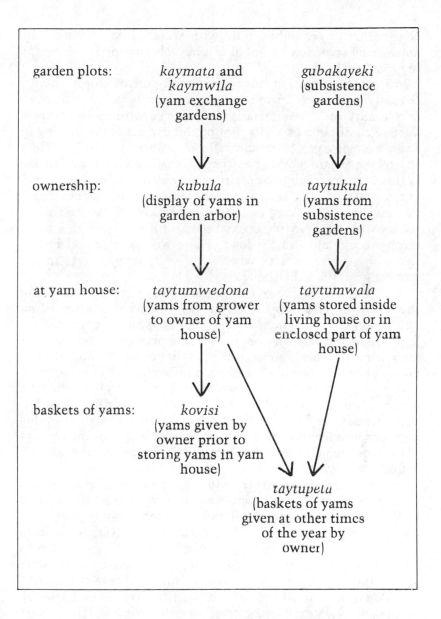

Figure 10. Terms for various stages of yam growing and exchange

boy's father or any other male with whom a boy resides. The house itself stands as a symbol of a boy's beginning involvement in formal exchanges.

In the transformation from living with parents to peer living, the activities of boys begin to be noticed by others. Now the power of beauty and attractiveness is reinforced with the actual productive ability of a boy. His first productive act is the making of a yam exchange garden for the male with whom he resides. When an aggressive hard-working boy begins a garden for a male, he also begins to make small presentations of garden produce (yams and/ or taro) to his mother and to women who are his true or classificatory sisters. No cooking is done in a bachelor house, and these sisters will often provide cooked food for him, although a boy's mother cooks most of his food. These women also collect any items of women's wealth which the young boy receives in the women's mortuary distributions.

The first yam exchange garden that a boy makes is for one of the following men: his father, an older married brother, or an older married male "kinsman." This last category includes a male kinsman who is in a boy's own *dala* or in his father's *dala* or who is married either to his father's sister or to his mother's sister. If a boy has lived with and been raised by one of these men, substituting for his father, this man receives yams from the first garden a boy makes. While a boy's mother's brother is included in this category, in this situation a boy has been adopted by his mother's brother and makes a garden for him within the context of an older male married kinsman, rather than because of any avunculocal residence rules.

In order to receive rights to land use, a young man must attach himself to an older male who has already established his own right to reside in a particular hamlet. In each hamlet, garden and hamlet lands are controlled by one man; however, sometimes two men (usually brothers) each control part of the land. A majority of men, however, *use* land rather than *control* it. Whether men reside on the land of their own *dala* or on that of someone else's *dala*, they must validate the right to live on that land by producing a yam exchange garden for either the hamlet manager or a linking intermediary male. Kinship can also be fictively created through a *dala* manager, but in all cases kinship becomes an active relationship through yam production. In return for the production of a yam exchange garden, the hamlet manager gives all resident men use rights to plots of garden land and the right to place a house foundation in the hamlet.

The key to the core of male/male relationships within a hamlet lies in the dynamic interaction between labor, land, and yams. Labor ensures a man use rights to any *dala* land. But the man lending these rights does not have to be a hamlet manager. A man can live on his father's land and work for his father, thereby securing his own rights to remain on that land.[7] Schematically (see fig. 11) a hamlet is composed of individual clusters in which younger men are linked to one older man.[8] Each man who is head of a cluster is linked directly to the hamlet manager.

A boy receives seeds for his first yam exchange garden from the male to whom the harvest will go. Therefore, a young man works a garden for an older male, and the presentation of yams at harvest is a presentation of *service* rather than *object*.[9] Thus the gardens a man makes for someone else are not gifts in the way Malinowski implied. The yam harvest from these gardens represents labor; the yams themselves are not a gift. Women and men prepare seed yams from their own yams for other men to plant for them. The yams, once planted, continue to propagate for the following year's harvest. Throughout the years, additional seeds are added and seed yams can be purchased from other men with a stone ax blade or money.

Every year, at the filling of the yam house, food (*sasova*) is prepared and presented to each worker by the recipient of the yams. The kind of food varies according to a man's wealth. A man with a very large yam house (which means that he has several gardens being worked for him) is expected to distribute pork at this time. Men with small yam houses usually distribute cooked yams and taro, betel nuts, and tobacco, but do not kill a pig. Rice, tinned fish, and tea are now favorite additions for those who have cash to spend in the trade stores.

A valuable (*vayuvisa*) is given to a man who makes an exceptionally large yam exchange garden by the recipient of the yams. This valuable (a stone ax blade, shell decorations, a clay pot, a small pig, or cash) is periodically given in return for very hard productive work. When a man plants larger quantities of seed yams, which the recipient of the yams has either accumulated or bought, he expects to receive a valuable for his labor.[10] The valuable is not only payment for labor, it also encourages the man to continue to work hard and plant a garden of the same size again. The valuable binds the relationship tighter, and the annual harvest is increased. In six or eight years another increase might be added: a larger harvest cultivated and another valuable received. Figure 12 represents the way in which seed yams, raw yams, and

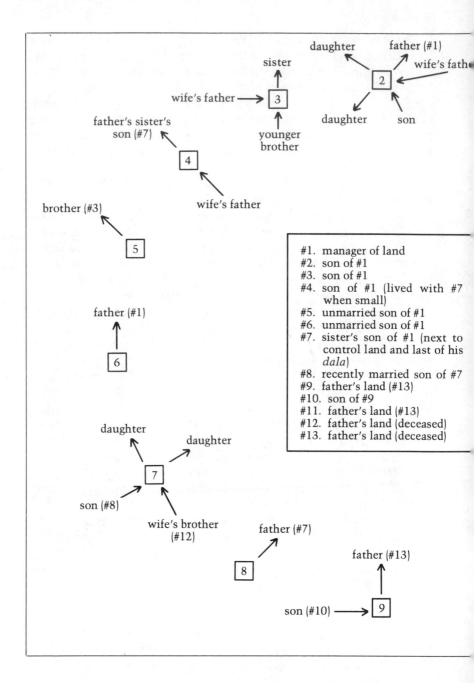

Figure 11. Circulation of yam exchange gardens in one hamlet. An arrow equals one yam exchange garden.

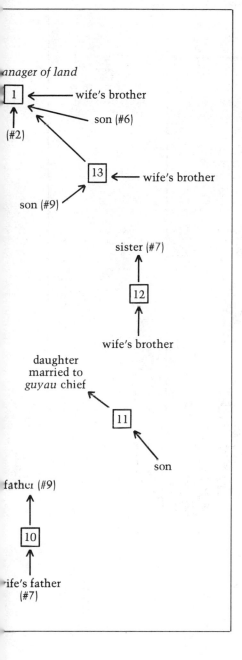

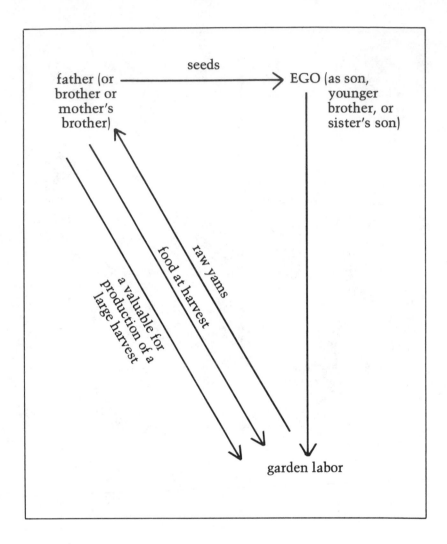

Figure 12. Direction of exchanges in a male/male yam exchange garden

the reciprocities due flow between the men involved in cycles of exchanges which link together primary male/male relationships.

Circumstances occur whereby a boy or man will make a garden for his older brother even though his father is still alive (see fig. 11). This usually occurs when there are four or more brothers, the oldest of whom is married. What this progression accomplishes is to spread out the wealth, assuring older married brothers an "income." (See table 1 for a list of exchange gardens made by Kwaibwaga men.) Therefore, men using younger brothers begin to establish their own field of interaction without leaving their father. As in many other aspects of the culture, older children usually have a distinct advantage over younger ones. But, as long as all brothers reside together with their father, a younger brother who is making a garden for an older brother rather than for his father still retains rights to residence, land use, and protection through his father. In addition he also has rights to some inheritance at his father's death.

Table 1. *Yam exchange gardens made by total male Kwaibwaga population*

Gardens made for male relatives		Gardens made for female relatives	
Father	23	Sister	11
Elder brother	16	Daughter	15
Male relative	16	Total	26
Total	55		

Even when a boy has been raised by another male relative, for whom he makes a first garden, he will often make a second garden for his true father, if his father has been a "good man" to him. Being a good man means being generous. Whenever I asked anyone why they made a garden for their father, I always received the same answer: "My father always gave me anything I asked for when I was a small boy, and always he gave me things for nothing. So now I make a garden for him to pay him back."

Men—through labor for their fathers—are investing in future rights to their fathers' knowledge and property. Even when a man leaves his father to return to control his own *dala* land, his father remains important. If a man desires to remain in residence on his father's *dala* land when his father dies, he must contribute large quantities of yams to the owners at his father's mortuary ceremonies. A man's participation in these events with his father's kinsmen demonstrates his right to "take the place of his father" in residence and land use.[11] He must also begin to make a yam exchange garden for the new manager. In cases where a man's father controlled his own land, he can achieve a position of strength within the hamlet unit. Further, if he has married a woman from his father's clan, he will be able to repeat the same process and secure a place for his own son. This son makes a yam garden for his father. When his father dies, he too may remain if he performs in mortuary distributions and makes a garden for the hamlet manager.

In general, the transactions which follow from the labor a man expends on any male garden involve two men who are in an asymmetrical status relationship to each other—that is, son to father, sister's son to mother's brother, younger brother to older brother. In other cases a fictive relationship can ensure residence rights. A man can also live in his sister's hamlet if he makes a yam garden for her husband.[12]

Viewed from the position of the older man A, the lending of land and seeds entitles him to an increase in workpower and therefore in control over additional resources. From the position of the younger man B, the amount of labor expended is usually proportional to A's other possessions. By increasing the size of the garden, B can obtain valuables from A in payment for his additional labor. The performance and inheritance of magic spells and the introduction into *kula* roads are all possibilities that can accrue from the yam relationship between A and B. Therefore, older men afford younger men the opportunity for security and access to objects and knowledge (i.e., valuables, magic, *kula*) that only older men possess.

For example, the amount and kind of magic spells that men teach their sons are relative to the strength of the yam exchange relationship that a son enters into with his father. Men transmit to their sons magic that they have learned from their own fathers. Men also purchase magic spells with valuables from anyone, except their fathers, who wants to give the spells. This occurs when men need a stone ax blade or a pig and have only the knowledge of magic as a comparable commodity to exchange. Thus, men with valuables are always patiently waiting for someone to find himself in circumstances where he will be forced to "sell out." In addition, "new" magic purchased from men on other islands is always circulating in the Trobriands. Every Trobriander has an individual store of spells. Today most villagers keep these spells recorded in notebooks, hidden in the recesses of their houses. Spells that are *dala* property form one part of a man's total inventory. Men are not torn between teaching their spells to their sons or to their sisters' sons, as Malinowski thought (see Fortes 1957, who correctly analyzed this situation).

Under all circumstances men do not learn valuable kinds of magic spells from other men until they have proven themselves to be strong married men. The spells that men learn from their mothers' brothers depend upon their birth order. The oldest son of a man's oldest sister has more chance to learn *dala* magic, but there is often extensive competition. The teaching of all *dala* spells (i.e., the spells that came from the founders) must be directly paid for in valuables by a man's sister's son. Only when a man automatically takes over control of a hamlet (i.e., because he is the last male of his *dala*) is magic transmitted without payment. But the magic spells that a man learns from his father are never directly purchased.

Thus the most significant and primary relationships between men evolve out of the interaction between men of two generations. Regardless of the specific kinship ties, older men attract younger men into a relationship. Similarly, younger men must attach themselves to older men in order to gain access to those commodities which older men control. Whether or not a man eventually takes over the managership of *dala* land, his first stage of male interaction takes place through his father. If the chance for control of his own land is minimal, his father remains the best source for economic and political growth. In time, if a man becomes the manager of his *dala* land, his father provides him with material gain in addition to what his mother's brother has to offer. In other words, a man remains his son's best agent for maximization.

III

_____

Another man appears on the horizon, and is called by the

154 Fathers, Sons, and Land

child kadagu *("my mother's brother"). This man may live in the same locality, but he is just as likely to reside in another village. The child also learns that the place where his* kada *(mother's brother) resides is also his, the child's "own village"; that there he has his property and his other rights of citizenship; that there his future career awaits him; that there his natural allies and associates are to be found. . . . He also sees, as he grows up, that the mother's brother assumes a gradually increasing authority over him, requiring his services, helping him in some things, granting or withholding his permission to carry out certain actions; while the father's authority and counsel becomes less and less important.—Malinowski 1929, p. 7*

The only men who gain any advantage from living on their own *dala* land are those who are heirs to the status of manager. These are the men who return to take up residence on their own *dala* land. Malinowski's analysis focused on the processes of land control, and he saw avunculocal residence as the rule of residence with noted exceptions.[13]

From the point of view of the continuity and control of land, *dala* identity and a mother's brother are important factors. But hamlet control applies to only a few men. In terms of land use, a man's father is the central figure. An analysis of an "ideal" system with lists of "exceptions" does not make good sense to a Kiriwina person. A man who lives with his father does not consider himself an exception to a rule. This is the place where he *should* live, unless he is next in line to claim control of his own *dala* land.[14] A more accurate description of residence patterns is that two conditions must be met: (1) continuity and control of land must be maintained, and (2) a way for any man to find residence and garden land must be secured. (See table 2 for male residence patterns in the six hamlets of Kwaibwaga.)

Theoretically, managerial status in one's own *dala* passes from the manager to his younger brother until the last sibling set has died. Then the status of manager passes to the oldest sister's oldest son. Thus many men are effectively disbarred from ever attaining this status; the sons of younger sisters in a sibling set stand very little chance of becoming managers. If a man's son is next in line to inherit the control of his own *dala* land, he is sent

Table 2. *Male residence patterns in the six hamlets of Kwaibwaga*

Hamlet	Male house owners who belong to same *dala* as hamlet manager	Male house owners who are members of *dala* other than that of hamlet manager	Total
Kwebagatola	4	1	5
Kwebagatola	3	1	4
Katagava	0	16	16
Oilavau	1	13	14
Yaluwala	3	9	12
Obulabula	1	16	17

Note: The difference in the totals between this table and figure 1 occurs because there are five houses in which widows reside alone.

by his father to live with his mother's brother. Often, a sibling set will be sent to live avunculocally so that a man will have support from his younger brother. Although he is living with his mother's brother, a man will often continue to make a yam garden for his father. Because wealth and opportunity vary from situation to situation, each dyadic relationship has its own limitations. Birth order is another limiting factor. But, although the oldest son, the oldest brother, or the oldest son of a man's oldest sister each occupy a preferred position, any possibility of becoming an heir can be undermined by younger contenders. If a man "returns home" to live with his mother's brother, he is potentially in a position to become an influential man. His father can provide support for him in addition to that of his own *dala*. In fact, if a man's son becomes powerful, his father might take up residence with him.

IV

What is interesting in Trobriand inheritance, especially of land and of magic, is that although it is the legal due of the younger man it has yet to be purchased by a special system of payments called pokala. *If, for instance, a younger brother or maternal nephew of the titular owner, i.e., his direct and immediate heir, or maybe heir once removed, wishes to acquire the title of* tolikwabila *or* tolibaleko, *he would offer his senior several substantial payments and the title would be, so to speak, gradually relinquished.—Malinowski 1935a, p. 345*

Malinowski noted that he did not understand why in some cases payments for acquiring land were made to a man's mother's brother and yet at other times the land was transferred without any payments (1922, p. 185). A man does not automatically take control of his own land unless he is the last male in his *dala*. In this case, the land passes to him without any payment being necessary on his part or without the need to make a yam exchange garden for the manager.

As long as there is more than one heir, a man must secure his rights to control by making a yam exchange garden for his mother's brother and by making *pokala* payments. The following is the way in which *pokala* was once described to me.

> The first time I go to my *kadala* [mother's brother] and I take him some fish. I say to him, "*Kadala*, here is your fish."
>
> Maybe one week or two weeks later, I return to this man and I give him some money. This time I say nothing about the money; I just give it to him without talking.
>
> The third time, I take that man some fish and I just leave it for him in his house.
>
> The fourth time I take some calico, but if I want many things from this man I take a *beku*. This time, my *kadala* says to me, "Stay and we will eat together." We eat together and then we have a conversation. My mother's brother says to me, "What do you want? You have given me many things. What do you want? Magic? Land? Areca palms?"
>
> "I want some land," I say.
>
> My mother's brother gives me a parcel of land to use, but, if I continue to make *pokala* to this man, later he will give me magic, more land, and coconut and areca palms.

According to my informants, all *pokala* transactions between *dala* members are enacted in this manner. The most important part of making *pokala*, I was told, is not to say the word *pokala* aloud when giving things to someone. To make *pokala*, a man gives and then he waits. To talk about *pokala* is a shameful thing to do and can often detract from success. To do *pokala* for land a man must be strong (*bulukupeula*), because presentations must continually be made to the manager of the land. (See figure 13 for a summary of *pokala* exchanges for rights to control hamlet and garden lands.)

If there is competition for control of the land between several men of the same *dala* (i.e., brothers or sons of several sisters), then the strongest man—the man with wealth, magic, and/or a strong father and affines—has the best chance to make extensive *pokala* for the land. In cases where two strong men compete for land, both may receive a parcel of land.

Figure 14 presents the genealogical history of a *dala*'s land for four generations. There are five important points concerning land tenure which this case history illustrates. (1) Sometimes there are two men who have the means to be competitive, and therefore they divide control of the land (see items B, C, and D; G, H, and I). (2) Living with the manager of the land and making a yam exchange garden for him each year are significant ways to gain control of the land when he dies (see item G). (3) Sons can continue to use their father's land after he dies (see item Q). (4) The last member of a *dala* automatically gains control of the land without making any payments of *pokala* or making yam exchange gardens (see item O). (5) When the last *dala* member dies, sometimes a fictive identity is arranged and a "new" man—one who is not a true genealogical member of the *dala*—moves into control of the land (see items P and R). Under some circumstances, a man whose founders came together with the original *dala* founders will take control. In other instances, a man's own sons will control that land.

Situations occur whereby other hamlet managers seek additional garden land for themselves and the residents of their hamlet. Hamlet managers try to become controllers of garden lands—*tolibaleko*—other than their own by making *pokala* payments. Often this means that high-rank men make *pokala* to men of lesser rank. In figure 15, I have diagrammed the direction of exchanges of land and valuables in *pokala* transactions for land tenantship (the use of garden land by managers from other hamlets). The initial *pokala* transactions follow the same pattern that a man

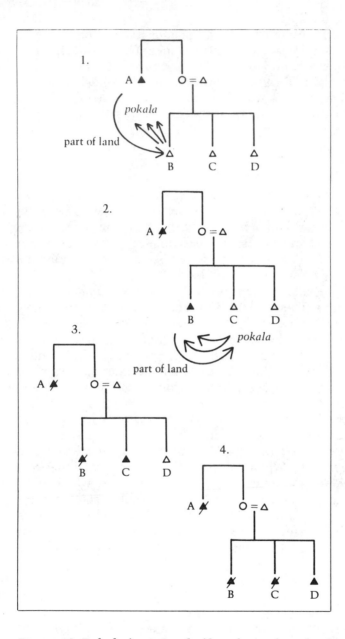

Figure 13. Pokala *for control of hamlet and garden lands in one's own* dala. *(1) B makes* pokala *to A. A gives B part of land. (2) A dies. B controls all of land. C makes* pokala *to B. B gives C part of land. (3) B dies. C controls land. D does not make* pokala *because he is the last man in his* dala. *(4) C dies. D controls land.*

uses to gain control of land in his own hamlet. But in this case further obligations are necessary. If a man wants to gain access to and retain use of a parcel of garden land which belongs to another hamlet, he must be wealthy enough to present valuables to the man who gave him the use of the land each time a death occurs in his own *dala*.[15] In other words, if a man who controls his own *dala* land decides to give a parcel of garden land to another hamlet manager from another *dala*, the first hamlet manager has the right to reclaim his garden land at the death of someone in the tenant's *dala*. But, as long as the tenant continues to do *pokala* each time someone dies in his own *dala*, then the men of the owning *dala* can only demand return of the land after the tenant himself has died.

The requirements are such that only hamlet managers usually do *pokala* for land from other hamlet managers. In this way, a manager can increase the size of his own yam and taro exchange gardens which other men (affines and sons) make for him. At the death of a manager, the true *dala* members of the leased land come to reclaim their land. But all claims on land require wealth presentations by the men of the *dala* to whom the land belongs. Taking one's own land back also entails a display of verbal strength and a long waiting period until the mourning for the deceased is finished. The following example, which occurred after the death of Uwelasi, a chief from Tubuwada village, illustrates the conflicts inherent in such a system of detachment and recall of land.

In the past, Uwelasi had made *pokala* for three large parcels of land from three other hamlet managers in his clan. Now that he was dead, the men who controlled their *dala* lands came to the first mortuary ceremony (*sigiliyawali*) to reclaim their land. At the end of the mortuary ceremony (see p. 74), the transactions for the land took place. There were about one hundred men sitting in the center of Uwelasi's hamlet. Monoyawa, who was the last member of Uwelasi's *dala*, was leaning against one of Uwelasi's full yam houses. Six men walked in single file to where Monoyawa stood and presented him with A$4 and four clay pots. The man in front of the line, who controlled his *dala* land, said to Monoyawa:

> Today, I find you and I do *sagali* for you. When Uwelasi was sick, you cooked food for him. [Monoyawa had killed a large pig for Uwelasi.] When you fed Uwelasi, he said to you, "When I die, Monoyawa, you must look after

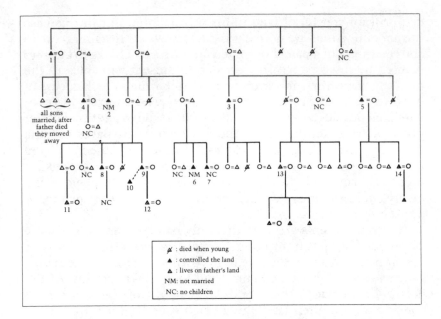

△ : died when young
▲ : controlled the land
▲ : lives on father's land
NM: not married
NC: no children

Figure 14. Genealogy of dala *land for four generations. Today all the people are dead except 10, 11, 12, 13, 14, and their children.*

A. *1 was controller of the land*
B. *2 made* pokala *for the land to 1*
C. *3 made* pokala *for the land to 1*
D. *1 gave some land to 2 and some to 3*
E. *3 made* pokala *again to 1 with the help of his brothers*
F. *1 gave 3 most of the land, and when 1 died 3 had almost all the land except the part given to 2. 5 controlled the land when 3 died.*
G. *4 and 6 made* pokala *to 2; 6 lived in the same hamlet with 2 until 2 died*
H. *2 died, and 4 and 6 controlled his part of the land*
I. *4 died, and 6 controlled his land*
J. *8 and 9 lived with 2 until they married; 2 lived to be a very old man*
K. *7 made* pokala *to 6 and controlled some of his land*
L. *6 died, and 7 received all his land to control*
M. *8 and 9 made* pokala *to 7 for the land*
N. *7 died, and 8 and 9 controlled all his land*
O. *8 and 5 died, and 9 got all the land and did not* pokala *because he was the last man of his* dala
P. *10, a young man from another* dala *of the same* kumila, *lived with 9*
Q. *11, 12, 13, and 14 now live on their fathers' land*
R. *9 died, and now "new" man 10 controls all the land*

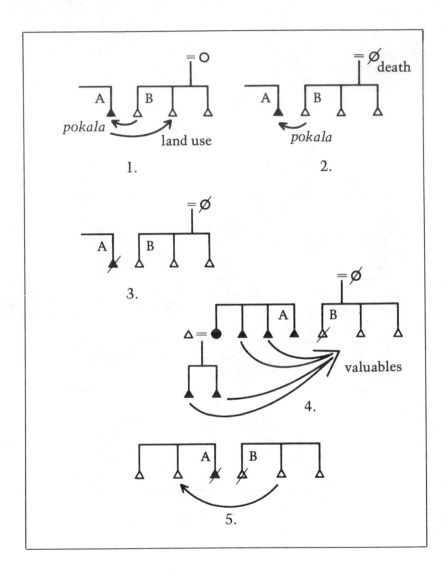

Figure 15. Pokala *for use of land in another* dala. *(1) B makes* pokala *to A. A gives B land to use. (2) Someone in B's* dala *dies. B makes* pokala *to A to continue to use land. (3) A dies. B continues use of land. (4) B dies. A's kinsmen bring valuables to B's successor at B's* sigiliyawali. *(5) At the end of the mourning period, B's heir returns land to A's heir.*

all the land in Tubuwada." I knew that Uwelasi was going to
die and I also knew that no one would look after all the garden land and hamlet land except you, Monoyawa. So I
came today and now I do *sagali* for you. I want my
land and I take it back.

Then Monoyawa said:

> Already you did *sagali* for me and that is finished. Do
> not worry about your money and clay pots. I will not eat
> your money. I will just keep it for a while; I will wait with
> it. When my uncle Uwelasi got sick, I only cooked food for
> him for four days, and then he died. He did not tell me
> which part of the land is mine. He just said, "If I am
> going to die, you must control all the land; it is your
> *karewaga* "

Monoyawa explained that he did not know the division of all
the land and that only Uwelasi's son knew about the land. He explained that he would take the valuables and keep them for a year
until Uwelasi's son stopped mourning for his father. When the
mourning period was over, Uwelasi's son would advise Monoyawa about the boundaries of all the land.

Later, my informants told me that Uwelasi's son had always
lived with his father and knew all about the land: which land belonged to Uwelasi and which belonged to other people. Therefore,
his son would remain on his father's land and live in his father's
hamlet, continuing to use his father's land.

This example not only illustrates the dynamics of *pokala* for
garden land but again introduces the importance of the relationship between father and son. By living with his father, a man not
only has possibilities for access to material things, he also gains
knowledge which makes him important for the continuity of his
father's landholdings. The waiting period which Monoyawa used
to delay the return of the land is an important mechanism for
understanding one aspect of the long mourning period. Not only
does time allow people to reorganize, but time keeps all the relationships which the deceased has established from falling apart
too quickly.

Despite the system of land control there are always situations
in which land is lost. Sometimes land loss occurs because the
dala is lost. When the women of a *dala* do not give birth to sons,
the land does not continue with the *dala*'s name. Sometimes a
dala name continues publicly, but a man from a different *dala*

controls the land. In this situation, the *dala* transfer is considered private and secret knowledge, and men go to great lengths to avoid a public discussion of the genealogy of the land. In other cases, the land is lost because men have made "mistakes," and out of fear they never reclaim their land.

About seventy years ago, men from two high-rank *dala* lived in the same village, but *dala* A was of higher rank than *dala* B. A man from *dala* B committed adultery with a woman who was the wife of an important man from *dala* A. When their secret was discovered, the hamlet manager of *dala* B moved out, along with his two brothers, because he was afraid the men of *dala* A would poison him and his kin.

Unfortunately for the men of *dala* B, but luckily for the men of *dala* A, there were large tracts of garden land near the village that belonged to *dala* B. The chief of *dala* A made *pokala* to the chief of *dala* B for all this land. Because of great fear and anxiety over the situation, all of *dala* B's land was used by the chief of *dala* A. Under normal circumstances, *dala* A had only gained the right to use the land and the men of *dala* B could have reclaimed their land when the chief of *dala* A died.

The men of *dala* B, however, were afraid to reclaim the land. When the chief of *dala* A died, his successor made *pokala* to the hamlet manager of *dala* B, who lived in another village, having made *pokala* for the use of his new hamlet. Again, when the second chief of *dala* A died, the third chief to control *dala* A made *pokala*. After another death, and *pokala*, the chief of *dala* B told the chief of *dala* A, "Already you made *pokala* for my land three times and now I say that that land is finished. It is your land and you do not have to make *pokala* again." In figure 16, I have diagramed these transactions.

Some mistakes can be serious, and in this situation adultery was a mistake that caused the loss of a *dala*'s land. The chief of *dala* B never gained more political power than the chief of *dala* A, and finally the only option open was default of the land. (The people who committed adultery left the island for a time and then returned to another hamlet.)

In a village hamlet, the last man to control a *dala*'s land (*dala* 1) died. Several years before, a young man from another *dala* (*dala* 2) of the same clan was brought to live with the manager of the land. Genealogically, these two *dala* were unrelated, but traditionally the men of these two *dala* had always helped each other, and land had been lent between *dala* 1 and *dala* 2. Historically, the origin story of *dala* 2 described the way in which the women and men of

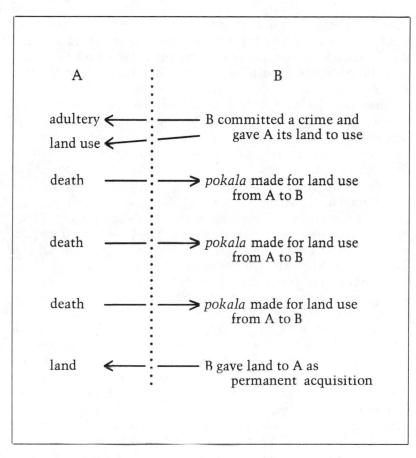

Figure 16. History of land exchange between dala *A and* dala *B.
For each death that occurred in* dala *A, the chief made* pokala *to*
dala *B for continued land use.*

dala 1 had helped them when they first arrived by canoe in Kiriwina. They were fed by the people who belonged to *dala* 1, and
thus began a long tradition of relationship between the two *dala*.
Thus they considered each other *veyola* (kin from the same place
of origin).

When the last man from *dala* 1 died, his "sister's son"—the
young man from *dala* 2—became the "new" man (*tovau*), and he
now controls the land (see fig. 14, items P and R, for a diagram of
this situation). An interesting aspect of the history of this land is
that four men are living on the land who have rights to the use of
the land through their deceased fathers, who were all members of
the original *dala* (see fig. 14, item Q). They each make a yam exchange garden for the "new" man, and by these exchanges they
validate their own rights to the use of the land. At the same time,
they are keeping the options open for their own sons to remain on
the land after they die. On the day that each man presented the
produce from his yam garden to the "new" man, I asked each one
why he was giving away yams. Their answers were all the same:
"I am taking the place of my father."

At the moment, the power situation for the "new" owner is not
yet secure. These four men have much to say about the organization of the land. They told me that their fathers had said, "If that
man is not a good man, then send him away." Recently, the
"new" owner gave some land to his brother-in-law to use, but one
of the four men had planned to use the land himself. They had an
argument over the land, and the "new" owner said that they
should go to court to settle the dispute. The other man cautioned
him, reminding him that if a court case developed he would have
to tell the true story of the land, and then the "new" owner would
lose the land because it was not truly his.

The court case was cancelled, and the use of the parcel of land
went to the man whose father was in the original *dala*. The
"new" man said that if they had had a court case it would have
"spoiled the name of the entire village."

Dala land is identified with one or two men who are in control of the land. If the genealogy of the land is incorrect in terms
of shifts in *dala* control, the history of the land remains private
knowledge, only becoming public when censure demands it. The
corporateness of land relates to its history from the time of the
founders. The importance of the origin story is that it described
men and women of the same *dala*, each of whom at one time
found land and then had the power to control the destiny of that
land. People identify themselves with their own land, but saying

"this is my land" does not have the same meaning as "I control this land." It is *dala* identity which is corporate; the history of the land for as long as the *dala* lasts is corporate, but the actual control of the land is ego-centered and the use of the land is diverse.[16]

Land is lent out for others to use. The primary return for land use and residence is yam production. In cases of *pokala*, tenantship of land brings returns of valuables for the manager of the land. In this latter exchange, residence with the land manager is not a factor. Thus, land is detached by the managers, lent out, and finally reclaimed in the name of the *dala*. In the process of the circulation of land, men either attach other men to themselves and control of workpower is organized, or wealth is transferred in the form of valuables.

Men detach decorations and names identified with their own *dala* heritage and lend these symbols of *dala* identity to their children. A similar process occurs with land in that again men detach that which carries the name of a *dala* and give it to others to use. An understanding of the way residence, yam production, and land use are integrated explains the resolution of two problems inherent in land tenure and the development of power: continuity of *dala* land through time and land for all men to use. Because the system of land control only admits a few men, most men find themselves using other *dala* land. The men who control land become strong men by being able to manipulate appropriations of land, thereby attracting other men.[17] Continuity through time is partially achieved by the significance given to origin stories. Knowledge of these stories gives men the right to claim land and to maintain their authority over land.

But, although men overtly reclaim their own land or politically manipulate claims to land, women are the ultimate reclaimers of the land. As long as there are women from a particular *dala* who give birth to sons, *dala* and land continue. Without sons, land is transferred either to the identity of a new *dala* or to "new" men who assume the identity of the old *dala*. Only women make the continuity of land a true historical tradition.

Chapter 7
Marriage: From Beauty to Objects

I

In the ordinary course of events, every marriage is pre-
ceded by a more or less protracted period of sexual life in
common. This is generally known and spoken of, and is re-
garded as a public intimation of the matrimonial projects
of the pair. It serves also as a test of the strength of their
attachment and extent of their mutual compatibility.
—Malinowski 1929, p. 67

When a boy is established in his own quarters (the bachelor house), he makes fundamental exchanges with men. Also at this time he very slowly begins to cultivate, through exchange, social relationships with female relatives who will help him throughout his life. Now a boy begins to look for partners for sexual relationships, one of which will eventually lead to marriage (see plate 18).

For most people the tradition still remains that an unmarried boy should take a single girl to his bachelor house at night. It is considered very shameful for a boy to sleep with a girl in her parents' house. One boy from Kwaibwaga was forced to leave his hamlet and live elsewhere because he was found sleeping with a girl in her parents' house. His actions caused his own relatives great shame. One night an angry argument broke out and, in self-defense, the boy ran away from Kwaibwaga. Several days later, some of his relatives from another village came and carried his house away to Omarakana, where he has now established a new residence for himself.

Occasionally, girls will occupy a house which is temporarily vacant, as happened when some people in Kwaibwaga went to live in another village for several months to mourn for a relative who had died. In their absence three sisters lived together in their

Plate 18. An unmarried Kwaibwaga boy makes himself
attractive for Kwaibwaga girls

house, but usually a counterpart to a bachelor house does not exist for young girls.

The separation of youths from their parental homes is publicly enacted for boys, while the separation for girls is a much more private and flexible affair. During the daytime, young girls still live with their parents. Superficially at least, no one should note a girl's nightly absence from her parents' house.

Young people still conform rigidly to the rules described by Malinowski (1929, pp. 73–75), in which girls are not to be seen entering or leaving the houses of their lovers and must never eat food in front of their lovers. Even at a large feast with hundreds of people milling about, a girl must hide in the bush to eat her food if her current lover is at the feast. Everyone knows who is sleeping with whom, and everyone except a girl's father and her brothers gossips and talks about the liaison, but the public act of sitting and eating together in the boy's hamlet radically alters the meaning of the relationship.

One of my closest young friends in Kwaibwaga was Boiyagwa, who was sleeping regularly with a young boy from Omarakana. Some mornings, Boiyagwa would not appear in Kwaibwaga; when this happened, my neighbors would tell me that "perhaps she was already married and staying in Omarakana." Each time this happened, however, Boiyagwa finally returned late in the morning or early in the afternoon. She told me that she had slept too late in the morning, when the other villagers were already walking about. She therefore had to wait inside her lover's house without food until all the people left for the gardens, so that she could leave the house without being seen by anyone.

In addition to these taboos, there are other strictures placed on who sleeps with whom. Most liaisons should occur within the village or neighboring villages. But this rule is enforced by one's peer group. If a boy from Kwaibwaga begins to sleep with someone from another village, and a girl in Kwaibwaga wants that boy for herself, then Kwaibwaga unmarried girls organize and wait for the unsuspecting villain to walk along the paths between the villages. The village girls spring out of their hiding places along the path and attack the boy with knives. I bandaged several boys who had been attacked in this manner by Kwaibwaga girls, and shortly after such incidents the boy was sleeping with a Kwaibwaga girl.

Boys also profess anger when a Kwaibwaga girl sleeps with a lover from another village. But boys do not physically assault a girl.[1] Neither do they engage in a fight with her lover, for fear of potential repercussion which would expand into intervillage feuding. Although their elders place few restraints on the sexual adventures of the young, these amorous affairs are often surrounded by anxiety and the attempt by peers to control each other's behavior.

Young boys, much more than girls, need friends to help them arrange meetings. They need some means to find objects such as tobacco and betel nuts: tokens to entice the girl they want as a lover and tokens to give their male and female friends for their help. A boy's father is the major provider of these things and therefore, when a boy takes up residence in a bachelor house, he remains dependent on others. Thus, being young and free involves fighting, secrets, teasing, finding friends to act as go-betweens, and the constant fear of losing a lover to someone else.

Only magic provides a solution to the insecurity generated by the inability to transform rejection into desire. In the enchanted eyes of the beholder, the ugly become handsome, the weak become strong, and even the old become young. Giving tobacco and betel nuts as tokens of intent and having exchange and friend relationships and even physical beauty carry no absolute guarantee of success. Through any of these means, Trobrianders believe that "there is no way to control the mind of another person." Thus nothing is more powerful than the use of love magic to induce desire in another person.

All boys have their private stock of love magic. Spells are recited over flowers and into coconut oil, with which they adorn themselves. When girls see the flower stuck in a boy's hair, or a glistening body, the response should be immediate desire. Girls also use these elements to attract. More potent in terms of control is the spell said by a specialist who breathes the words directly into a betel nut or tobacco. A friend of the suitor offers the impregnated object to the girl. Once ingested, the released words "spoil her mind," for now she can no longer think freely.

The following is a small part of a love spell recited into a betel nut or tobacco. It was told to me by Mekiyasi, a man renowned for his knowledge of powerful love magic.

Gala tegamu tegamu tegiliwali.
Gala tegagu tegagu tegababa.
Gala tegamu tegamu tegababa.
Gala tegagu tegagu tegiliwali.
Tuli yokwa, baba yegu.

Igilugilunanomu ikaleguyaya nanomu.

Lokugisegu lokukwoma kamu.
Gala kugisegu kasikaukaw kosibunukwa.
Kusuvibwala kuvilamu.
Kuloya keda kutigili.
Kuloya keda kutigili.

No, your ear, you do not hear [the advice of your relatives].
No, my ear, I am deaf.
No, your ear, you are deaf.
No, my ear, I do not hear [the advice of my relatives].
You are deaf, I am deaf.

Your mind becomes weak, your mind dies.
You see me, you eat food, eat.
If you do not see me, you throw your food to the dog. You throw
   your food to the pig.
You go inside your house, you cry.
You walk to the road, you cry. [You wait for me.]
You walk to the road, you cry. [You wait for me.]

II

There is, further, the natural inclination of a man past his
first youth to have a house and a household of his own. The
services rendered by a woman to her husband are naturally at-
tractive to a man of such an age; his craving for domesticity has
developed, while his desire for change and amorous adventure
has died down. . . .
   The woman, who has no economic inducement to marry, and
who gains less in comfort and social status than the man, is
mainly influenced by personal affection and the desire to
have children in wedlock.—Malinowski 1929, pp. 81–82

When a girl remains in her lover's house in the morning, so that
other people in the hamlet see the two of them sitting eating food
together, they are publicly on view as partners in a new marriage
(*vegilevau* means "newly married"). Their public appearance sig-

nifies a forthcoming change in their life style, because now a woman as wife (*kwava*) and a man as husband (*mwala*) will gradually begin full participation in formal exchanges.

Prior to the moment when a boy and a girl decide to announce their intentions, evaluations and discussions concerning the talents and abilities of each partner are ongoing topics of conversation and gossip. The criteria used in the judgments are approximately the same for either a girl or a boy, but the dynamics and the people involved in making decisions are very different.

The father of the boy and the father of the girl are the *karewaga* of the subsequent marriage exchanges. But their public and private performances differ dramatically. A boy's relatives make their decision regarding the forthcoming marriage *before* the marriage becomes public knowledge. (I use the term "relatives" or "relations"—following my informants' use of *veyola*—to include members of a woman's or a man's *dala* and her or his father.) Most boys have a special first-love relationship, but this is rarely the person whom they finally sit with and eat with and, thus, marry. One day a married man told me the following story:

> Today I saw G on the road. This girl G used to be my
> very best friend. I gave her some tobacco because she and
> I were first friends. My father told me I should marry B in-
> stead of G. He said B worked very hard with her mother and
> she knew how to make mats and skirts very well. So I
> married B but always I remember G, and whenever I
> see her I always give her a present of betel nuts or to-
> bacco.

Other men told me similar stories.

A boy's father must approve of his marriage or the marriage does not take place. The only way to escape a disapproving father is to take up residence with another man and sever the exchange connections with one's father by making a yam exchange garden for another man. In Kwaibwaga, one boy moved to live in the same hamlet with his married sister and her husband because his father, living in another hamlet in Kwaibwaga, did not approve of his son's marital choice. A boy's father controls his marriage, and the only way to escape his final judgment is to escape from the relationship itself.

For a girl, control by elders remains at best ambiguous. Prior to the announcement of marriage, a man cannot discuss his daughter's forthcoming marriage. Although information concerning who is sleeping with whom is common knowledge, it is assumed that a girl's father and her brothers do not have any knowledge of her sexual liaisons. It is extremely shameful to discuss the sexual adventures of a girl with either her father or her brothers. A father learns of his daughter's marital arrangements *after* she has been seen sitting with her lover in his hamlet. At that time, the girl's mother goes to her daughter's brothers and father and tells them that the girl is already married.

These data differ from Malinowski's interpretation in that he inferred that a man usually makes prior arrangements for his daughter's marriage:

> It is remarkable that, of all the girl's family, the person who has most to say about her marriage, although legally he is not reckoned as her kinsman (*veyola*), is her father. . . .
>
> When two lovers have decided on marriage, . . . perhaps her father will, on his own initiative, say: "You sleep with my child: very well, marry her." (1929, pp. 84–85)

According to my informants, a father is most important to his daughter's marriage, but only *after* the marriage is made public.[2] Malinowski (ibid.) placed emphasis on the importance of the father prior to his daughter's marriage, because he said that a girl's mother's brother cannot have anything to do with arranging her marriage because of the extension of the brother-sister taboo regarding sexual matters to all of a sister's maternal relatives.

The brother-sister taboo operates between a brother and sister in their own personal lives. It does not extend to relationships between a mother's brother and a sister's daughter. A girl's mother's brother admonishes her in public for improper behavior concerning her affairs with boys. I attended several village court cases held in Kwaibwaga in which young unmarried girls were reprimanded for inappropriate behavior (e.g., pp. 178–179). The men spoke very openly about the problems which had developed regarding the sexual liaisons of their sisters' daughters. These arguments took place in front of the girls' mothers, sisters, and other mother's brothers. Absent from the court cases were the girls' brothers and fathers.

A girl's mother's brother leads the gossip about the value of a marriage between his sister's daughter and a boy before the marriage is publicly proclaimed. The girl's father is not part of this gossip. Covertly, a girl's mother's brother has very much to do with approval or disapproval *prior* to the marriage, but the decision is not made public until the girl's intentions are publicly dis-played and she remains in her husband's hamlet. Then her father acts in her behalf. If the marriage is unacceptable to the girl's kin (now including her father) she is physically taken from the house of her lover by both her parents and brought back to her own residential hamlet. Situations of this nature occurred while I was living in Kwaibwaga, and Malinowski (1929, pp. 85–88) gives several very similar accounts. In all the cases I heard about, the boy was called "ugly," "lazy," and "weak" by the girl's relatives.

In summary, the girl's relatives either allow the marriage to become formalized by bringing raw yams to the boy's relatives, or they publicly stop the marriage by removing their daughter from the boy's hamlet as soon as the marriage itself becomes public knowledge. But, in the words of one of my informants, "A father has everything to say about what his son does, whom he marries, where he goes, but a father says nothing about his daughter."

Overriding all the public and private approvals and disapprovals, however, are the wishes of the young girl. If a girl does not want to marry someone, she does not, regardless of the pressure of her relatives. Or, if she finally acquiesces, she may later leave the man her parents favor and return to live with her mother and father. Conversely, if a girl decides to marry a man who is objectionable to her kin, she has ways to finally win out over any opposition. Although, at first, her parents will drag her home from the village of her spouse, she can leave her own village and meet her lover at the beach. There they will live together for two or three days, and the marriage is a *fait accompli*. The exchange of yams and valuables must follow, for not to enter into the appropriate marriage exchanges is shameful for both sides.

In marriage, clan exogamy is the rule, but there are a few cases in which villagers have married a clansperson. Economically, these marriages are disadvantageous because the mortuary payments at the death of a spouse occur within a clan rather than between two clans, thus splitting segments of a clan rather than uniting segments. Villagers attach great shame to clan endogamous marriages, and the situation cannot be discussed with any of the wife's or husband's relatives. In all cases, other people told me that "the girl wanted to marry him. She cried and she would not eat. And so they married."

A young girl is aggressive in seeking liaisons with lovers. She can reject a boy. She can take advantage of his tokens of admiration without succumbing to his advances. With counterspells she can even disengage herself from the force of the magic enclosed in a betel nut. Further, her activities are given a protective cloak under which she remains autonomous. Unlike boys, who separate from living with parents, girls remain at home, publicly at least. Once a boy takes up residence in a bachelor house, his responsibility and accountability to adults place constraints on his behavior. Although young girls help their mothers in making skirts and bundles, this help is not obligatory, because there is no reciprocal return for such service.

Young girls who are accorded an extensive degree of independence must finally make up their minds and choose a spouse. Just as young boys must choose the setting and the words with which to publicly speak their minds in political matters, girls must decide when to be seen eating with a boy. Thus girls through marriage and boys through politics are encouraged by an older generation to make their thoughts public. But, in these areas, encouragement is not control: only the young themselves can make such statements.

III

And the only really substantial gifts from the bridegroom's family to the bride's . . . [valuables] . . . exert a definitely binding force on the husband, for if the marriage be dissolved, he does not recover them save in exceptional cases. . . . But this present from the husband must emphatically not be considered as purchase money for the bride. This idea is utterly opposed both to the native point of view and to the facts of the case. Marriage is meant to confer substantial material benefits on the man. . . . It is an anticipation of the benefits to follow, and by no means a price paid for the bride.—Malinowski 1929, p. 93

When a girl and boy make their intentions public, the girl's own kinsmen and her father first bring baskets of yams to the boy's relatives. The placing of yams in front of the boy's father's house by the girl's father is called *katuvila*. The organizer and owner of this exchange is the girl's father (or, if she does not have a father, her mother's brother); it is his *karewaga*. He and his wife's brother collect their own yams and yams from other kinsmen of both *dala*.

My informants said that the boy's father (also called *karewaga*) takes each basket of yams to one of the boy's *dala* kinsmen. Every man who receives yams must return a valuable (a stone ax blade, a shell necklace, a clay pot, or money) to the boy's father.[3] He then distributes the valuables to the girl's relatives who gave the yams. This return exchange is called *takola*. These are the first transactions between the boy's father and his own *dala* relatives and the girl's father and her own *dala* relatives.[4]

A boy must be assured that valuables are forthcoming, for, if he is accepted by a girl's relatives, then his side must reciprocate valuables for yams. If a boy's father disapproves of his son's choice, his disapproval signals the unavailability of valuables. A boy does not sit and eat openly with his "friend" (*lubegu*) until he knows that his father will approve of his friend's becoming a wife.

The significance of valuables was illustrated in the following village court case. Two young girls were reprimanded for interfering with another girl's relationship with a boy. The two girls were sisters, and the following was spoken by their mother's brother, Bunemiga:

> Remember, if you get married, then we take some
> yams for you girls and give the yams to your husbands'
> relations and your husbands' relations give us valuables.
> We take those valuables to our houses and we look after
> them. You live with your husband for a long time, but your
> husband is always quarreling with you and he hits you. You
> come to our houses because you do not want to be married to
> him any more. Do you think we will believe you? No, we
> cannot believe you girls, because when you were single you
> began to be friends with that boy. We told you to stop sleep-
> ing with that boy, but you did not want to stop. You got mar-
> ried anyway, and now you want a divorce because you tell us
> that your husband's customs are not good.
> We are frightened of your husband's relatives because they
> gave us those valuables. When you come to our houses, we
> cannot stop you with your husband. We will send you back
> because, when we told you to stop sleeping with that boy,
> you married him anyway. That boy gave us valuables and we

must take care of him. If he hits you or quarrels with you, if he does not give you betel nuts or tobacco, you cannot say to us, "I do not want to stay with him because I made a mistake." We said "stop with that boy" and you did not stop.

If a second time you come to your mother and father because you left your husband, they will send you back again and you will have to stay there until your husband dies, because we have those valuables and we are frightened of your husband's relatives. Remember, if you are married and your husband is mean to you, how can we stop you, because we have those valuables. Before Europeans came here, our customs were like this. Today nobody can break the rules. Our customs are still like this.

Bunemiga's admonishment to his sister's daughters reflects less the actual control that elders exercise over young girls than the bind in which they find themselves as a result of the girls' ultimate autonomy both before and after marriage. Although ostensibly Bunemiga warns of the dire consequences that befall girls if they change their minds, his implicit concern is with the dire consequences that will befall him. A discussion of the nature of valuables is necessary to understand the predicament that Bunemiga foresees.

Of all objects of exchange, shell and stone valuables are inherently the most durable and permanent. Within the internal exchange system in Kiriwina, stone ax blades (*beku*) are the most valued. A man is called wealthy (*toesaesa*) if he owns such ax blades. The general term for *beku* is *veguwa*. Clay pots (*kuliya*), manufactured in the Amphlett Islands (cf. Lauer 1970a, 1970b, 1973; Malinowski 1922, pp. 282–286), are used as utilitarian cooking pots, but they are also used as *veguwa* for exchange. Shell valuables, such as those in *kula*, as well as shell body decorations are sometimes substituted for *beku* and are also classified as *veguwa*. Today, Western cash has become an important object in the *veguwa* classification. But, even though the stone for *beku* is not being quarried anymore, *beku* is still considered the primary wealth object.[5]

The sizes of the ax blades vary. Men say that the worth of a *beku* is determined by its length: hand, hand to elbow, and full arm length. *Beku* are undecorated and are not elaborated with any external markings of individual identification. The physical and aesthetic properties of the stone are in sharp contrast to the overelaboration and colorful decorations of *kula* valuables. *Beku*

*Plate 19. In this payment of stone ax blades (*beku*) during one transaction (*wayala kaybila*) in the first* sagali *after Uwelasi's burial, an argument occurred as one man claimed ownership of a* beku *that another man had just presented. The first man said several months ago the second man denied to him that he had the first man's* beku. *Now he could tell by the coloration of the stone that it was his* beku, *and he began to recite the history of all who had once owned the* beku. *The piece of folded paper is an Australian two-dollar bill, given by someone in lieu of a* beku.

are made from smooth, dark, flat stone, but the stone itself has streaks of lighter-colored stone. The colored markings and the size of the stone are the only physical criteria which men use to differentiate their own *beku* from *beku* which belong to others (see plate 19).

Stone ax blades can be converted through exchanges into a wide variety of other objects and services.[6] For example, *beku* are especially important as payment for having someone perform sorcery. *Beku* can be exchanged for pigs, magic spells, seed yams, and raw yams. Unlike yams, the virtually indestructible ax blade circulates for generations. Moreover, ax blades, unlike yams, are not home-grown. As with certain other valuables—for example, clay pots and shell decorations—ax blades are manufactured by specialists. Access to these manufactured valuables within Kiriwina comes about primarily through exchanges of pigs, yams, and magic spells.[7]

In overseas *kula*, men have the opportunity to find additional objects of wealth: clay pots, shell valuables, and stone ax blades. Some necklaces and armshells (*soulava* and *mwali*) are collectively called *kitoma* because they are *not yet* part of any *kula* road. These shell valuables provide some of the keenest competition in *kula*. Men try to obtain as many of these *kitoma* as possible. Success presents a man not only with prestige but also with several options. A man can put *kitoma* into the *kula* ring, thereby establishing new partners or strengthening old ones. Also, the *kitoma* valuables can be given as wealth within Kiriwina, or they can be given to one's children for body decorations.

Access to valuables is of the utmost political importance. Hamlet managers, whether of high or low rank, constantly need valuables in order to keep making payments (*pokala*) for continued land use. Men who control workpower need valuables to repay other men for large yam gardens. Men need valuables for the marriages of their sons, brothers, and sisters' sons, and men need valuables when a death occurs. If *kula* is the most expedient road to find wealth objects for one's own use, then I suggest that the search for valuables remains a driving force behind the *kula* exchange of an armshell or a necklace.[8]

Just as *kula* valuables move from place to place, so too do stone ax blades. *Beku* "walk around," I was told, and the history of each *beku* is a history of its travels. Figure 17 traces the actual history of one *beku*, which traveled away from its owner for seven years and was finally reclaimed. As this diagram shows, the *beku* is released by its owner either as payment in specific exchange relations (i.e., marriage or mortuary distributions) or when other objects such as pigs, betel nuts, or yams are needed. Once a *beku* is set into circulation, it may travel from one man to another, and with each transaction each donor of the *beku* receives another commodity in return. But stone ax blades should never become alienated from their original owner. Although *beku* "walk around," an owner should be able to trace his *beku*. By making an appropriate exchange of yams, betel nuts, or pigs (called *ibasi laveguwa*), an owner reclaims his own *beku* from the last man who received it.

As one would expect, there are innumerable quarrels and court cases concerning the true ownership of *beku*. Ax blades "walk" very far, and sometimes men have problems reclaiming their own *beku*. Other men might substitute a different ax blade, which is then reclaimed by its legal owner when the *beku* is used in a public exchange such as mortuary ceremonies. At other times, a man will say that he does not remember ever having the *beku* which is being requested. A man must be strong and well respected (i.e., feared) to be assured of recapturing his own *beku*. Several men told me how they lost their own *beku* because the last man who had the *beku* told a different story of its history and won the resulting court case.

Once a *beku* is sent on its way, it should return, but there is

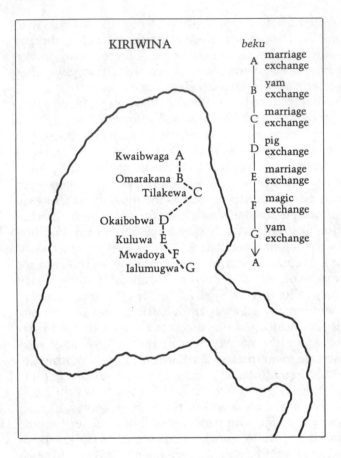

Figure 17. Seven-year history of the travels of one beku. *The map shows the villages in the northern part of Kiriwina through which the* beku *traveled. (1) A owned the* beku. *A's son married a girl whose father was from village B. A received yams from B. B received the* beku *from A. (2) B had the* beku. *C needed a* beku, *and he gave B yams. B gave the* beku *to C. (B and C were relatives.) (3) C had the* beku. *His son married a girl whose father was from D. D gave C yams. C gave the* beku *to D. (4) D had the* beku. *D wanted a pig because his son was coming from Port Moresby and D wanted to prepare a feast. D asked E for a pig. E gave D a pig and E received the* beku. *(5) E had the* beku. *E's son married a girl whose father was from F. F gave E yams. E gave F the* beku. *(6) F had the* beku. *F wanted magic to make* kuvi *yams grow very long. F received magic from G. G received the* beku. *(7) G had the* beku. *A wanted his* beku *back. A found G and took yams and betel nuts to G. G gave the* beku *to A.*

never a guarantee of this. Winners in the game of exchange must be strong men; the more workpower, magic, and objects a man controls, the more certain he is of success in all his transactions. A *beku* does not return automatically to its owner: the owner must walk after his *beku*, going from village to village to retrace its movements. The circulation of stone ax blades involves releasing one's own wealth in order to obtain something else, but the burden of return lies with the owner. Therein lies the problem for individuals: the *beku* might be lost to someone else and never return to its owner.

Thus the symbolic meaning and use of a *beku* constitute a paradox. In its economic use, a *beku* elicits direct reciprocity. Even when a man reclaims his own *beku*, he must make payments for its return.[9] But there is more to *beku* than economic value. What makes a man identify with a particular *beku*, as opposed to any other of equal exchange value? What is the nature of the "spirit of the gift" (Mauss 1954; see also Sahlins 1972), which causes men to walk far to follow their own *beku*?

One possibility lies in the fact that, when a man dies, his *beku* live after him. Each *beku* has its own genealogy, consisting of all the names of its owners. Men are known by their valuables. The names attached to the genealogy circulate beyond a man's lifetime: "When I die, people will remember my name because of my *beku*." Men also told me this about *kula* valuables. Thus, for a man, valuables contain an element of generational time. Valuables are male wealth, but as an objectification of person they assume symbolic elements of male regeneration.

Informants told me that there are two primary roads for valuables: (1) *kula* and (2) yam exchanges which involve married women. When valuables are presented to a girl's relatives in marriage transactions, they are "paid for" by yams. After approximately one year of marriage (or at the next harvest season), the girl's relatives make a large yam presentation (*vilakulia*) to her husband's father. He in turn divides the yams and distributes them to each man who originally gave a valuable.

Women's wealth is also exchanged at this time. When the girl moves to her husband's hamlet, her husband's sister (*tabu*) presents three or four colorful skirts to the new bride. The bride must immediately try on each skirt and stand while her husband's *tabu* cuts each skirt (*litutila doba*) to its proper length. Now the bride must wear her skirts at knee length rather than at the short miniskirt length that marks an unmarried girl.

During the waiting period, prior to the payment of the valuables with yams, the new husband and wife live together in a small house in the husband's hamlet. The young couple live in a house that does not have a hearth. The girl does not perform any cooking tasks for herself and her husband, for the husband's mother brings food daily to the newly married couple. Food is brought into the house in one bowl, and both wife and husband sit and eat together from the same plate. No one is invited to join them while they eat, and they remain secluded inside their house during the course of the meal. According to custom, they should eat one yam at a time, cutting it in half, before eating the next yam.

At the end of the year, usually concurrent with a presentation of a second round of yams from the girl's relatives, the man's mother brings three stones into the house and places them in position for the preparation of the hearth. From the time that the hearth is created, a woman cooks her husband's food and she serves her husband in his own bowl. Other men and unmarried boys should always be invited to join her husband in his meal, because it is considered shameful for a man to eat alone. Husband and wife never again eat together from the same bowl; they are now called *vavegila* ("married") instead of *vegilevau* ("newly married").

At this time cooked yams are sent from the husband's relatives to his wife's relatives as a "gift" (*bobwelila*) for the second presentation of yams. Informants said that, when cooked food is given after exchanges which involve valuables, the cooked food is a "present" or is "free."

Nothing is expected in direct return for the "gift" of cooked food. But it seems that cooked food in these instances signifies that one set of exchanges is finished and that a new set of exchanges will eventually transpire.

The rules and ethics concerning food and its distribution and consumption indicate quite clearly that the emotional content which we in our own culture place on "breaking bread" is no less significant than is sharing *kaula* ("good food") in Kiriwina. For example, when a man goes on overseas *kula*, he cannot sit and eat with his *kula* partner until the exchanges between them have been consummated. A visiting *kula* friend will spend the night on the beach, eating alone, if his tactics to obtain a valuable have been unsuccessful. The following day, if the exchange is finalized, the two friends then sit and eat together.

Eating together between husband and wife marks the beginning stage of marriage. But, with the establishment of a hearth, that stage is finished. The initial marriage exchanges of yams/valuables/yams are also completed. Now, each year, a girl's father or her brother makes a yam exchange garden in her name. See figure 18 for a list of marriage exchanges.

The valuables have been repaid, but the fact that they were presented constitutes a long-term exchange relationship between a woman, her father, and her husband. The strength of the newly formed relationships can only be determined through time as each party demonstrates, through formal exchange channels, its intent.

IV

Cross-cousin marriage is, undoubtedly, a compromise between the two ill-adjusted principles of mother-right and father-love; and this is its main raison d'être. The natives are not, of course, capable of a consistent theoretical statement; but in their arguments and formulated motives this explanation of the why and wherefore of the institution is implicit, in an unmistakable though piecemeal form. . . . "To marry a tabula *(cross-cousin) is right; the true* tabula *(the first cross-cousin) is the proper wife for us."—Malinowski 1929, p. 101*

Concerning marriage choices, my informants told me the same thing that Malinowski (ibid.) was told: "A person should marry his or her *tabu*."[10] From my data, I found that in fact no one in Kwaibwaga has married his true father's sister's daughter. Malinowski found the same discrepancies in his census. What does occur is that usually both women and men marry someone who is a member of their father's clan. Therefore a man marries into the same clan into which his mother married.[11]

If a girl is from the same clan as a boy's father and that boy wants to sleep with her, he calls her *tabu*, the kin term for father's sister's daughter. My informants were very concerned that I understood the "trick" of the word *tabu* in this particular context. A special vocabulary exists for verbal communication between a boy, a girl, a man, or a woman for establishing sexual

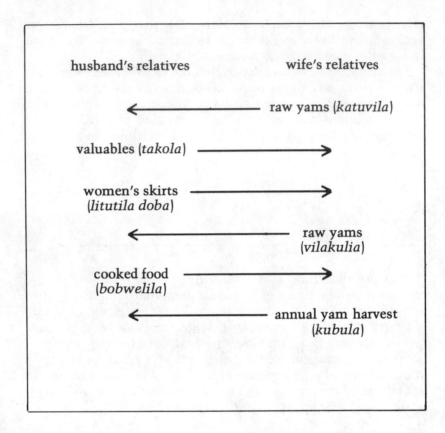

Figure 18. Marriage exchanges. The husband's relatives include his father, true brothers, and mother's brothers. The wife's relatives include her father, true brothers, and mother's brothers.

relationships which are more lasting and more meaningful than liaisons in the bush. To call a girl *tabu* means that a boy wants to take her to his house and sleep with her there, thus signaling a relationship with a chance for longevity.

Of the fifty-three current marriages in Kwaibwaga as of 1972, 55 percent of the men married women in their fathers' clan, and 51 percent of the women are married to men belonging to their fathers' clan. In 23 percent of the marriages, none of these relationships between clans appears with spouses and fathers, but the husbands' fathers belong to the same clan as the wives' fathers. In this latter category, 12 percent of the marriages were either to *guyau* men or women, and/or men married women from the same clan as their mothers' fathers, thereby continuing the *keyawa* relationship through time betweeen *dala* in two clans. In 8 percent of the marriages, there was no apparent relationship between the clan of the spouse and the clan of the spouse's relatives.

By keeping marriages stabilized between *keyawa* of two clans, the majority of mortuary distributions unite individual *keyawa* within one clan and oppose *keyawa* of one clan against those of another clan. Thus, segments within two clans operate as dual exchange categories, where the directions of payments shift. Whether through the first ascending generation (his father) to ego or through the second ascending generation (ego's mother's father), all continuing links are through men who are fathers.

There is a strong effort to keep impending marriages contained within the village population and, if not within the village, then at least within neighboring villages.[12] In figure 19, I present the marriages in Kwaibwaga as they relate to natal kinship and spatial distance of the female spouses. Of the fifty-three marriages in Kwaibwaga in 1972, thirty-one women lived in the village before they were married; either they were born in Kwaibwaga or, as young children, they came there to live with adoptive parents. Thirty of these women moved from one hamlet to another at marriage, but one woman married a man who lived in her own natal hamlet, and she and her husband remained there after their marriage. Twenty-two of the fifty-three married women came from other villages, but eleven came from neighboring villages less than one mile away. Only two of these women did not have kinship connections with someone in Kwaibwaga other than their spouses. Eleven other women came from villages not more than seven miles away, and only four of these women did not have any prior kinship affiliation with anyone in Kwaibwaga. The men, however, to whom these four women are married do not

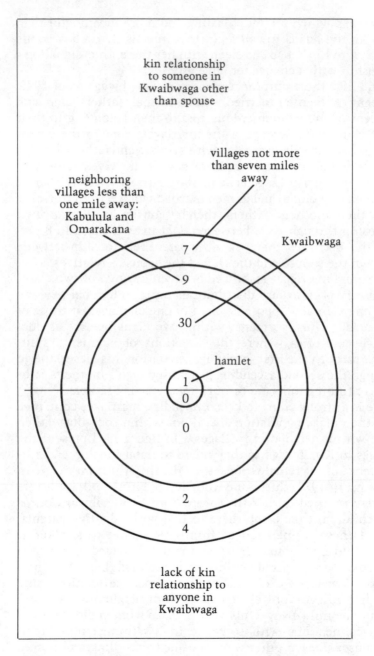

Figure 19. Natal spatial and kinship distance of female spouses living in Kwaibwaga in 1972. There are fifty-three marriages.

have any current status of importance or any potential for power.

Marriages between hamlets in one village (and neighboring villages) mean that almost an entire village is related through affinal bonds. Therefore, when someone dies in the village, the mortuary ceremonies will involve most people within a village. In most cases women do not move very far from their primary kin: mother and father. The relationships created through marriage serve to solidify a woman's own importance and position within her own *dala* and her father's *dala*.[13]

V

But among people of lower rank, also, there are many instances of a woman leaving her husband simply because she does not like him. During my first visit to the Trobriands, Sayabiya, a fine-looking girl, bubbling over with health, vitality, and temperament, was quite happily married to Tomeda, who was a handsome, good-natured and honest, but stupid man. When I returned, she had gone back to live in her village as an unmarried girl, simply because she was tired of her husband. A very good-looking girl of Oburaku, Bo'usari, had left two husbands, one after the other, and, to judge from her intrigues, was looking for a third. Neither from her, nor from the intimate gossip of the village, could I get any good reason for her two desertions, and it was obvious that she simply wanted to be free again.—Malinowski 1929, p. 144

During the court case described earlier concerning the young girls in Kwaibwaga, Bunemiga, the girls' mother's brother, discussed the hypothetical situation concerning his obligation to take care of a girl's husband because he has received a valuable from her husband's relatives. The care, Bunemiga told me later, referred to annual yam presentations and the ramifications in terms of reciprocity and services which follow. By maintaining his sister's daughter's marriage, the future cycle of exchanges remains open and active. Divorce is not easily effected, and relatives on both the girl's side and the boy's side are often instrumental in repairing a marital separation.

Marital separations sometimes stem from conflicts between the marriage partners and sometimes from pressures from relatives on either side (cf. Malinowski 1929, pp. 142–147). Adultery is by far the most prevalently stated cause for a separation. But I also learned that adultery is a very effective mechanism to effect a divorce when relatives prefer a divorce. At other times, in cases of adultery, a man might serve a few months in jail or a woman might be attacked and cut up by a jealous wife, but the marriages continue.

In divorce, a woman leaves her husband and returns to her native hamlet, and it usually appears as if the woman precipitates the separation. Men, however, have ways of creating situations which force their wives to leave them. Informants told me that, when a man hits his wife, she knows that her husband does not want her any more, and she will usually pack her things and return to her mother and father. Often a lover's bite marks on her husband's skin or the loss of eyelashes which a lover has bitten off is all the evidence a woman needs to leave her husband. If a woman finds betel nuts or tobacco hidden under her husband's pillow or underneath his bed, she knows immediately that he must be planning to meet another woman.

Wives and husbands watch each other. When a woman thinks her husband is hiding betel nuts and tobacco, she begins to follow him to the garden and to watch the women with whom he stops to talk. When a man returns from the garden, he might find his wife saying to him, "Today I saw you take betel nuts and give them to that woman in the garden, so you stay with her and marry her. I am taking my things to the house of my mother and father." At the same time, men watch to see how quickly their wives return from the water holes or from the gardens. One man in Omarakana went to the gardens to look for his wife, because she had gone alone to her garden several hours before. He found her working, but he also saw a man working close by. He attacked the man with his knife, accusing him of having slept with his wife.

If a man sees that his wife is always chewing betel nuts or tobacco, he becomes suspicious and demands to know from whom she received these things. A clever woman will give the betel nuts or tobacco she has received from her lover to her mother or a young unmarried sister, asking them to hold them for her and give her only a little bit at a time. In this way, a wife can then say that she went to visit her mother, who gave her a present. Women also use the promise of a liaison to obtain betel nuts and tobacco from men without ever fulfilling the promise. Most women are very shrewd in their seductive abilities.

Sometimes a spouse does not suspect her or his mate of having an affair, but relatives of the unknowing spouse discover a liaison. These relatives (female relatives of a wife and the mother of a husband) come and say, "All the time you stay alone in your house and your husband [wife] is sleeping with another woman [man]." The result of this gossip can be separation, angry bloody fights, and a native or administration court case. According to tradition, the many wives of *guyau* chiefs are supposed to allow their husbands free rein in their sexual liaisons. But I have seen the resulting scars on several women who were attacked by the jealous wives of one of the most powerful Tabalu chiefs.

All my Kiriwina friends told me confidential stories of past intrigues, and everyone was in agreement that adultery was all right as long as no one discovered the liaison. Under the suspicious watchful gaze of Kiriwina people, however, secrecy is almost impossible to maintain. Moreover, finding out someone's secret can be just the proper weapon for ending a marriage, but many times the relatives on both sides attempt to repair a marital separation.

When a woman returns to her natal hamlet, she waits; even if her husband marries someone else, she still waits. She sleeps with other men, but the dissolution of her first marriage is not complete. If her husband's second wife has "good customs," then in fact the marriage is over, but many times her husband's second marriage only lasts a few months. "The second woman's customs were not very good," my informants said, and the husband chases his second wife away. In this case, the first marriage is still very much alive.

A man's relatives (his father, mother, and mother's brother) tell him they want him to return to his first wife because she had "good customs." "This woman," they say, "knew how to make mats very well, and she always called other people to come and share the food she cooked. Why do you want to divorce her?" Often his relatives will give him a special kind of love magic (*kalakasina*) to use to bring his wife back.

But the husband tells his relatives that he is frightened of his wife's father and mother because she has been staying with them for a very long time. The man's relatives then collect valuables (stone ax blades, a clay pot, and money), now called *lula*, and they take them to the relatives of his first wife. Sometimes the wife will run away to another house when the husband and his relatives appear with valuables, and she will refuse to return with her husband. Her own relatives, if they want the marriage to continue, tell her husband not to worry: "You return home and later we will send her to you because we do not want her to marry anyone else." But even then a woman still has the option to refuse. Sometimes, when a man brings valuables, they are immediately rejected: "Take those valuables back" (*"Lula bikeimalisa"*), the woman's relatives say, "you are too late, because she wants to marry someone else." Then a man will resort to love magic.

If a woman does marry another man, her new husband must present a valuable to her first husband (see Malinowski 1929, p. 147); this exchange is called *mapula*. A woman's own relatives never have to repay the valuables they received from her first husband, and it is this transaction which finalizes a woman's separation from a previous marriage. If, however, the first husband marries before she does, then there is never a presentation of a valuable, because, if a man marries first, it means that "he does not like his wife, he does not want her back, the marriage is truly finished."

But, when a man's wife remarries first, he might refuse the valuable presented by her second husband and instead ask for a child. For example, M lived in Kwaibwaga, and she was married to the brother of a man who controlled the land in one of the Kwaibwaga hamlets. According to village gossip, M was very lazy, and she did not work hard in the garden. Her husband's brother, who had a very large yam house and who was a feared and respected man, was not happy about the marriage. He discovered that M was sleeping with another man, and M ran away from Kwaibwaga and married the other man. M had a ten-year-old son from her first husband. Therefore, her first husband demanded—and received—the son instead of the valuable.

Although the people I questioned told me that a man would ask for a daughter to remain with him, in the three cases I recorded in Kwaibwaga the child who stayed with the father was a boy. The boy remains identified with his mother's *dala* in name, but his allegiance, his services, and his future are centered in his father.

The fact that, in divorce, children can be substituted for valuables is further confirmation of my suggestion that a valuable contains a symbolic element of male regenerative capacity. In marriage, valuables given to the woman's relatives elicit a continuous return of yams and a new generation of children. Both female and male valuables are given from the boy's side to the girl's side. Yams always follow a reverse pattern. Thus yams move with women; valuables move with men. It seems in this instance that yams and women constitute natural reproductive cycles, and valuables (both male and female) constitute a cultural manifestation of reproduction.

Bunemiga's fearful discourse over divorce in the speech previously recorded now seems a very significant concern. Divorce blocks the benefits of fertility; the initial valuables are not returned. Only another round of valuables can revitalize the original contract.

In all these exchanges, women—not men—remain the autonomous force. Women represent sexuality and fertility but also danger. Control over women is not so easily effected. Women have a degree of freedom because they encounter fewer societal restraints on their sexual behavior. Unlike our society, Trobriand women are accorded full respect for the power of their sexuality. That men pay women for sleeping with them both before and after marriage does not indicate men's use of women, as Malinowski and Lévi-Strauss suggest. Rather, women use their sexuality to full advantage because they and everyone else recognize the full value of sexuality.

From this view I suggest that the concept of "virgin birth" is used as a protection for the innate value of women. For a woman to become pregnant and have a man reject her is an ultimate shame, publicly destroying her potency. The pregnancy itself is not the cause for shame, for many women are married when they are five or six months pregnant. The alarm then is that the man refuses the marriage. Thus "virgin birth" shields the value of women, giving them a public position of even greater power: the ability to conceive alone.

Chapter 8
Yams and Women's Wealth

I

*We now come to the most remarkable and, one might
say, sociologically sensational feature of Trobriand marriage. . . . Marriage puts the wife's family under a permanent tributary obligation to the husband, to whom they have
to pay yearly contributions for as long as the household exists.
From the moment when they signify by the first gift that they
accept the marriage, they have to produce, year after year
by their own labour, a quantity of yams for their kinswoman's family.—Malinowski 1929, p. 121*

The first year of marriage is a publicly marked period of time in
the life cycle of each spouse. They no longer participate in the
peer activities of adolescence, yet they have not assumed the full
responsibilities of adults. A woman cannot cook food, since she
has not been given a hearth. Her husband grows yams for another
man; no yams have yet been given to him. Each day, the couple
share their common food, yams, the only time in their lives they
will eat with an adult of the opposite sex. Eating together demonstrates that the kin of each spouse have fulfilled their initial obligations, thus sanctioning the marriage. Now the spouses must
demonstrate that they can fulfill each other's needs as individuals. The exchanges, inherently hazardous, do not begin again until the end of this trial period. During this year, the first child is
often conceived.[1] Thus, by the end of the year, the reproductive
cycle is regenerated and the yam cycle is reconstituted.

For all Trobrianders, at any time in their lives, open discussions
concerning the sexual relations of a husband and wife are strictly
taboo in their presence. Although banter among adults and even
small children often takes the form of "fuck your mother," "fuck
your father," and so on, the most horrendous insult, with dire

consequences, is to say to a man "fuck your wife."[2] In Kwai-bwaga, a young man was forced to move to another village be-cause, in the heat of an argument with his mother's brother, he screamed at him, "Fuck your wife!" In the context of this taboo, the sharing of yams between wife and husband seems to come closest to any public statement regarding their sexual union. Yams symbolically represent fertility, fertility which combines both female and male elements.

The importance of the union of maleness and femaleness is made explicit in the magic spells for yams. In the first stage of gardening, when the concern is with fertility of the soil and the development of the yam under ground, the cycle of gardening spells contains repetitious use of such phrases as "the belly of my garden swells as with a child" and "swell out, O soil, swell out as with a child" (Malinowski 1935a, pp. 101, 102). In preparation for the range of spells to be chanted at this time, ceremonial *beku* are covered with herbs containing special magical qualities. But the herbs are placed between the ax blade and a strip of dried banana leaf carefully folded over the ax (ibid., p. 95), thus enclosing the herbs between the ax and a strip of *nununiga* (bundles of banana leaves). Later in the gardening cycle, when the vines begin to break through the ground and wind around the poles erected over each yam plant, the metaphors and metonomy in the spells change (see ibid., pp. 142–148). The emphasis is now on such movements as "come out," "shoot," and "anchor," elements of male sexuality.[3] The growth stage of the vines is further drama-tized by the building of large erect poles (*kamkola*).

It seems especially significant that wife and husband do not merely share food, but that they cut each yam in half and together consume the one Trobriand symbol representing the union of both male and female complementary powers of fertility.

At the close of the trial period, if the marriage remains in good standing, a woman's kinsmen make a final confirmation of the contract by bringing a yam harvest to the husband's kin in pay-ment for the valuables already given to them. Shortly thereafter, a woman's father prepares a yam garden in her name.

Yam exchange gardens from a man to a married woman. A man makes his first female exchange garden (*kaymwila*) for his married daughter and continues to present his daughter with yams each year until one of his sons takes over this production. When other daughters marry, or when a man grows old, and/or when a man's sons marry, a woman's brother begins to produce the annual garden for her. Usually, the association in birth order provides the link between a particular man and his sister: that is, eldest brother makes a garden for his eldest married sister, next-eldest brother for the next-eldest married sister, and so on. If a man has many daughters, he himself will not always initiate gardens for his youngest daughters. This responsibility falls to one of her brothers. If she has no brothers, her mother's brother will usually take on this role.

Fathers and brothers give yams; husbands receive yams. These yams provide a man access to a larger and more significant set of social relationships than he has been able to cultivate before. Now, for the first time, a newly married man is able to make independent decisions beyond the pale of the father/son relationship. Through the annual presentation of yams made to him by his wife's kinsmen, a man moves into an adult role. He now controls his own supply of yams, the basic medium of exchange.

In a sense this process does seem as sensational as Malinowski described. But Trobriand marriage is far more complex than is seen from Malinowski's assertion that marriage places "the wife's family under a permanent tributary obligation to the husband" (1929, p. 121). The yams given to a man by his wife's kin can be used by him, but eventually he must reciprocate. These annual yams are grown by a woman's kinsman in a garden marked in her name. When the yams are arranged in front of her husband's yam house, they are presented in her name. In a titular sense, she is the owner of the yams. With the receipt of yams, a man is not obligated to his wife's kin but to her directly.

Reciprocal exchanges from a man to his wife. Although a woman is able to manufacture skirts and bundles alone, she needs far more wealth than she can accumulate herself in order for her to participate as a major distributor of wealth in a mortuary ceremony. The major responsibility of a man to his wife is to provision her with additional wealth. A man supplies his wife with wealth in two ways. First, a man's "sisters" formally present bundles, skirts, and now pieces of calico and Western clothing to his wife just prior to the start of the women's mortuary ceremony. Each "sister" gives wealth because she is reciprocating for the baskets of yams that her "brother" gives her each year. Although a man's "sisters" publicly give wealth to his wife, they do so only when they themselves have received yams from him. These transactions, described in chapter 4, are called *kabiyamila*. In the women's mortuary distribution, women walk in a line across the center of the hamlet, carrying objects of wealth to their "brother's" wife. This line of women (from eight to fifty women)

publicly symbolizes the size and extent of a man's range of female help. Second, through *valova* (exchanges of pigs, valuables,
Western trade goods, etc., for bundles and skirts) a man assists his
wife in accumulating women's wealth. Her huge filled baskets at
the start of the distribution and her ability to contribute bundles
to every exchange during the day are public statements of her
husband's support and wealth. The significance of *valova* is reflected in the following statement, made by one of my informants.

> We watch our sister's husband carefully to see how fast
> he helps her get ready for the women's mortuary ceremony.
> If he does not help her quickly to collect her things, then we
> say that man is not a good husband and we do not want
> to make a garden for our sister any more.

Thus a man reciprocates the annual yam presentations by con-
verting his own male wealth into women's wealth for his wife.
His wife's wealth, in turn, is distributed on behalf of her kin, including her father.

Women's performance in mortuary distributions. When a man
makes a garden for his married daughter, he is ensuring her support in any mortuary distributions which members of his *dala*
perform. A woman will continue to support these distributions
even when her brother takes over the production of her garden. A
man's presentation of yams through his daughter to her husband
is indirectly securing his son-in-law's service for the members of
his own *dala*. The return service is exhibited through the amount
of wealth a man's daughter contributes to a distribution; therefore, her husband, in return for yams, should help his wife accumulate this wealth.

The performance of women in mortuary distributions at the
death of their fathers can be especially significant for their brothers. A man's contributions of raw yams to his father's mortuary
distributions are essential for continued residence on his father's
dala land (or his father's father's land). But the amount of yams he
has contributed to the full range of distributions is never publicly
documented until the women's mortuary ceremony. In the important set of transactions called *kaymelu*, women pile up the
largest amounts of skirts and bundles for those men who have
contributed the most yams. A woman's lavish performance during *kaymelu* establishes publicly the fact of her brother's contribution of yams and validates his claim to continued land use
from the hamlet manager of his father's *dala* land.[4]

Once a woman receives yams from a man, she has obligations that remain throughout her life. The man from whom she received yams may die, but she performs mortuary distributions for him until she is too old or until she dies. Usually, a woman's daughter will assume her deceased mother's obligations and "take the place of her mother" at mortuary distributions. A bond is created which is never broken or forgotten. In one magic spell for yam growing, the shadows of those yams which were once piled in the houses and eaten are called upon to return to the garden and teach the growing yams how to become larger. The remembrance of past yam exchanges continues to elicit reciprocity from the woman who received the original yams.

Baskets of yams from a man to married women. In addition to making a formal yam garden for married sisters or daughters, men make smaller presentations of yams, supplemented by taro, to other sisters. These yams are selected from the pile displayed in front of his yam house at harvest time. He puts fifteen or twenty yams (called *kovisi*)[5] into various baskets. He then gives these baskets to the women, who may be true sisters or may stand in a classificatory or fictive "sister" relationship to him.

When a man gives a basket of yams to a woman, her husband is obligated to return a valuable (a stone ax blade, a clay pot, or money), and as in marriage exchanges this valuable is called *takola*. At the next harvest, the original giver of yams again returns yams, now called *vewoulo*.[6] These yam presentations are much larger in size (150 to 300 yams) than the first presentation. *Vewoulo*, according to my informants, is payment for the valuable. Once this set of exchanges (yams/valuable/yams) is completed, a close relationship between two men as brothers-in-law and one woman as wife and sister has been established. Year after year, this same woman will receive baskets of yams from a man as true brother, classificatory brother, or some other kinsman.

Each man establishes his own individual network of "sisters," and each network varies in size depending upon the power and talents of individual men. These women reclaim their "brother's" *dala* names from his children; they perform beauty magic for his children; they perform the most important mourning and burial rituals when their "brother's" child dies. And finally, as previously mentioned, they give women's wealth to his wife at the start of the women's mortuary ceremony. (Figure 20 diagrams the two ways a man helps his wife at mortuary ceremonies.)

Taro gardens from a man to married women. In addition to yams, raw taro plants (*uli*) are used to supplement and/or expand

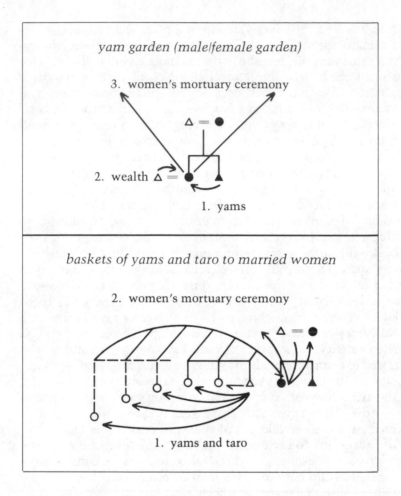

Figure 20. Ways a man helps his wife accumulate her wealth. Yam garden (male/female garden): (1) Yam garden made by brother (or father) for married sister (or daughter). (2) Sister's husband gives objects to be converted through valova *exchange into women's wealth. (3) Sister distributes bundles and skirts at a death in her own* dala *or in her father's* dala. *Baskets of yams and taro to married women: (1) A man gives his married "sister" baskets of yams and taro. (2) A man's "sisters" give women's wealth to their brother's wife on the day of the women's mortuary ceremony, when their brother's wife is a major participant in the women's mortuary ceremony for her own* dala *or her father's* dala.

exchanges to networks of women. Men prepare taro gardens (*gu-bwauli*) twice a year, and each garden site is marked for a particular woman. As with yam exchange gardens, no one else may use the taro growing in a marked garden. Unlike the one yam garden a man makes for a woman, he makes many taro gardens for many women. A man plants between twenty and fifty taro plants for each woman who is part of his personal network of "sisters." The entire taro plant is presented in these transactions.

II

Thus the chief's urigubu *became a tribute levied on a number of village communities, but always levied in virtue of his position as a glorified brother-in-law of the whole community.*
—*Malinowski 1935a, p. 192*

The procedure for making a yam exchange garden for a woman changes when her husband is a chief. Chiefs have the right to be polygamous, but a chief must be powerful in the eyes of other people in order to attract wives. A few men, who live in Omarakana and are identified as members of a particular *dala*, act as bodyguards or messengers for the Tabalu. The choice of a wife (except for a chief's first wife, whom he himself chooses) is made by these men. They decide which *dala* is strong in workpower. They then go to the hamlet manager of that *dala* and throw a spear with four coconuts tied to the top into the ground in front of the manager's house. Without words, the spear and coconuts denote the request: one woman who belongs to the manager's *dala* is requested in marriage. Each coconut represents the number of main gardens that must be made annually by the woman's relatives. Usually the chosen are her father, her mother's brother, her brother, and any other kinsmen (*veyola*). Included in the kinsmen category are both blood (*veyola tatola*) and origin (*veyola*) kinsmen.

Yaulibu from Kwaibwaga was married to Mitakata, the former Tabalu chief who died in 1961. When Mitakata was alive, seven men made gardens for Yaulibu. Four of the men belonged to her own *dala*, and the others belonged to a *dala* whose founders came from the same place of origin with Yaulibu's founders. Her father also made a garden for her, but he died shortly after her marriage.

Each marriage to a chief begins with four *kaymata* (main) gardens. Men may choose to increase the number of gardens for their kinswoman. If a chief is generous and becomes a strong man, other men desire to attach themselves to him. But men are also competitive in regard to their own sister vis-à-vis a chief's other wives. Each woman has her own yam house in front of her private living quarters. A chief has his separate house (*ligabu*) built in a prominent place in the hamlet (see plate 20). Neither a woman nor any man except members of the Tabalu and the Mwari *guyau dala* may enter his house.

Although all men making gardens for a kinswoman married to a chief receive benefits from her spouse, the polygamous practices of chiefs prevent hamlet managers from achieving their full potential. When a kinswoman marries a chief, men who under other circumstances would be making large gardens for the hamlet manager now only make small gardens or give *urigubu* (pigs, coconut and areca palms) or baskets of yams to the hamlet manager. But a woman's kinsmen are not paying "tribute," as Malinowski and Powell described, for chiefs incur the same formal reciprocal obligations to their wives as do all other men. These chiefs must use their resources to provision their wives with women's wealth. Using yams, they too cultivate networks of "sisters." Aside from the formal reciprocity which every man has to his wife's kinsmen, chiefs are in a position in which their resource control is often under challenge.

For example, when a chief clears his garden and asks his wife's relatives to come and help for the first time, he must be prepared for a challenge from his affines. While the men are working in the gardens, one of them says, "I smell pig excreta." The etiquette involved requires that no one ever overtly asks to eat pork. When the host hears his visitors discussing pig excreta and sees them sniffing the air to smell it, he must then kill a pig and present the men with pork. If he refuses the challenge, the men will not return to help him again.

Men carefully consider whether or not to comply with the request made by the throwing of the spear. If the chief is strong and is believed to have access to powerful magic, then the decision is usually quickly made in the affirmative. When Mitakata died, his successor Vanoi and Vanoi's successor Waibadi had problems on

*Plate 20. In the center of Omarakana stands Vanoi's house,
newly built, painted, and decorated in 1971*

the occasion of their first attempts to find wives. Men of several
dala refused to give them their women and their support in workpower. But, shortly after the rejected offers, a serious drought occurred which lasted several months. It was thought that Waibadi
had caused the drought because he had magic to control the sun
and the rain. Waibadi himself made his actions publicly known.
At the end of the drought, wives were forthcoming, and it was
agreed that the Tabalu of Omarakana were indeed still powerful.

A man's power, however, even at the Tabalu level, must be
constantly reaffirmed. Throughout the length of the marital relationship, there always exists the possibility that the relatives of
the wife might withdraw their support. During the political crisis
in 1972, there was talk of affines refusing to make gardens for
both Vanoi and Waibadi. In an intensely dramatic political meeting concerning this crisis, Waibadi fought for the supremacy of
his power in an emotionally charged speech in which he again
proclaimed sole control over the sun and the rain.[7]

For each woman that a chief marries, he establishes a relationship with men from two different *dala*: the woman's own *dala*
and her father's *dala*. In figure 21, I have diagramed the differences between the numbers of gardens which polygamous men
have made for them and the way in which monogamous men gain
workpower.

Tabalu "chiefs," however, have additional means for gaining
control over resources. To begin with, there is *urigubu*. *Urigubu*
consists of pork, the nuts from coconut and areca palms, and betel pepper plants. Unlike the extensive garden preparations for
yams and taro, *urigubu* does not require extended preparation. In
one respect, *urigubu* is a redundant presentation, serving to reenforce a relationship already created through other transactions.
Urigubu is presented from time to time to someone for whom
the giver already makes a yam exchange garden. There does not
seem to be any special time sequence. Rather, when a man has
something extra to give and when he wants to make a further
statement about a relationship already established, he makes *urigubu*.

In another use of *urigubu* and in contrast to the notion of re-
dundancy, *urigubu* is given to take the place of giving yams to
someone. If a man makes a garden for his older brother, and his
father is still living, he might give *urigubu* to his father. If a man
makes a yam garden for one married sister, he might give *urigubu*
to another married sister for whom he cannot make a yam garden.
Or, if a man has other obligations and cannot make a yam garden

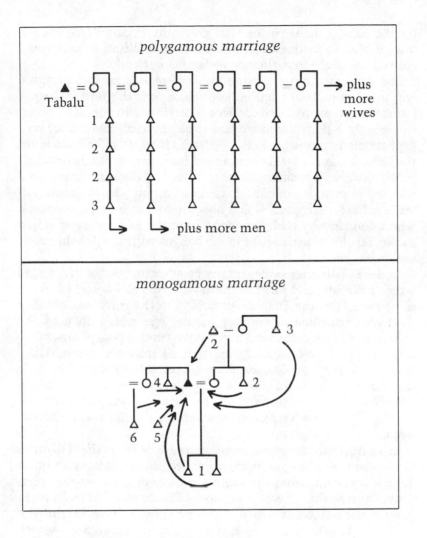

Figure 21. Differences between the yam gardens that polygamous and monogamous men receive. Men who make yam gardens for a man in a polygamous marriage: (1) each woman's father; (2) men of the same dala as the woman (veyola tatola); (3) men of the same clan who are descendants of those who came from the same place of origin as the founders of the woman's dala land. Men who make yam gardens for a man in a monogamous marriage: (1) ego's sons; (2) ego's brother-in-law (or father-in-law); (3) ego's wife's mother's brother (sometimes); (4) ego's younger brother (sometimes); (5) adopted "son" or fictive relative; (6) sister's son (sometimes).

for the hamlet manager, he will give him *urigubu*. *Urigubu* allows a man to utilize other resources in addition to cultivated crops in order to strengthen or widen his networks.

Bopokala includes the same kinds of objects as does *urigubu*, and this has probably caused confusion over the terminology. I found that some men use the words *urigubu* and *bopokala* interchangeably, but men who are said to be knowledgeable make very explicit distinctions between the two terms. *Bopokala* includes the same kinds of objects exchanged for *urigubu*, but, unlike *urigubu*, *bopokala* exchanges are explicitly between ranked and nonranked men. *Bopokala* (glossed as "tribute" by Malinowski)[8] are continual exchanges which obligate Malasi hamlet managers, whose founders by tradition came from the same place of origin as the Tabalu, to participate in exchanges with the Tabalu chiefs of Omarakana.

In the Tabalu origin story, many people came out of the ground with the Tabalu, and some of them—the Malasi—belonged to the same *kumila* as the Tabalu. According to the story, each Malasi man who remained in another hamlet was called upon by the Tabalu to furnish them with areca nuts, betel pepper plants, coconuts, and pork. Waibadi told me that all the *dala* of the Malasi *kumila* who are not Tabalu but who came from the origin hole near Labai with the Tabalu are called *wasesi* (*wosa* is the singular). *Wasesi* people (essentially the hamlet manager), from the time of their founders, gave *bopokala* to the Tabalu of Omarakana.

In addition to *bopokala* from nonrank Malasi, the Tabalu of Omarakana also have exchanges, called *guyapokala*, with other Tabalu who came from the same place of origin. After the emergence from the hole near Labai, some Tabalu traveled to different parts of the island but, when they parted from those Tabalu who settled in Omarakana, they lost some of the decorations which only the highest-rank Tabalu have the right to wear. Therefore, in the origin story,[9] the Tabalu of Omarakana retained all the decorations, but simultaneously the other members of the Tabalu entered into *guyapokala* exchanges with the Tabalu of Omarakana. These exchanges function exactly like *bopokala* exchanges except for the difference in rank.

Today, *wasesi* people still give *bopokala* to Vanoi and Waibadi. Waibadi told me that he and Vanoi get things in two ways: from *kubula* (yam gardens) given by affines and from *bopokala* and *guyapokala*. From the first category, they obtain yams; from the second, pork and the fruits of trees.

The origin story as told today by the Tabalu serves to verify their right to these exchanges. In some ways the actual acting-out of the transactions looks very much like "tribute," because *bopokala* is usually collected prior to the filling of the Tabalu yam houses. In this way, Vanoi and Waibadi acquire betel and pork to entertain and feed their affines, who work to fill their yam houses.

One example of *bopokala* exchange will illustrate the mechanics of these exchanges. Peter, who belongs to the Malasi *kumila*, is the land manager of one hamlet in Kwaibwaga. Six years ago he gave one of his areca palms to Vanoi for *bopokala*. Today the palm rises high in front of Peter's house; around the upper part of the palm is tied a woven coconut mat to indicate that no one is to climb the palm. In times past, white cowrie shells should also have been tied about the upper reaches of the palm so that, when the winds blew, people would hear the noise and know that the palm belonged to a *guyau*.[10]

Each time the areca nuts ripen, Peter takes all of them to Vanoi. The first year that Peter presented Vanoi with areca nuts, Vanoi returned a clay pot as *takola*. Peter is obligated to give Vanoi all the nuts from this palm until it dies. Peter may then give Vanoi another palm, and for this he will receive another *takola* in return. *Bopokala* or *guyapokala* does not end there, however, because these direct exchanges also include indirect reciprocity.

The Tabalu of Omarakana and their sisters and mothers are obligated to participate through distributions of women's wealth in mortuary ceremonies for anyone who dies in those *dala* with whom the Tabalu of Omarakana have *bopokala* and *guyapokala* exchange relationships. Although the demands made upon others by the Tabalu through *bopokala* and *guyapokala* at times appear to be tribute, and even feel like tribute to those who must produce goods and food continually upon request, these two exchanges establish long-term relationships which have positive exchange feedback for the original donors. Following a death, when each man related to the deceased must accumulate as much as he can, those men related through *bopokala* and *guyapokala* receive help from the Tabalu of Omarakana.

Similarly to *bopokala*, when men give *urigubu* they receive a return of a valuable, and from then on areca nuts or coconuts are taken periodically to the recipient. But, when a man gives *urigubu* to his married sister and receives *takola* from her husband, he must then prepare a large harvest of yams (*vewoulo*). This chain of exchanges follows the same pattern as marriage exchanges and baskets of yams and taro presented to a married woman (see fig. 22). Each woman who receives *urigubu* must help the donor's wife in mortuary distributions.

At this point, the question posed earlier—what does a man return to his wife's kin for the annual yam presentations made to him in his wife's name?—has been partially answered. A man returns wealth to his wife and through his wife to her kin. Throughout his married life, he continually works for his wife to support her economic position. By provisioning a woman for participation in mortuary distributions held by members of her *dala* and her father's *dala*, a man is indirectly contributing large amounts of wealth to these people. She, on the other hand, does not distribute large amounts of wealth for her husband when a member of his *dala* dies. A woman does not stand with the owners of her husband's *dala* as she does in mortuary distributions for someone in her father's *dala*. However, there are times when she may contribute small amounts of wealth to the women's mortuary ceremony organized by her husband's *dala*. But this help is given because the deceased is from the same clan as her father (or her mother's father). A woman says, "I am helping my father's *kumila*." Therefore, when a woman marries a man from the same clan as her father, members of her husband's *dala* will be included among those people in her father's clan with whom her father maintains mortuary obligations.

A woman's continual efforts on the part of her own kin in mortuary ceremonies indicate the error of assuming that she has been given to her husband. In fact, she is merely *on loan*. Although women physically move at marriage to live in their husband's hamlets, structurally women never move out of their natal situation: identified with their own *dala* and united with their fathers and their fathers' *dala*.

In the Trobriands, the opposition between brother and sister is culturally and publicly maintained through a wide range of taboos associated with sexual and social separation. At the same time, sister and brother have a strong private bond between them, as evidenced in the support and exchange of such "gifts" as cooked food, tobacco, and betel nuts. Publicly, a woman helps her brother in duties performed for his children. Politically, she demonstrates her brother's position through her performance in women's *sagali*. A woman also recovers *dala* property lent by her brother to his children. Finally, the reproductive powers of women establish the continuity of *dala*. From this view, a sibling set of brother and sister seems to constitute the basic core of all kin-

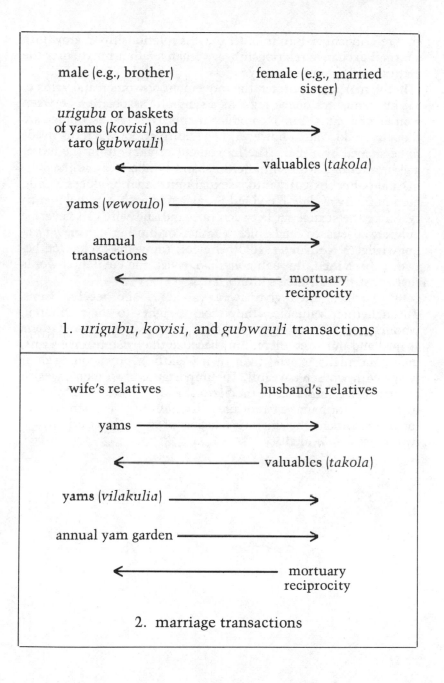

Figure 22. *Exchanges from men to married women*

ship relationships. But, in order for this relationship to grow into a formal exchange relationship, a woman's father must enter the picture, and she must marry.

In the marriage contract, the movement of women and yams to the husbands' residence suggests a symbolic association between women and yams. Yams reproduce themselves, just as women are thought to do. Yams, however, need cultivation as a fetus needs to be shaped by a man. The movement of yams from the father and brother of a woman to her husband symbolizes the transformation of her sexuality into a sexual union that produces a child born not only of *dala* blood but provisioned with paternal identity. Since the sexual act between husband and wife can never be publicly discussed, and since a father or brother can never acknowledge a woman's sexual behavior, the yams exchanged between these men, through a woman, speak the elemental words that constitute all men's immortality.

In marriage, men give away valuables and receive yams. Through their valuables, they receive rights to their children, whom they develop and provision just as their own fathers shaped and nurtured them. But, because they also receive yams, men continually expend their own wealth in provisioning their wives with women's wealth. The importance of women's wealth exceeds the importance of the historical time controlled by men. In their performance of mortuary distributions, women control for all Kiriwinans the ahistorical aspect of time: the continuity of *baloma* and *dala* identity.

Chapter 9
The Nature of Trobriand Exchange

I

... the final goal, of which an Ethnographer should never lose sight ... is briefly, to grasp the native's point of view, his relation to life, to realise his vision of his world. We have to study man, and we must study what concerns him most intimately, that is, the hold which life has on him. In each culture, the values are slightly different; people aspire after different aims, follow different impulses, yearn after a different form of happiness ... To study the institutions, customs, and codes or to study the behavior and mentality without the subjective desire of feeling by what these people live, of realising the substance of their happiness—is, in my opinion, to miss the greatest reward which we can hope to obtain from the study of man.—Malinowski 1922, p. 25

Malinowski sought to find cultural meaning in subjective desire. To understand the Trobriander's mind it was necessary to conceptualize events through the "native's point of view." Subjective desire as a motivating force for behavior could then be articulated into logical structures of Trobriand reality. For Malinowski, the reduction of such motivation to psychological phenomena became the primary reference point from which to describe and explain the Trobriander's "vision of *his* world."[1] While Malinowski realized that the system of exchange could provide him with insights into the psychology of the Trobriand people, he failed to realize that the system serves much the same function for the people themselves. Trobrianders regularly use the particulars of specific exchanges to read and send messages about each others' states of mind.

In this study, I too have been concerned with subjective desire. But, unlike Malinowski, I have attempted to read objects of exchange as the Trobrianders' symbolic representations of their own thought. In the Trobriands, where exchange is the basic framework around which formal patterns of social interaction are organized, objects become highly significant because in their manner of presentation—quality, quantity, and the like—they can be read as an objectification of desire and intent.

In order for Trobrianders to read specific exchanges as reflections of the thoughts and feelings of the participants, they must possess a system of interpretation. Ethnographers have assumed that this system can be understood by eliciting the rules for specific exchange events. But the system described in this way allows only two messages; either participants adhere to the rules and "all is well," or they do not follow the rules, in which case "something is wrong." Among the Trobrianders, however, I observed a much wider range of communication through exchange acts. Trobrianders evaluate each others' thoughts and feelings in light of the value of specific exchanges, and they take care that the dispositions they wish imputed to themselves will be correctly read by others.

Each person is accorded some degree of autonomy in all social relationships. Therefore, the danger in exchange is that relationships remain at best tenuous. The persons with whom one exchanges can change residence, divorce, or not work too hard in the gardens. Through conflicts, a man may lose his yam house or a woman will be able to produce only a meager supply of her wealth. Here, as elsewhere, there exists a strong ethic of *equivalence*, despite rank and other status differentiations. People are not free to command each other. They cannot effect their will over another person. But Trobrianders believe that it is possible to *influence* the disposition of others. Such influence, however, has limitations, and the process is notoriously fallible.

Giving things to others and the use of magic spells are the two most effective persuasive devices available to every individual. Magic spells are an attempt to gain control over objects and persons through powerful verbal persuasion (see Tambiah 1968). The dynamics of exchange embody similar, though less powerful, attempts at persuasion. While magic, when successful, can directly control the mind of another, exchange, even when successful, depends on a general ethic of generosity. In exchange, the giver must demonstrate generosity even as she or he attempts to exploit it.

The central contradiction, which I suggest has implications for a general theory of exchange, is that exchange mediates the opposition between the self and others, while simultaneously it reenforces the very same opposition. Every individual believes himself or herself able to negotiate some measure of control in all relationships; yet recognition of the inherent limitations of control is just as immanent.

Thus, whereas Lévi-Strauss saw exchange as the mediator of fixed opposed categories of relationships, I am suggesting that Trobriand exchange creates and reinforces oppositions of self-interest at the same time that those oppositions are momentarily overcome. Trobriand exchange prevents the identity of one person from being totally absorbed by another; the untenable extremes of complete autonomy from others and total dependence on others are avoided through the mechanism of exchange. Exchange allows social space to be negotiable at the same time that personal space (one's autonomy) is inviolable. In contrast, magic is a mechanism that allows one person to intrude upon the personal space of another. Were magic rather than exchange the *modus operandi* of daily social interaction, the split of society into two classes—controllers and controlled—would be complete. This speculation suggests the social value of exchange. The possibilities of gaining power over other people are limited, but the liabilities are also limited. Individuals are constrained by exchange, but they also maintain their personal autonomy within its framework.

Because everyone believes in her or his own independence and because control is constrained, self-interest must be disguised. The constraints on the system demand that self-interest not be expressed in words; hence, in the Trobriands, desire and individual intent should not be overtly stated. As in the case of *pokala* and marriage exchanges, verbal statements of intent are withheld until it becomes clear through the nonverbal medium of exchange that one's expectations will be fulfilled. Villagers read exchange events by treating the objects and styles of exchange as evidences of attitudes and expectations. In this way, objects communicate what words cannot. Objects change hands in formal settings, publicly announcing one's expectations but keeping the calculations verbally silent. The transaction usually states an accomplished fact while allowing each participant to subvert that fact. Exchange does not alienate the donor, as Marcel Mauss and Karl Marx implied (see Sahlins 1972, pp. 180–181), but gives scope to an ongoing process wherein the donor and the recipient may continually reevaluate the other's and their own current condition or states of being in the system.

But words have their own power; in terms of conflict, words are more ominous and therefore ultimately more powerful than objects. Words, unlike objects, directly and immediately challenge the balance between control and personal autonomy. This I suggest is the reason that the spoken words of magic spells contain the power to swiftly effect one's desires, desires that cannot be accomplished through the formal channels of exchange. The words of magic spells are the fantasies of private thought and, when spoken, these words are the projection of power. The practice of magic extends the strength of one's creative and manipulative intent to control and publicly displays one's autonomy.

Exchange objects must also be displayed. But, in this case, display establishes one's ability to maintain relationships through the formal channels of reciprocity. Throughout life, an individual is dependent on resources obtained through others. Ascribed birth rights must be fortified and expanded by achievements, which are continually validated in public display. Given the Trobriand milieu, this achievement is indeed a great accomplishment. All objects demand constant care and watchful control for, in one way or another, all external property can be lost. Goods, including land, are in constant circulation, providing avenues for conversions of one kind of resource into another. In the course of these conversions, increases in control can be effected. But to maintain these controls as a steady or increasing state demands constant surveillance. Again we see another contradiction in the process of exchange: an elaborate system with an ever-constant propensity toward loss. Such loss is, however, a control on an ever-expanding system. In actual practice no man can ever rest on his laurels. Even the strongest men cannot escape from the danger inherent in the game they play.

Thus, if exchange is the fundamental road to all relationships, it is also a difficult road to travel. A man spends his life trying to hold his relationships and objects together. Building a yam house is a testimony to this ability, for he can only do so if another man is making a large garden for him. The elaborate construction of a yam house, the symbolic significance of its decoration, its permanence and prominence in the hamlet—all combine to visually symbolize the actions of people vis-à-vis each other. A yam house is the personification of the complete transformation of power from the beauty of youth to the power of objects now displayed in a permanent edifice, symbolizing the power of a man who knows how to make relationships work. Year after year, yams must be produced. The supply is always being converted into something else or eaten and therefore destroyed. The demand remains constant. A yam house, whether full or empty, stands as a symbol of both past and future relationships with women and men, a symbol which, like a myth, aggrandizes the continuity of those relationships in the face of reality which understands thoroughly the tenuousness of all social relationships.

At the death of its owner, a yam house must be dismantled. The only part of the structure that remains is the four coral boulders forming the base. The yam house is an external symbol of the power of a man; it is not a symbol of *dala* because it is only permanent until the death of its owner. At death, all yam roads must be constructed anew. The deceased's stored yams are distributed after the first *sagali*; these yams cannot be used as formal mortuary payments, nor can they be passed on to successors. Further, when a man loses the allegiance of other men, he must remove the symbol of that relationship and take down his yam house.

Motawoli, whose father is dead, lived with Todai—his classificatory mother's brother—and made a main garden (*kaymata*) for him. Todai also received yams from a very small garden (*kaymwila*) made by his wife's brother. Todai had a reputation for being a miserly man, totally lacking in generosity. He and Motawoli constantly quarreled over betel nuts and coconuts, which Motawoli said he had a right to take from Todai's palms because he made a garden for him. Todai always objected. One day they had a bitter quarrel over betel nuts, and Motawoli became angry and carried his house away to another hamlet.

Motawoli went to live with his "sister" (they both had the same mother's mother's mother) and her husband. Motawoli immediately began to make a large garden for Masawa, his sister's husband. When all this happened, Todai had to take down the poles of his yam house, and now there is nothing in front of his living house except four coral stones. The yams that Todai receives from his affines are few in number, and he stores them in the interior of his living house. There is little public pride in these yams and much shame.

Even the relationship between a man and his son can be precarious. This is the reason men watch young men so carefully. No man can be forced to work hard in the gardens. The amount of labor expended is of one's own choice. A man, unhappy about a relationship, will say, "I am tired this year and I cannot work so hard in the garden for you."

In this milieu, where even the most seemingly permanent control over others can be lost, all men—and women—use magic in an effort to retain and maximize their own situation. The power of magic is exploited at the highest political level, and every individual attempts to build up her or his own personal repertoire of magic spells. When people believe in the forces of magic, magic becomes the most creative and powerful tool that anyone can wield. Magic is calculated to serve the right cause at the right time. Sometimes its use is deliberately withheld, while at other times magic is accompanied by great ritual and political display.

Malinowski contrasted technology and magic. According to him, when technological skills run out because of the limits of his empirical knowledge, primitive man turns to magic to allay his anxiety, built up out of the realization that he lives in a hostile, uncontrolled *physical* environment.[2] Malinowski's (1925, pp. 30–31) classic example supporting this view was that men who fish in the safe waters of the lagoon do not use magic, while open-sea fishing necessitates extensive use of magic spells. My point of departure from Malinowski begins with a collapse of the ideas summarized in the following quotation.

> Magic is to be expected and generally to be found whenever man comes to an unbridgeable gap, a hiatus in his knowledge or in his powers of practical control, and yet has to continue in his pursuit. Forsaken by his knowledge, baffled by the results of his experience, unable to apply any effective technical skill, he realizes his impotence. Yet his desire grips him only the more strongly. His fears and hopes, his general anxiety, produce a state of unstable equilibrium in his organism, by which he is driven to some sort of vicarious activity. (1931, pp. 638–639)

The words of Trobriand spells contain explicit references to all manner of objects, birds, animals, and so on, in the environment which are called upon as agents to perform the actor's will (see Weiner n.d.). The use of metaphor and metonymy in the spells illustrates the subtlety and sophistication of the Trobrianders' knowledge of their physical environment (see Munn n.d.*b*; Tambiah 1968). To distinguish categorically between the logicality and the irrationality of magic is invalid (see Tambiah 1973). For, in the Trobriander's "vision of *his* world," magic is a resource rationally conceptualized and powerfully exercised. While it is true that the use of magic occurs at an "unbridgeable gap," the gap does not result from the kind of impotence suggested by Malinowski. The hostile environment is not the physical surroundings, for through the spells that environment becomes a powerful part of one's resources. Rather, the "hiatus" is a result of the lack of knowledge of what is in other people's minds, the possibility that others' interests will conflict with one's own interests, and the consequences these factors have for the Trobriand system of power.

The physical world proves hazardous only when it has been rendered so by someone else's magic. Others' magic spells will be directed against oneself only when one's actions have had (or threaten to have) undesirable consequences for someone else.[3] By the same token, a Trobriander uses magic whenever the actions of others have consequences for herself or himself, and there is reason to believe that these consequences do not agree with one's own interests, or when one's own interests may be advanced by fulfilling the expectations of others.

Exchange obligations are an example of the latter case. Thus, according to my informants, men *do* use fishing magic in the lagoon when they need to fulfill an exchange obligation. Further, fishing on the northern coast for *kalala* necessitates a more extensive use of magic than does any other kind of fishing (see Malinowski 1918). *Kalala* fishing occurs in the shallow water along the beach, a place not physically dangerous. However, the fishermen of Labai must produce large amounts of *kalala* because this fish is exchanged with the Tabalu of Omarakana in an obligation that goes back to the Tabalu origin story (see chap. 2). Moreover, a man uses garden magic *only* in those gardens which he grows for someone else; no one uses magic in subsistence gardens, for this produce is immediately converted into food and does not facilitate the maintenance of extended formalized social relationships.

Therefore, the hostile environment is one's social milieu with the inherent threat of rejection. In order to retain control, men must constantly draw on and publicize their own internal resources, their personal knowledge of spells. Nowhere is the contradiction between need and fear dramatized so impressively as in *kula*. For men, *kula* is very like the game that adolescents play where competition and jealousy are rife and the game of attraction is paramount. When men embark on overseas *kula* expeditions, they leave behind the symbols of their power: their yam houses, wives, sisters, and children. The only objectifications of power men take are themselves, their canoes, their beauty, their decorations, and their magic. On *kula*, men return to and draw on the power of youth: the use of the self as the primary mechanism for attraction. Love magic is used as if one were seducing a *kula* partner, for, as Vanoi once told my young friend Dabweyowa regarding *kitoma*: "Remember, a *kula* shell is like a young girl; she looks over every man until she decides which one she likes best. One man is chosen and the others are sent away."

Thus magic must be understood as a counterpart to the process of formal exchange. The knowledge of spells and their use demonstrate perhaps better than any other aspect of Trobriand life the opposition between dependency on others and the fear of personal autonomy. Magic is not only used against others as an exertion of power, it is also used to coerce others into believing in one's sincerity and good intentions. Magic represents both love and danger, need and fear, and the trauma of illness and death. Magic in its use value has the power to change a person's thoughts and, for the person who has knowledge of a magic spell, the use of that spell has the power to make the owner's ambitions a reality. The power of spells gives access to those areas where the device of exchange is insufficient for control and also allows the intent underlying reciprocal obligations to be publicly demonstrated. If objects of exchange effect limited control over others, then knowledge of magic spells, residing within a person and therefore not subject to the same kind of loss as objects, effects the strongest possible control at the moment that the spells are spoken. For the power of magic, unlike exchange, lies in spoken words.

Magic resides in the belly,[4] fortifying a woman or a man with something that cannot be lost. Magic does not rot, nor is it lent out and retrieved or lost like stone ax blades or land. It must be periodically displayed to affirm one's power and the complete knowledge of the spell. For, when magic does not work, it is thought that part of the spell was not transmitted by the former owner. In old age, magic is given away line by line so that a man or a woman who owns magic continually receives support from someone who wants the magic. Magic, therefore, is only lost across generations, when someone dies before she or he has shared the complete knowledge of the spells. On the other hand, "new" magic from other islands is always being sought and imported.[5]

The power of magic and its concomitant uneven distribution and ownership produce anxiety in others so that a closed circle of forces is formed. Magic breeds fear of others, and fear of others is overcome by magic. Technical skill in the garden is essential for producing yams, but the production of yams is related to networks of relationships. People are far more difficult to control than yams—a fact no Kiriwina person ever forgets.

From this perspective, I propose the following premises that seem to underwrite the dynamics of Trobriand exchange. (1) It is essential for people to control human behavior, but this control is constrained by formal rules of social interaction. (2) Despite formal rules, complete control over others is never assured because every individual is accorded some measure of autonomy. Thus the nature of control and autonomy introduces an element of danger into the relationship. (3) This danger is further intensified because of the cyclical nature of Trobriand exchange. The attempt to control is not limited to the sociopolitical sphere but includes a cosmic order of time and space. Individuals are concerned not only with present situations but with a past and a future in which death is made less threatening. To ensure that order rather than chaos is maintained, the "social construction of reality" (Berger and Luckmann 1966) is built up on the dialectical opposition between personal desire and the social and cultural ordering of events and persons.

Thus human thought must be recognized as a partial distortion of reality, a reordering in which myths are created from the fabric of desire. Death, the use of magic, and instances of political confrontation most dramatically explode these myths, leaving exposed for a moment the fact that others' personal autonomy has collapsed. At these moments all effort is marshaled to bind the rupture, but such a moment also serves to reenforce the continued need for disguise.

Marcel Mauss, drawing heavily on Malinowski's Trobriand ethnography, introduced the concept of exchange as "total social phenomena" containing elements at once social, economic, legal, moral, aesthetic, and so on. Mauss analyzed exchange by separating the acts of giving, receiving, and repaying. In order to expose the structure of exchange, reciprocity as a total concept was fragmented into discrete categories. Mauss's reciprocity was a major step toward a general theory of exchange, but the segmentation of reciprocity was a major conceptual error (see Lévi-Strauss 1966b; Sahlins 1972).

In analyzing Trobriand exchange, I have indicated that if exchange events are described within a single dimension, that is, transactions of gift and countergift, the processes of social interaction then appear to be determined by principles of cause and effect. The mistake here is to reduce exchange to an act seen within the limitations of the present rather than to analyze exchange events as comprising a system of regeneration in which the temporal context of generational continuity carries as much weight as economic and political factors.

Mauss's concept of exchange effectively emphasized the importance of understanding the concrete totality of social life, the need to explore beyond a framework of discrete institutions. But, although Mauss seemed to be searching for broader boundaries than those of institutions, his use of the words "social" and "gift" appears to so set the frame of analysis that later theoretical perspectives still focus on social boundaries in terms of the traditional anthropological institutions of kinship, marriage, economics, and politics. Further, conflict and the practice of magic as the counterpart of exchange have not been integrated into a "total" view of exchange. The Malinowskian dilemma of "giving for the sake of giving," followed by other ethnographic accounts of giving for "love" or "generosity," has tended to obscure the nature of power and controls underlying exchange events.

The view of primitive exchange as primarily social in nature because of the generalized character of reciprocity and kinship (see Sahlins 1965) seems unsatisfactory. By continually emphasizing the primacy of exchange as social rather than economic, anthropologists have tended to ignore exchange as part of a power system. We must push exchange beyond the level of our view of the social world and seek to understand exchange as the means, however limited, of gaining power over people and control over resources in the widest sense (see Adams 1975). Lévi-Strauss, a proponent of the social view of exchange, wrote: "From an economic viewpoint, no one has gained and no one has lost. But the point is that there is much more in the exchange itself than in the things exchanged" (1969a, p. 59). The "more" is the social relationship established, the tie of obligations that "makes one obligated, and always beyond what has been given or accepted" (p. 59).

What seems missing from an approach emphasizing the social nature of exchange *as a form* of social organization is an understanding of exchange as action—action engaging donor and recipient in games of control which transcend the purely social, economic, and political domains. In a sense Malinowski's emphasis on the context of situation and Mauss's call for a study of "total" behavior are the points to which we must return. But we must see context through a temporal perspective and must view exchange events as actions of control in the widest sense. Thus we must expand social fields of action to include what Hallowell has called a "total culturally constituted environment," making the boundaries of analysis conform to informants' concepts of time and space, rather than imposing a priori largely ethnocentric social categories.

The basic force that gives momentum to the processes of human interaction is control over the circulation of goods, over workpower, *and* over the final regeneration of persons through social and cosmic time. From this perspective, self-interest is not simply a calculated part of exchange (see Firth 1967); self-interest is *paramount*. Trobriand children do not merely grow up, marry, and die. Rather, from the moment of conception, recognition of the potential of that child-to-be predominates and is measured in social and political terms that include controls over the reconstitution of each Trobriand self. Therefore, the processes of exchange must of necessity accommodate relationships that will extend over long periods of time. This extension of time, introducing the importance of cyclicity in exchanges that create and maintain fundamental social relationships, reenforces the danger in the system because, regardless of the relationship, power over others remains inherently weak.

If we return for a moment to the anthropologists who have devised theories about exchange, we find an interesting series of dependencies. The Trobriand informants who say they exchange for "love" or "generosity" are following a myth that serves in their society to hide a reality of self-interest. The anthropologist who then insists on labeling this act as a "gift" seems to be perpetuating the Trobriand natives' myth. But this is probably only incidental to what she or he is doing. In weaving the "gift" myth, is not the anthropologist hiding a reality that concerns *his* or *her* role in *his* or *her* society? Is he or she not perpetuating and creating an image of "the primitive" as a person, or "primitive society" as a way of life, that has survived on some fundamental principle *other than self-interest*? Although Sahlins initially seems skeptical about claims of altruism in primitive exchange, nevertheless he formulates a model of exchange that relies on altruistic, nonexploitative behavior among close kin as the central principle.

"Generalized reciprocity" refers to transactions that are putatively altruistic, transactions on the line of assistance given and, if possible and necessary, assistance returned. The ideal type is Malinowski's "pure gift." Other indicative ethnographic formulae are "sharing," "hospitali-

ty," "free gift," "help," and "generosity." Less sociable, but
tending toward the same pole are "kinship dues," "chiefly
dues," and "noblesse oblige" . . . This is not to say that hand-
ing over things in such form, even to "loved ones," gener-
ates no counter-obligation. But the counter is not stipu-
lated by time, quantity, or quality: the expectation of
reciprocity is indefinite. (1965, p. 147)

Why is the emphasis wholly on reciprocity and obligation? Could
it not be on investment and risk taking and on fear as well? Is not
the "indefinite" quality of the "reciprocity" more meaningful if
seen as the uncertainty inherent in risk taking? And, following
Elizabeth Colson (1974), is not the "obligation" psychologically
an expresion of fear of this uncertainty?

Clearly, without the logically prior obligation of reciprocity,
there could be no investment, no risk, and so on. The possibility
of using the system to advance self-interest is wholly contingent
on the norm of reciprocity. It is for this reason that reciprocity
and generosity have been emphasized by Lévi-Strauss, Sahlins,
and others. But logical priority does not necessarily imply structural centrality. Norms of reciprocity do not exist outside of and
prior to the members in society. Rather, norms must be constantly negotiated and renegotiated in the arguments and justifications
surrounding specific acts. Logical priority serves the purposes of
argumentation because norms are only invoked in the particular
cases of compliance or noncompliance.

In order to secure individual claims, people disguise their self-
interests by arguing that any failure to reciprocate in a particular
instance might establish the precedence of a counternorm of
selfishness. Therefore, it is in the interests of the exchange partner to sustain the norms so that he may take advantage himself at
a later time. In an oral tradition, norms do not exist apart from
the occasions of their use.

If norms are abstract formulations, effective apart from their
articulation, then every failure to comply must count as a breach.
If, however, norms are part of the rhetorical equipment people
draw upon to be persuasive, no act (or failure to act) need constitute a failure to comply, if it is allowed to pass unnoticed by all
the parties involved. This ensures that people need not be shamed
by default on either side and allows for the possibility of individual withdrawal.

Throughout this book I have alluded to the use of disguise in
rhetoric and in certain social taboos as protection for participants

in a social relationship with long-term intent. The most important "close" relationships are those between a woman and her brother, a man and his children, a woman and her husband, and a woman and her children. Exchange events condition the stability of these relationships at every turn in the life cycle, continuing beyond death. The danger exists because no one can wield complete constraint. Thus fear of what others may do must be recognized as an integral part of the action of exchange. As Colson argued, "Fear, to most of us, seems a poor basis on which to found a society or develop a system of law. But we are unrealistic if we ignore the fear and concentrate solely on the advantages people see in their associations. A dynamic picture must include them both" (1974, p. 45).

In his analysis of Choiseul Island kinship, Harold Scheffler has shown the importance of seeing the rhetoric of kinship as "one of the ways of 'getting the work of society done,' or organizing and 'steering' action" (1965, p. 300). In the Trobriands, the rhetoric of exchange serves just this purpose. Thus the "trick" of *tabu*—the use of the term *veyola* (kinsperson) for those who are privately recognized as nonkin—the deception of "virgin birth," and the exchanges given in the name of "love" and "generosity" are not ideals, nor are they norms. Rather they serve as a disguise, presenting people with a degree of freedom in behavior while simultaneously communicating the significance of the game without confusion in anyone's mind.

At the same time, the fear of conflict always lies just below the surface. The personal space, or autonomy granted as each individual's due, includes thoughts, desires, intentions, and a continual evaluation of others. Magic provides a unique resource, individually acquired and manipulated. It is feared that behind each masked face lies uncontrollable danger that will defiantly erupt into a public confrontation. When this kind of drama occurs, the façade of the myth is sharply torn asunder. The contradiction between autonomy and control is flagrantly exposed and every villager is witness to his or her own vulnerability.

In the most climactic political meeting I attended, the question to be resolved was the continued support of the Local Government Council, controlled by Waibadi as president, or the transfer of support to John Kasaipwalova and his newly organized Kabisawali movement. About four hundred men gathered near the mission station in Omarakana. Following almost two hours of individual debate, Waibadi strode into the center in great agitation and announced his mother's name:

My mother is Kabwenaya. She gave birth to me and
she called my name Waibadi. When I say once, it is once.
No one can stop me. Whatever I say, I do. Nobody can stop
me or change my mind. I know two kinds of fibers for binding canoes. One is called *momulukwausi* and one is *momuyobikwa*. You people are going to vote for which one you like
and which one you do not like. *Momulukwausi* is my fiber.
If it goes bad, I can change it and put on a new one and then
retie it. Other people who live near the lagoon [part of the
opposition side] have *momuyobikwa*. They tie it for a
long time on the canoe and only then can they change it.
But, for me, I tie my fiber maybe for two weeks and then
I am going to change it. Come on, vote, and then we
will find out which fiber is stronger.

With these last words, the meeting exploded. Several men pro-
tectively pulled me back from the center. Fighting was about to
occur and men were shouting in all directions. "This is the Kiriwina way," my friends told me. Waibadi, remaining impervious,
left the meeting site, and everyone thought he had gone to get his
spear. In his absence the other chiefs restored some degree of
calm. They said that one of Waibadi's kinsmen (a young man
known for his radical views) had "spoiled" Waibadi's mind. Waibadi returned, *sans* spear, but his sister pulled him away again.
She shouted that no one had "spoiled Waibadi's mind. No one has
the power to control Waibadi." The meeting was over and no vote
was taken.

The fiber that Waibadi used to metaphorically circumscribe his
position of power referred to his knowledge of sun and rain magic,
magic that could destroy crops for the entire island. He argued
that his kind of magic (the *momulukwausi* fiber) was unlike the
weather magic which a few other people were known to own.
Like the fiber on his canoe, the force of *his* magic could be
changed at will. Thus he alone had the power to use his magic
spell in a destructive way that far surpassed anyone else's power.
And in so saying, however metaphorically, Waibadi was issuing a
clear threat.

The danger in this confrontation was Waibadi's public declaration, which compelled the formal taking of sides in a vote. The
power of his magic was always known and its effects had been
demonstrated on other occasions (see chap. 8). In fully exposing
his intentions, Waibadi precipitated a vote in which individuals
had to choose sides not on the basis of formal exchange relation-

ships but in response to fear and individual power. Informants said that taking Waibadi's side or opposing him publicly was dangerous because one became dependent once one committed oneself. I was witness to many situations of individual power confrontations from the hamlet level to the level of this large political gathering. All these fights erupted because angry words were spoken and response was immediate and hazardous.

Confrontation lifts the mask of myth, and all individuals are made to face the reality of power with which they must cope. This revelation reaffirms the danger of social interaction while simultaneously confirming the need to contain competition within lines of exchange so that individual intent remains balanced by the constraints of exchange. Thus exchange is not merely a "treaty of peace" (see Lévi-Strauss 1969a; Mauss 1954; Sahlins 1972) but is a particular kind of treaty, giving full recognition to what has seemed to be the paradox of the other as opposition. From time to time, the treaty of peace must momentarily be broken. But in these moments myth is reformulated once again out of fear of reality, a reality of power.

Within this frame of reference, death can be seen as a disruptive event, totally unpredictable and uncontrollable. It can therefore be depended upon to occur with some randomness—sufficient to bring about the periodic alignment of personnel and the public taking of sides which must be reenforced from time to time. Death precipitates the accumulation and loss of all resources. Distribution is publicly accountable in precise economic and political terms. The fear generated by death becomes fear *written large*. This most antisocial occurrence is read by villagers as an individual attack against not just one person but against the strength and the continuation of *dala* identity and property.

I return for a moment to the movement of an individual through a life cycle in order to more fully present the context in which death must be viewed. In the Trobriands, a person is born identified as a member of a particular *dala* through the essence of *baloma*, the blood of a woman, and her nurturing milk. Blood, milk, and *baloma* therefore constitute basic resources. But ascribed birthrights must be fortified and expanded by things achieved through relationships with others. Each infant only becomes a social being as it claims ties with others beyond *dala* identity. From birth, social ties to the father's *dala* are symbolically stated when a father's name is given and when holes are pierced in the earlobes of the infant. The functional acquisition of the father's "property" necessitates significant social relationships with the father's "sisters," thus commencing the growth of the infant into a fully social being. In life this process continues as the locus of power shifts through time from the power of one's physical self—the power of youth—to objects external to one's self. After marriage, the display of objects becomes more important and denotes a wider range of relationships than did the display of self. As one ages, one's own private individual power, such as knowledge of magic and land and origin stories, grows inside one's body. Knowledge within the self enables a woman or a man to maintain and expand social networks, even when the objects outside the self diminish. At death, the full range of individual achievement is dramatically portrayed in the women's mortuary ceremony. On that day, the magnitude of the worth of the deceased to other living members of the society can be traced through each individual exchange event.

Thus the dynamics of the rituals of death encapsulate that "fleeting moment when the society and its members take emotional stock of themselves and their situation" (Mauss 1954, p. 77). In taking stock, the system of power is dramatically revealed in both its negative and positive aspects. Individual power, the cause of death, demands the display of group power, but this latter statement is made through giving away all resources, thereby reversing complete autonomy to its proper balance—a balance produced by the nature of Trobriand exchange.

Chapter 10
Women of Value, Men of Renown:
An Epilog

I

Another sociological feature, which forcibly obtrudes it-self on the visitor's notice is the social position of the wom-en. Their behavior, after the cool aloofness of the Dobuan wom-en, and the very uninviting treatment which strangers receive from those of the Amphletts, comes almost as a shock in its friendly familiarity. Naturally, here also, the manners of women of rank are quite different from those of low class commoners. But on the whole, high and low alike, though by no means re-served, have a genial, pleasant approach, and many of them are very fine-looking.—Malinowski 1922, pp. 52–53

One of the underlying themes of this book has been to view the Trobriand universe within a perspective that gives as much weight to the cosmic order as to the social order. By collapsing traditional analytical categories of social, economic, political, and so on, I have shown that exchange is a process that holds a system of power relationships in balance. With this approach, I have been able to support the thesis that the individual human being in Trobriand society is accorded great value. I have shown that this value is reaffirmed in the symbolic qualities embedded in Trobriand objects of exchange, for these objects carry significata denoting elements of fertility, sexuality, and immortality.

From this perspective, the power of Trobriand women can be seen to circumscribe the most vital area of concern for women *and* men: regenesis. But the controls which women exert at the two ends of the life cycle—both at birth and in death rituals—are given greater significance through the objectification of their power into wealth objects: skirts and bundles. Therefore, Trobriand women have power which is publicly recognized on both sociopolitical and cosmic planes. Beyond the ethnographic data, however, the "discovery" that Trobriand women have power and that women enact roles which are symbolically, structurally, and functionally significant to the ordering of Trobriand society, and to the roles that men play, should give us, as anthropologists, cause for concern. In all major areas within our discipline, we have reevaluated and reformulated nineteenth-century theories of society and culture. But we have accepted almost without question the nineteenth-century Western legacy that had effectively segregated women from positions of power. We have subjected early missionary and travelers' documents to a careful evaluation of their bias toward the "native." But have we equally considered the effects of their bias toward women? We have allowed "politics by men" to structure our thinking about other societies; we have led ourselves to believe that, if women are not dominant in the political sphere of interaction, their power remains at best peripheral. We unquestioningly accept male statements about women as factual evidence for the way a society is structured. We argue the problem of emic and etic, but not with reference to women's perception of their roles. From this view, since we compare women to men in the context of politics, we should not be surprised that we arrive at the almost universal notion that women's status is secondary to that of men.

It then becomes a matter of course to assume that women's roles correspond to the "nature" side of a universal nature/culture paradigm or to argue that women are only one of many objects exchanged at marriage. But these views can be as devoid of cultural substance as the above quotation from Malinowski, in which he described Trobriand women as friendly, pleasant, and "fine-looking." To devote only one chapter of an ethnography to women or to produce a book about the kinship system of a particular society from only male informants' points of view is to reduce the study of society and culture to an impoverished view of human interaction.

Any study that does not include the role of women—as seen by women—as part of the way the society is structured remains only a partial study of that society. Whether women are publicly valued or privately secluded, whether they control politics, a range of economic commodities, or merely magic spells, they function within that society, not as objects but as individuals with some measure of control. We cannot begin to understand either in evolutionary terms or in current and historical situations why and how women in so many cases have been relegated to secondary status until we *first* reckon with the power women do have, even if this power *appears* limited and seems outside the political field.

Equally important, we must analyze, where it is appropriate, such cosmic phenomena as notions of ancestral substances or objects which regenerate property or human beings as part of a society's resources. Too often, what seem to us to be natural phenomena are an integral part of the "culturally constituted environment" of a particular people (Hallowell 1954, p. 86). This view enables us to delineate the controls which women and men exert over a wider range of resources than sociopolitical phenomena. Women's control over certain resources can then be seen as articulating with male controls rather than as having negative value when measured against male power. Politics, then, does not appear as the ultimate measure of power but as power of a particular nature that operates with differing manifestations contingent upon the nature of the resources that women control.

The Trobriand situation presents an impressive example of the importance of this view. Both Malinowski and Powell deemed Trobriand women unworthy of careful study. They paid lip service to the high status of women, but their studies took for granted the inconsequentiality of the role of women. Lévi-Strauss extracted an example from Malinowski's Trobriand data to support his view that "the total relationship of exchange which constitutes marriage is not established between a man and a woman, where each owes and receives something, but between two groups of men, and the woman figures only as one of the objects in the exchange, not as one of the partners between whom the exchange takes place" (1969a, p. 115).

Malinowski described the presents of betel nuts, tobacco, and other small objects that a boy or man must give the woman with whom he sleeps. Following these observations, he concluded that "sexual intercourse . . . is a service rendered by the female to the male" (1929, p. 319). Therefore, sexual intercourse is not an "exchange of services in itself reciprocal. But custom, arbitrary and inconsequent here as elsewhere, decrees that it is a service from women to men, and men have to pay" (ibid., p. 320). Rather than examine these transactions as indicative of the power of women and the general nature of human interaction (see chap. 7), Lévi-Strauss concluded that "the lack of reciprocity which seems to characterize these services in the Trobriand Islands, as in most human societies, is the mere counterpart of a universal fact, that the relationship of reciprocity which is the basis of marriage is not established between men and women, but between men by means of women, who are merely the occasion of this relationship" (1969*a*, p. 116).

Clearly, as I have shown, the value of Trobriand women expands at marriage to encompass her own socioeconomic power in the production and distribution of her wealth, her control over the regeneration of *dala* identity, and the recovery of certain kins of *dala* property. The power of a woman to conceive and the importance of children to her husband are significantly valued. At marriage, women and men begin to negotiate their relationship *with each other* through cyclical exchanges which have importance for a wide network of relationships *with other men and women*. Through annual harvests of yams and women's activities in mortuary distributions, women are given public recognition for the active, pivotal role they play, a role demonstrating the worth of men in their lives and, equally, their own sociocultural value. Throughout a marriage women and men have equal negotiating power. Such power, of course, has implications for the relationships between men, but women are not "merely the occasion" of these relationships, as Lévi-Strauss so emphatically claimed to be a "universal fact."

Marriage in the Trobriands is a relationship through which men establish a range of social relationships not only with men but with women (i.e., their sisters, their daughters, *and* their wives). For a woman, marriage provides the context in which she can display, manipulate, and channel the power of her Trobriand womanness. The power of a Trobriand woman, from a cultural view, is not merely a fact of biology. Rather, the value of womanness is identified through the cultural symbols of her wealth—skirts and bundles which serve to objectify this transformation. *The value of womanness, not women*, is what men gain at marriage, and and this value is now exploited in a positive sense by women themselves on every level. The question to be posed now is whether the Trobriands are unique in this regard or whether we, as anthropologists following the Malinowskian tradition of paying merely verbal homage to the status of women, have too often been victims of our own cultural bias.

At the outset we must recognize that one must understand the power structure in which Trobriand women operate in order to understand how Trobriand men perceive themselves. Nature exists in order to be shaped and transformed to serve one's purposes. All manner of human resources and energy is turned to this effort. The basic premise on which this effort is sustained is the regeneration of human beings. The symbolic qualities of exchange objects mirror the preoccupation with the developmental cycle of life and death. Stone ax blades (male wealth), skirts and bundles (female wealth), and yams (the composite of male and female wealth) constitute the basic artifacts of Trobriand exchange, and each object symbolically represents some measure of regenesis.

Trobriand exchange objects, unlike Western money, cannot be detached from the human experience of regeneration and immortality. They are not alienated from the basic concerns of society, and therefore social relationships are not merely relations between impersonal things, in Marx's terms, but remain relations that reify the cyclicity of life, death, and rebirth. Thus, Trobriand women and men, exemplified in the objects they exchange, perceive the value of each other through the interface of the value of human beings and the value of regenesis.

Therefore, an understanding of matrilineality, as suggested by this analysis of Trobriand society, requires that we see matrilineality not in the context of descent but in terms of the value that a society places on the regenerative processes of human life. Beyond the fact of matrilineality, the Trobriand concern with regenesis gives Trobriand women their primary place of value. The importance of such a view has explicit consequences for understanding the value placed on women in other societies.

Trobriand women control immortality through the recapitulation of *dala* identity. Thus women's power over cosmic (ahistorical) time is singularly within their own domain. Women, through their wealth, also enter into the historical domain of men. But here their power is less complete because they share the stage with men. Women do not control male objects of wealth (*kula* valuables and *beku*), but they do operate within their own sphere of influence in mortuary distributions. Men, however, cannot enter into the ahistorical domain of women, in which the continuity of *dala* identity is recapitulated through unmarked time; nor can men reclaim *dala* names lent to others; nor can men alone secure the indigenous reconstitution of *dala* hamlet and garden lands. From this view, Trobriand women participate on both the social and cosmic planes, but men are limited to the social. Even on the social plane, women are an integral part of control and power. Men can only control objects and persons which remain totally within a generational perspective of social time and space. Men, therefore, remain destined to seek their measure of immortality through perpetuating individual (as opposed to *dala*) identity.

Individual male identity seems more singularly encapsulated in male objects of wealth. These are the only objects which carry a man's name outside *dala* control and circulate beyond his lifetime. Peter once told me that "men on Fergusson Island do not know my face, but from my *kula* valuables they know my name and my father's name." Another man said that he found a new *kula* partner because, although the other man did not know his face, he recognized his deceased's father's name from the former circulation of a large *kula* armshell. But male valuables demand the recording and memory of names for their personal articulation with the activities of the living, and male valuables are often lost to others. In *kula*, partners are easily attracted to stronger men and to more advantageous possibilities. Genealogies of ownership are changed to hide the "theft" of *kula* valuables, as valuables are lost forever from one's control. Women cannot reclaim valuables for men in this political sphere. Although I have some evidence that indicates that women play a part in the exchange of *kula* valuables within Kiriwina, women cannot recapture a valuable in the way they can reclaim *dala* property. Thus male valuables, made from shell and stone, the least perishable artifacts in the Trobriand corpus of exchange objects, carry a man's name only as long as he can demonstrate his power over other men. Thus a son may inherit his father's stone ax blade or *kula* road but, in the course of his own transactions with other men, he may easily lose his rightful inheritance. The tenuousness of male/male relationships seems to mirror the fragile nature of men's attempt to artificially produce individual immortality beyond the parameters of *dala* identity.

Especially within the limits of *dala* property, men's struggle against the danger of loss is constant. The concept of *dala* embodies the male dilemma. *Dala* refers both to identity conceived through women and to property (i.e., land, decorations, and names) controlled by men. But, in the male domain, this property is lent to others of different *dala* blood. Without women to recover property and reproduce, *dala* property is lost. Further, the men controlling *dala* land must remember a genealogy of the detailed exploits of specific people. Therefore, land does not provide a transcendental identity in the way that women's regenerative ability maintains the continuity of *dala* identity. Within the female domain, the power of immortality is not subject to loss through misfortune and miscalculation. Women do not need to talk or memorize to demonstrate their control, but men must commit to memory the facts of the founding of land. In order to maintain control, men must be ready to publicly display this knowledge. Land genealogies, unlike personal genealogies, are used for political advantage, and *dala* land is subject to the same vicissitudes of loss as other property that men control.

The founders of land differ significantly from ancestral beings. The former are individuals with specific identities who are associated with specific historical events. The latter have lost their personal identity and only recapitulate *dala* identity through unmarked time, which remains outside specific generational time. Origin stories are political dogma used by men not only to verify their rights to land but to establish their prerogatives to taboos, rank, and in some cases to polygamous practices. In this way, origin stories constitute ideology as superstructure. Conversely, the shallowness of the details of genealogy, the movement of a *baloma* spirit through unmarked time, and the power of women alone to reproduce *dala* identity function apart from the politics of men. The elements that women control cannot be conceived as political ideology. Rather they form the very *base* of Trobriand society.

Thus, in the Trobriands, male power over others is limited and the male search for immortality can only be fully achieved through women's control of *dala* identity. Men's attempt to achieve individual immortality must always remain an imitation of women's control over the regenesis of human life. Men seek to imitate regeneration through control over property, which allows them to construct power hierarchies composed of women and men. But danger of destruction lies close to the surface. Most dramatically, the shattering of a hierarchical network is exemplified at death, as men must literally pick up the pieces (parts of the deceased's body) and work on the construction of another network.

In summarizing a passage from Simone de Beauvoir's *The Second Sex* (1953), in which de Beauvoir discussed the negative value placed on women's role as procreator, Sherry Ortner wrote:

> In other words, woman's body seems to doom her to
> mere reproduction of life; the male, in contrast, lacking
> natural creative functions, must (or has the opportunity to)
> assert his creativity externally, "artificially," through the

medium of technology and symbols. In so doing, he creates
relatively lasting, eternal, transcendent objects, while
the woman creates only perishables—human beings.
(1974, p. 75)

Trobriand women, with their complete control over the continuity of life and death, never confront a possible loss of their control. The structure of time and space that women control must be
seen as fundamental to the organization of the Trobriand universe. Equally significant, it also serves as a model for the structure of time and space that men control. The fact of matrilineality gives women a domain of control that men can neither emu-
late successfully nor infiltrate with any degree of lasting power.
But, if the power of Trobriand women is reflected in matrilineality, it becomes essential to explore the relationships between
womanness and the cultural value attached to all Trobrianders.

Since individual human beings in the Trobriands are valued,
the autonomy granted all people does not produce the kind of
alienation found in Western society. Fear, self-interest, and danger exist, but they exist in a milieu where freedom and control are
delicately balanced and individual production and knowledge are
in no sense deemed worthless. Of equal importance is the fact
that the female domain, the regenesis of human life, is accorded
primary value.

In the Trobriands, recognition is given to the perishability of
human beings, but, rather than diminish the inherent value of
human beings as a means for achieving immortality, this recognition, especially enacted in death rituals, stresses the value placed
on the continuity of life. In this way, the perpetuation of life or
human survival is given far more transcendental significance
than is the kind of immortality found in objects or in "cultural"
survival. Therefore women, innately tied to the continuity of life,
remain the locus for the means by which human survival transcends itself.

Because of the exigencies of political events, Trobriand men,
through their artificial objects, can only achieve a limited degree
of immortality. But all major exchange objects remain symbolically tied to the process of life, death, and rebirth, so that immortality can only be achieved through this cycle or a replication of
such a cycle. From this view, men must follow women. The objects men "create" do not transcend the fundamental concern for
human survival.

In Western society, the objects men create are alienated from symbolic referents to individual concerns with origins and death. In his discussion of the "fetishism of commodities," Marx describes the way the social character of a producer can arise only through the exchange of commodities: ". . . the relations connecting the labour of one individual with that of the rest appear, not as direct social relations between individuals at work, but as what they really are, material relations between persons and social relations between things" (1906, p. 84). From this view, social relations become objectified, but they are objectified through the commodity itself, which does not carry any subjective referent to human life in terms of continuity and perpetuation.

Thus, in the creation and production of resources that are free from the processes of a life cycle, objects become depersonalized and a shift occurs in the relations between persons and things. It seems imperative for us as anthropologists to consider these views in the light of Western society before establishing analytical categories for the study of non-Western societies. For example, in our own society, has religion as an institution assumed control over the formulation of an ideology of the life and death processes, and therefore at some point have men become free to pursue the means to their own immortality through objects, symbols, and scientific exploration that have little to do with regenesis? Within this trend, I suggest that, when men seek avenues to create their own transcendence that are free of assurances for the perpetuation of life, the value of women declines, tied to the decline in the value placed on life itself.

Conversely, but in a sense not so differently, in some non-Western societies—other areas in Melanesia, among the Australian Aborigines, and in other parts of the world—objects carry a symbolic value of fertility and regeneration, but men attempt to control all such objects. Therefore, we find the physical segregation of women from men's cult houses and ritual secrets and myths often explaining the way men once stole power and control over objects from women. In these societies, the power of men is continually expended in attempts to assume and incorporate the power of women. Here we must question whether control over others is of such a nature that men, despite the overt separation of the sexes, cannot symbolically separate themselves from the biological *and* cultural regenerative powers that women possess. But, in order to begin to restructure the questions we ask of our data, we must begin to objectify the processes in our own historical tradition that have effectively denied both the biological and cultural powers of women.

The questions that this perspective raises are questions of power. As men in Western societies seek to gain greater control over others and thus destroy the value of individual autonomy, does this alienation create a disregard for the subjective nature of human beings? When human life is only valued as something to be controlled and when, for example, religion as an organized institution provides substitute security, or power in its own right, in terms of individual immortality, women's concern in life, death, and regeneration is marginalized, displaced by men's part in the sociopolitical sphere. Does men's clutching after immortality through objects incapable of regeneration merely serve to devalue human beings and women's role in the perpetuation of life? In the drive for the only kind of power they can get, men effectively separate themselves from women and thereby contribute to a myth that denies the fundamental power of women, preventing womanness from becoming publicly valued as being equal to or superior to the power of men. Only by unmasking that myth, by placing the value of universal womanness within a sociocultural context recognized as powerful within its own right, will the importance attached to the perpetuation of human life have a chance to be restored.

The Trobriand islanders, geographically and technologically removed from the mainstream of the history of human societies, recognize the value of womanness and by extension the value of human beings and the continuity of life. Since the turn of the century, they have provided anthropologists with classic ethnographic examples which now form the base of much anthropological theory. However, despite all that has gone before, the Trobrianders still provide us with the means to reevaluate our thinking in order to formulate theories more significantly sound and less ethnocentrically biased and chauvinistically conceived. On many levels, we have much to learn from them.

Appendix 1
Body Decorations for *Guyau* and *Tokai Dala*

I. Shell decorations
   A. Raw material
   1. *Buna*: white cowrie shells
      of various sizes
   2. *Soulava*: spondylus shells
      polished into beads
   3. *Kaloma*: spondylus shells
      about the size of a nickel,
      polished flat
   4. *Mwali*: cone shells polished
      into arm bands
   5. *Doga*: shells polished flat
      like a boar's tusk. A boar's
      tusk is also used.
   B. Body decorations

Guyau	*Tokai*
1. *Sedabala*: band of *kaloma* worn around head with smaller shells attached	Band of *kaloma* worn around waist
2. *Segadula*: either *kaloma* or *soulava* worn as a long hair tail with *buna* at the bottom. Only Tabalu *giyobubuna* can wear a long *segadula*. Tabalu of all other ranked *dala* can wear a shorter *segadula*.	Cannot wear
3. *Kesapi*: large *buna* tied to each wrist. Only Tabalu and Mwari *dala* can wear *kesapi*.	Cannot wear
4. *Tabala*: *soulava* with shells attached, worn crisscrossed over chest	Worn around neck only
5. *Wakala*: band of four or five rows of *kaloma* worn at waist	Worn below waist with only one row of shells
6. *Luluboda*: string of small *buna* worn below each knee	Cannot wear

	Guyau	*Tokai*
7.	*Bunadoga*: belt of small *buna*	Same
8.	*Mwali*: cone-shell arm band of various sizes	Same
9.	*Doga*: boar's tusk or a shell polished to resemble a boar's tusk, worn around the neck with *kaloma* added	Worn around neck without *kaloma*
10.	*Kuwa*: spondylus short necklace with black beads added, worn by *guyau* big-men and unmarried girls and boys	Worn by those whose relatives are *kula* men (now made of plastic beads and worn by many people)
11.	*Paya*: earring of polished tortoise shells. For girls red *kaloma* are attached at the end of the brown tortoise shell. *Guyau* usually have more individual shells than others.	Same

II. Other decorations (There are many other decorations connected with magic spells.)

    A. Feathers

1.	*Umakata*: red parrot feathers. Tabalu can wear four feathers, other *guyau* only two. Feathers worn stuck into hair in center of head, surrounded by white cockatoo feathers.	Can only wear one *umakata*

    B. Woven bands

1.	*Kwasi*: fibrous woven arm band worn on upper arms and legs, four to six inches in width	Only two to four inches in width
2.	*Duliduli*: woven waist band, often imported from other islands for *guyau*	Woven with native fibers, except for *kula* men who import others
3.	*Mituwetuwa*: woven armlet, only worn at wrist by *guyau*	

Appendix 2
The Manufacture of Bundles

In making bundles, the banana leaf is split along the midrib, and strips of each half-section of the leaf—measuring four to six inches wide and ten to twelve inches in length—are cut. Using a flat wooden board (*kaidawagu*), which comprises part of the household inventory of every married woman, and either the sharpened lip of a shell or a cutting tool (*kaniku*) made from the edge of an empty tin of fish, women and girls scrape the outer epidermal layer of the leaf, removing the bright green fibers. Each strip is scratched first in a horizontal direction and then in a diagonal direction, giving the strip a patterned texture. Then the strips are left on the ground in a sunny spot to dry.

The drying-out process changes the original color of the leaf to a very light tan. After drying, each strip is further divided into narrower strips, each about an inch wide, called *yapwepuya*. About twenty-five of these narrow strips are placed together, making a round thick bundle. The bundle is securely tied at one end near the top, and the edges are trimmed with a knife. Following this procedure, the top is held in the left hand and inverted so that the loose ends are now at the top. Each strip is pulled downwards as one would pull back the petals of a rose. Then the tied part is inverted again and each strip is again pulled down, making the bundle about ten inches wide at the bottom and a bit puffed-out in the center. It takes fifteen minutes for a woman to tie the strips together and make one finished bundle.

Appendix 3
The Manufacture of Skirts

It takes one day for a woman to weave a skirt, but it takes several days to prepare the fibers from the banana leaves and an additional several days for the fibers to dry out in the sun.

The first step in making skirt fibers is to split a banana leaf in half down the midrib. Next, using the same tools as are used in the preparation of bundles, each half-leaf is finely fringed. When the fringing is finished, the fibers are spread out on the ground to dry. The process of fringing is important because there are special distinctions made between lengths of fibers.

Most skirts are made from small segments of the fringed half-leaf. These segments are called *katelawa*, and they are used for the underneath part of skirts. Fibers which have been dyed bright colors—traditionally red and purple, now also yellow, blue, and green—are added on top of the *katelawa*, and pieces of bleached pandanus are used as decorations around the waists of the skirts. *Guyau* women will sometimes add small white cowrie shells around the belts of the skirts.

Lengths of banana-leaf fibers are woven into the belt of the skirt. Only one end of the midrib is tied into the belt; the rest hangs perpendicular to the belt. In other words, the midrib of the leaf does not form the belt of the skirt. In this way various lengths in fibers are achieved. Dyed fibers are woven directly into the belt of the skirt in bunches and, therefore, colored fibers are always shorter than natural-colored fibers before the length of the skirt is trimmed for its wearer.

Traditionally, coloring substance was taken from the root of the *noku* plant. In times of famine, the fruit of this plant was also used as an important starvation food (Malinowski 1935a, p. 160). Today, the *noku* plant as food or dye is seldom used. With the increase in Western cash, women have the means to buy commercial dyes in the trade stores. As a result, there is much more variety in the colors of fibers used for making skirts. The *noku* plant provided only varying shades of red, but, even today, red is the predominant color used for skirts presented in the exchanges at mortuary ceremonies.

To weave a skirt, a woman sits on her veranda with her legs extended straight out in front of her. She places three pieces of string, the skeleton of the belt, around the back of her waist. She ties the ends of the strings together and loops them over her extended foot; in this way, the belt is held taut. Each small section along the strings is finished before the weaving of the next section begins. In this way, the belt becomes a thick, heavy cord containing the ends of all the fibers which have been woven tightly into the three pieces of belt strings.

First, the woman weaves the natural-colored fibers into the strings;

then she adds the colored fibers. Additional colored fibers, which are shorter in length, are then added, and finally pieces of pandanus are woven into the layers of the colored fibers. If the skirt is a mourning skirt, only natural-colored fibers are used, but they are woven in the same way, with the fibers placed in layers on top of each other until the desired thickness is achieved. An important mourning skirt—*sepwana* —is also woven with the same techniques, but for this skirt the ends of one thousand or more fibers, each about ten feet in length, must be woven into the belt.

Notes

1. The Theoretical Framework

1. For the first week I stayed in the small Trobriand Hotel at Gusaweta. I was greatly aided in getting about the island through the kindness of Jannis Daris-Wells, the local A.D.C.

2. Etic analyses attempt to explain native behaviors and institutions in terms of whatever distinctions the analyst finds useful and applicable. Emic analyses attempt to explain native behaviors and institutions only in terms of the distinctions drawn by the informants themselves.

3. I basically follow Adams's definition of power and control: "Power is that aspect of social relations that marks the relative equality of the actors or operating units; *it is derived from the relative control by each actor or unit over elements of the environment of concern to the participants*. It is therefore a socio-psychological phenomenon, whereas control is a physical phenomenon" (1975, pp. 9–10; italics mine). In the Trobriand case, I stress the relationship of the cosmic environment to the circumstances of social controls and power. In speaking of control I consider controls to be exercised not just over technological resources but over such private psychological processes as knowledge and skills held by individuals.

4. When Abraham told me that the day's events were "women's business," I assumed at first that he was demeaning the value of what women were doing. Later, he explained he had meant only that women could tell me about their business much better than men because women were in charge of these distributions.

5. I do not mean to imply that the power women exercise has been totally ignored by ethnographers. See, e.g., Goodale's (1971) excellent study of the Tiwi and the contrast with Hart and Pilling's (1960) male-focused work on the same group. Important work on the power of Haitian women has been done by Mintz (1964, 1971). See also especially Goody 1973; Hoffer 1974; Matthiasson 1974; Stack 1974; Tanner 1974; and Wolf 1974.

6. My use of historical and ahistorical aspects of time and space is taken in part from Munn's terms "transgenerational plane" and "intergenerational plane" (1973, pp. 27–28), which she used for her analysis of Walbiri iconography.

7. It is beyond my concern here to enter into debates on the theoretical issues of the meaning of kinship (e.g., Beattie 1964; Geertz and Geertz 1975; Goodenough 1970; Leach 1951, 1961b; Lévi-Strauss 1963, 1966a, 1969a; Lounsbury 1964, 1965; Needham 1971; Scheffler 1966, 1973; Schneider 1964, 1968a, 1972). But my approach throughout this book is that kinship cannot be studied as a separate unit or institution; it must be understood in both its social and cosmic dimensions where relevant. In the Trobriand case,

only through an analysis of the cyclical nature of exchange can an understanding of kinship emerge that goes beyond the first principles of genealogy.

8. One of the major themes in the work of Hallowell was addressed to the importance of expanding social categories to include a cosmic frame of reference: "At any rate, if we assume the outlook of the self as culturally oriented in a behavioral environment with cosmic dimensions and implicit metaphysical principles, a great deal of what is ordinarily described as 'religion' is seen to involve the attitudes, needs, goals, and affective experience of the self in interaction with certain classes of objects in the behavioral environment. These classes of objects are typically *other* selves—spiritual beings, deities, ancestors" (1954, p. 92).

2. A Return to the Beginning

1. Two species of yams are extensively cultivated in Kiriwina: large yams (*kuvi, Dioscorea alata*) and smaller yams (*taytu, D. esculenta*). Throughout the text, unless otherwise noted, I use the word "yam" to refer only to the smaller *taytu* yam. Production of the larger *kuvi* yam is not treated in this discussion, but see Malinowski 1935a.

2. But, at the same time, the increase in the availability of Western cash has made villagers less dependent on exchanges of yams as the means to *all* other things.

3. See Miller (1959) and Krueger (1953) for brief descriptions of mil-

itary tactics involving Kiriwina. Powell (1956) gave some details of the war years and the years immediately following.

4. I have examined examples of Trobriand wood carvings from this early period of contact in the Museum of Mankind, London; the University Museum of Archeology and Ethnology, Cambridge; the Australian Museum, Sydney; and the Buffalo Museum of Science, Buffalo. All these collections contain some carvings which seem to have been strongly influenced by Western ideas.

5. See Malinowski (1935a, p. 20) and Austen (1945a) on the effects of pearling on the local population.

6. Even in the genealogies that are recited at the beginnings of magic spells, the term used is *tabu*, not *baloma*. But Malinowski (see especially 1916, pp. 198–200, 206–207) tried to equate *tabu* with *baloma* as used in the spells. My informants said that only the recently deceased are referred to as *baloma* in the genealogy of a magic spell. Malinowski also translated the last part of the genealogy of a spell as "recently deceased" where *baloma* is used following a list of *tabu* names (ibid., p. 198).

7. I was told that having someone else speak a chief's words in court cases was a traditional custom. But I only saw this custom (similar in some ways to the Polynesian "talking chief") observed in land claims.

8. See Malinowski (1926b, pp. 117–118; 1929, pp. 496–497; 1935a, pp. 342–343) for shortened versions of parts of this origin story.

9. Lévi-Strauss (1969b, pp. 52–

53), in his interpretation of Bororo myths, discusses the significance of the use of body adornments as a means for the creation of a discrete system which emerges with the destruction or removal of some decorations from the original whole. "Adornments and ornaments thus introduced divergences within the society (ibid., p. 52).

10. The villagers of Labai still catch *kalala* and take them to their "brothers" in Omarakana. See Malinowski (1918) for a detailed description of the magic and technology for *kalala*.

11. Today the Tabalu of Omarakana still maintain this food taboo. Whenever Vanoi and Waibadi came to visit me, some of my neighbors always checked to make certain that I served Waibadi and Vanoi food on plates that had not come into contact with their taboo foods.

12. *Guyapokala* is a special exchange between the Tabalu of Omarakana and Tabalu who live in other parts of the Trobriands. I discuss these exchanges in chap. 8.

13. See Seligman (1910, pp. 664–668) for a description of warfare between the Tabalu *dala* and the Toliwaga *dala*.

14. This confrontation was precipitated by the growing conflict between Kabisawali and the Local Government Council. Some of the *giyobubusi* Tabalu were on Kasaipwalova's side in opposition to the *giyobubuna* Tabalu of Omarakana.

15. There is, however, one situation in which decorations from one *guyau dala* are given to a man

from another *dala*. In warfare or in a fight when someone is killed, the *dala* members responsible for a death must repay the deceased's *dala* members. Sometimes this payment is a specific decoration which only members of one *dala* ordinarily have the right to wear.

16. In chap. 7, I describe marriage rules in greater detail.

17. The term *yawa* has been glossed as "in-law" by Malinowski and others.

18. My treatment of *kumila* as a way of dividing individuals who intermarry, exchange important material objects, perform ceremonial services, etc.—recruiting kinspeople from "opposite" *kumila*—is very like de Laguna's (1972) treatment of Tlingit moieties. She states that moieties are not aggregates of clans, even though informants explain them as such.

3. The Rituals of Death

1. *Lisaladabu* literally means "shaving one's head for mourning." Though this word was given to me as the name for the women's mortuary ceremony, the only term of reference I ever actually heard used was *sagali* or women's *sagali*. Therefore, for clarity, I use "women's mortuary ceremony" to refer to *lisaladabu*.

2. When a chief dies, the workers sit with the body on the chief's open seating platform rather than inside his house.

3. Sorcery and witchcraft cause sickness and death, but even accidents such as drowning are attrib-

uted to the evil intent of someone.

4. Today chemical poisons are imported from urban centers such as Lae and Port Moresby. Villagers often gossip about the increased dangers of *bwagau* now that "Moresby poisons" are prevalent in Kiriwina.

5. Forge notes that among the Abelam ". . . a man who is innocent of any suspicion of complicity in sorcery will have little influence and no chance of becoming a big-man" (1970, p. 273).

6. On Panaeati in the southern Massim, a husband makes a strong political statement when he buries his wife on his land rather than on her lineage's land (Berde 1974).

7. When Uwelasi, a chief, was buried, his grave was dug at the edge of the central clearing and his decorations were removed prior to burial.

8. Malinowski notes discrepancies among informants regarding distinctions between *baloma* and *kosi*: "These remarks show that, generally speaking, the question as to the nature of the *baloma* and *kosi* and of their mutual relationship has not crystallized into any orthodox and definite doctrine" (1916, p. 169).

9. It is difficult to gloss *sasopa* with one English word as it is used in the context of this exchange. The giving of the first valuable is a "lie" because publicly it looks as though the spouse's relatives are giving valuables to members of the deceased's *dala*, but the latter are the true givers in that they return the valuables with additional valuables on the following day. See Malinowski (1935*a*, p. 63) on the gloss of *sasopa*.

10. Many Kwaibwaga villagers have notebooks purchased at the trade stores in which they record magic spells. These books are called *bukela megua*.

11. *Veguwa* ("valuable") is the same word that Malinowski spelled *vaygu'a*. But a glottal stop is not present, and my change in spelling is closer to the way the word is pronounced.

12. This is the same kind of high bed used in childbirth, but then the bed is called *okavasasa*. However, in childbirth and following the delivery a fire is kept under the bed. For mourning purposes, a fire is not prepared. The term *libu* also refers to the mourning house and to the formal crying for the dead one.

13. This was the only *tadabali* that I observed.

14. I describe yam exchanges between men and women in chap. 8. Some of these exchanges Malinowski called *urigubu*, but *urigubu* (except in the most southern part of Kiriwina) refers to exchanges of betel nuts, coconuts, and pork, not to yam exchanges.

15. I use the term "lend" to signify those exchange events in which *dala* property or persons are used by members of other *dala* and later reclaimed by members of the original *dala*. While I was in the Trobriands, I did not consider the importance of this process and therefore I do not know if the Trobrianders have an equivalent word in their language.

16. See Goffman (1959, 1967) for the development of a framework in which the management of impressions in social interaction is analyzed.

4. Women's Mortuary Ceremonies

1. In a household survey of material culture conducted in 1971, I found the following amounts of women's wealth in a total of 53 houses in which Kwaibwaga married women lived: 248 *doba* exchange skirts, 108 mourning skirts (used in exchange, but not considered wealth), and 190 baskets of bundles of banana leaves with approximately 500 bundles in each basket.

2. I am indebted to Jerry W. Leach for the linguistic forms of the suffix -*niga*.

3. Among the Daribi in the Highlands, Wagner reported that "the banana is associated with growth and fertility, and the word for banana (*ta*) is the stem of the verb 'to copulate'" (1967, p. 64). Unfortunately, I did not collect enough data to verify any precise symbolic content in the banana fruit or leaves.

4. One thousand individual fibers measuring about ten feet in length are used to weave this skirt.

5. In northern Kiriwina, August is the time of the filling of the yam houses, but beginning in April yams can be taken directly from the gardens to use in mortuary distributions. The supply of yams tends to run out by the end of December.

6. During the *sagali*, *olopola* is the term used for the central area.

7. See Malinowski (1929, pp. 8–12) and Lévi-Strauss (1963, pp. 132–166) for discussions of the spatial arrangements of Omarakana. Malinowski said that, "without over-labouring the point, the central place might be called the male portion of the village and the street that of women" (p. 10).

8. In preparing taro pudding, women flatten pieces of taro on pounding boards. Men grate the coconut and collect the appropriate kind of firewood; only men cook the pudding. The pudding must be cooked in large clay pots which are often borrowed, and the owner of the clay pots receives a portion of the pudding.

9. I did not observe a women's *sagali* for a Tabalu or other persons of political importance. These *sagali* undoubtedly would exceed the wealth distributions of Obwelela's *sagali*. I also did not observe mourning activity for a child, but when a child dies, the *sagali* are small. The major exchanges pass from the child's kin to her or his father's kin.

10. See Malinowski (1922, 1925), who claimed that "flying witches" are female. In Kwaibwaga, one man was known to have the powers of a flying witch. Male flying witches, however, are not thought to be an aberrant phenomenon, although in terms of numbers more women than men are known as witches.

5. To Be Young and Beautiful

1. Following Malinowski's (e.g., 1922, p. 71; 1927, p. 23; 1929, pp. 179–186) theories of Trobriand paternity, the role of the biological and social father in Trobriand society has generated much debate, but it is beyond my purposes here to review these issues. The major discussants and critics have been Austen 1934; Barnes 1973; Leach

1966, 1967; Montague 1971, 1973; Powell 1968, 1969*b*; Rentoul 1931, 1932; Robinson 1962; Scheffler 1973; Schneider 1968*b*; Sider 1967; and Spiro 1968, 1972.

2. The valuable is not kept by the wet nurse but is eventually given to her own son or to another male member of her *dala*. Women do not own male valuables.

3. See Carroll (1970) for discussion of recent theoretical issues concerning adoption.

4. See Malinowski (1929, pp. 20–21) for a detailed description of the elaborate care a father gives his young baby.

5. In addition to the range of reciprocal obligations between a man and his children throughout their lives, a man receives public repayment in the women's mortuary ceremony when one of his children dies. See the *kalakeyala kapu* distribution in chap. 4.

6. Names which denote specific contemporary events are also given by a father. E.g., following an unsuccessful *kula* expedition to Kitava in 1970, Waibadi named his daughter Mwasila, meaning "shameful." Unfortunately, I do not know if these names are incorporated into the ancestral *dala* repository.

7. These women include true *dala* sisters and other women, not members of ego's *dala*, to whom ego gives annual presentations of yams. See chap. 8, pp. 196–199, for details of these exchanges.

8. Coconut palms, betel palms, or land use can also be given in this situation in place of the giving of a name. Land given is reclaimed by the *dala* hamlet manager when the receiver dies.

9. See the myth presented by Malinowski (1922, pp. 322–324), in which an old man breaks apart a *kula* necklace and gives the separate pieces as gifts to three stars who led him home.

10. Munn (n.d.*b*) has described transformations which occur in Trobriand myths when old age reverses to youth concomitantly with reversals of body tempo in accelerated situations such as dancing and sexual intercourse.

6. Fathers, Sons, and Land

1. In planting the large *kuvi* yams, however, an eye is usually removed for seed and the rest of the yam is cooked.

2. But there are several reports of harvested taro being kept for periods of up to two months (see Bulmer 1967, p. 13). As Chowning noted, this seems to have occurred only in Melanesia among the Karan of the New Guinea Highlands and the Maenge of coastal New Britain (1973, p. 17).

3. In one women's *sagali*, 1,130 yams and 360 taro plants were distributed. The deceased had not been a person of high rank or political consequence. For a person in these latter categories, the distribution of yams and taro would have been much greater.

4. *Urigubu* as a term designating yam exchange gardens made by a man for a married woman is used in the southern part of Kiriwina, where taro is more available and more important in exchange than yams. I discuss *urigubu* exchanges in chap. 8.

5. Malinowski devoted two vol-

umes (1935*a*, 1935*b*) to the processes of gardening in the Trobriands. I refer the reader to *Coral Gardens and Their Magic*, vol. 1, for a detailed description of the way in which yam gardens are technically prepared.

6. The large, communal bachelor houses described by Malinowski (1929, pp. 69–75) are no longer in existence.

7. Fortes, in a reinterpretation of Malinowski's data, correctly anticipated that there is some provision whereby sons may share their fathers' land (1957, pp. 182–185).

8. The residential pattern is similar to a "nodal kindred" which Goodenough (1962, p. 10) defined for the Lakalai of New Britain.

9. The giving of seed yams to someone in another *dala* to plant is in contrast to the process of yam planting in Dobu, where seed yams must remain within a *susu* and always be planted by a person belonging to the owning *susu* (Fortune 1932, p. 69).

10. Malinowski assumed that harvest "gifts" were repaid at irregular intervals by presents of valuables (1935*a*, p. 190). However, my informants said that a valuable is only given in payment expressly for the production of a large harvest.

11. A woman's distribution of her wealth during one part of the women's *sagali* verifies the contribution of yams made by her brother (see chap. 4, pp. 110–112, and chap. 8).

12. Malinowski (1935*a*, p. 198) assumed that brother and sister will inevitably reside in different villages after the sister's marriage.

In fact, in most cases this is not so. From my data, brothers will occasionally reside in the same hamlet with their sisters. Further, in Kwaibwaga, the largest percentage of marriages occurs within the village (see chap. 7, p. 187).

13. Powell (1969*a*, pp. 189–192) also noted many exceptions to avunculocal residence rules.

14. Richards (1950, pp. 207–251), in her analysis of four Central African matrilineal societies, has also been concerned to show that distinctions between the ideal and the norm are spurious. She demonstrated that in each of these societies a system has evolved by which potential clashes among requirements of residence, succession, and control are prevented.

15. If a man who controls the land dies, then his successor receives *pokala* from the tenant.

16. The system of land managership and land tenantship as it operates on the ground resembles what Goodenough (1955) and Davenport (1959) have called "stem kindred."

17. See Weiner 1974 for additional ways in which small parcels of land are given to men from other *dala* to use.

7. Marriage: From Beauty to Objects

1. This seems to be a recent constraint on boys' behavior. Malinowski (1929, pp. 272–273) reported that he was told stories of situations where boys sexually attacked the girls of their village on the girls' return from a formal party (*katuyausi*) held with boys

from another village. But Malinowski only mentioned this in reference to returning *katuyausi* parties, not to individual intervillage liaisons.

2. Robinson (1962), reinterpreting Malinowski's and Powell's data, quite accurately suggested the significance of ties of patrifiliation. She also demonstrated the priority of the father's interest in the marriage of his daughter.

3. Malinowski (1929, p. 89) presented a list of more extensive marriage exchanges, consisting of cooked food and fish interspersed between the primary exchanges of raw yams and valuables.

4. Malinowski (1935a, p. 190) described this gift as a valuable (*takola*) given at intervals to repay the harvest gifts, but my informants said that a valuable (*vayuvisa*) was only given in payment for the production of a large harvest. A gift of a valuable in an exchange called *takola* is given in other circumstances involving yam exchanges.

5. Traditionally, *beku* came from Sorogu on Woodlark Island, and the ax blades were polished in the Kiriwina villages of Okuboba, Omarakana, Wabutuma, and Wakesa.

6. The following are approximate rates of exchange for one *beku* about eight inches in length: two large clay pots, four or five small clay pots, one large pig, A$15, or two to five coconut or areca palms.

7. Sometimes, when *beku* are used in specific exchanges, they are not called by the general term *beku*. In each case, a specific name

is used. For example, in marriage exchanges a *beku* is called *giliwakuma*; to make an alliance with other men prior to warfare, a *beku* is called *vaila*; and to repair a marital separation or as a peace offering after a fight a *beku* is called *lula*.

8. In addition to Malinowski's (1920, 1922) classic description of *kula* and Fortune's (1932) study of *kula* from Dobu, see also Belshaw 1955; Brookfield with Hart 1971; Cunnison and Gluckman 1963; Forge 1972; Guidieri 1973; Harris 1968; Heider 1969; Lauer 1970b, 1971; Mauss 1954; Uberoi 1962; and White 1959.

9. Each time a *beku* is reclaimed by its owner, negotiation over repayment occurs. But since the renegotiation value usually represents a small difference, and the advantages could go to either party, informants do not regard the *beku* exchanges as the means for the accrual of interest.

10. Trobriand data have been used in analyses of patrilateral cross-cousin marriage, but discussion of these theoretical issues is beyond my purposes here. For a review of the problem see Homans and Schneider 1955; Leach 1958, 1961a; Lévi-Strauss 1969a; Lounsbury 1965; Malinowski 1929; Needham 1962; and Powell 1956.

11. There are three cases in Kwaibwaga where a wife and a husband were from the same clan. Both Malinowski and Powell also reported a few cases.

12. Neighboring villages include Kabulula, Omarakana, and Daiyagila, all within a mile of Kwaibwaga.

13. Powell (1956, p. 274) noted that women are not transferred but only attached to their husbands' *dala*. After marriage, women continue to remain full members of their own *dala*.

8. Yams and Women's Wealth

1. If a couple remains childless throughout their married life, villagers assume that someone has performed magic to prevent pregnancy. Ease of adoption, however, gives everyone access to children.

2. Malinowski also referred to this genre of insult: "Their attitude to this phrase is correlated with the rule that the erotic life of husband and wife should always remain completely concealed, and it has a special indecency *in that it refers to an action which does as a matter of fact take place*" (1929, p. 486; italics mine). In regard to the italicized clause, see Labov (1972), who made a similar point about the distinction between ritual (nonserious) and real (serious) insults among black American adolescents.

3. But cf. Munn (n.d.*a*), who analyzed the symbolic qualities of fertility in the magic spells for *taytu* yams exclusively as elements of female fertility. Tambiah (1968) suggested that Malinowski refused to recognize the relationship between human fertility and garden magic for *taytu* (see Malinowski 1935*b*, pp. 262–263), but Tambiah did not explore the specific nature of fertility. The relationship between male and female fertility and garden magic appears

more complex in retrospect than I realized while I was in Kiriwina.

4. See chap. 4, pp. 110–112, in which I describe this important part of the women's mortuary distributions. In this *kaymelu* exchange, both bundles (clean ones) and skirts are given to men who brought yams for all the mortuary distributions. Women who do not have large numbers of bundles save bundles so that they can use them for the specific men who have given them yams. Men's names are called out, but their wives claim the bundles and skirts. On Panaeati Island in the southern Massim, Berde (1974) described women's mortuary distributions of yams, which reenforce their husbands' lineages' claims to land.

5. Sometimes yams are presented at other times of the year, and then they are called *taytupeta* rather than *kovisi*. Both *kovisi* and *taytupeta* are also given to men for direct obligations not related to mortuary events, e.g., to repay land use, in exchange for an ax blade, to purchase a pig, or to establish an inland *kula* partnership.

6. In marriage exchanges, the valuables returned from the husband's kinsmen and father to his wife's kinsmen and father for a first presentation of yams are also called *takola*, but the return payment of yams for the valuable is called *vilakulia* rather than *vewoulo*. My informants said the word changes because, for marriage exchanges, the return harvest of yams (*vilakulia*) is divided among each man who contributed a valuable. The return of yams,

vewoulo, only goes to one person.

7. A year later, as the political crisis continued, the Tabalu did not receive any yams from their wives' kinsmen (Leach 1975*b*).

8. Cf. Powell (1969*b*), who supports the use of the word "tribute" for *urigubu* and *bopokala*.

9. See chap. 2, pp. 46–49.

10. The sound of shells clanging together is also said to be important when wearing *kula* necklaces.

9. The Nature of Trobriand Exchange

1. See Fortes (1957) for a discussion of the influence of Freud on Malinowski's work.

2. Malinowski's major writings on magic can be found in *Argonauts of the Western Pacific* (1922); "Culture" (1931); *Coral Gardens and Their Magic* (1935*a*, 1935*b*); and *Magic, Science, and Religion* (1954). Other interpretations include Evans-Pritchard 1929; Homans 1941; Munn n.d.*a*; Radcliffe-Brown 1952; and Tambiah 1968, 1973.

3. The actions of people in previous generations can also precipitate the use of sorcery on living kin, as explained in chap. 3.

4. One day I asked some men where magic resided. Bunemiga shook his head and said, "I think our ancestors made a mistake about that because they said magic stayed in our belly. If that were true, then when we defecated we would lose all the magic. Our ancestors were wrong about magic. I think it stays in our heads."

5. Traditionally and today magic from other islands of the Massim and from other parts of Papua New Guinea, especially Port Moresby, Lae, and Rabaul, circulates in Kiriwina.

Glossary

baku: central clearing in each hamlet where all meetings and such major events as mortuary distributions take place.

baloma: unnamed matrilineal ancestor spirit who departs from the body of the deceased and goes to live on the island of Tuma.

beku: stone ax blade used in Kiriwina as an important object of men's wealth.

bobwelila: gift of cooked food, tobacco, or betel nuts for which no obvious return is required.

bopokala: continual presentations of the fruits of coconut and areca palms, pork, and betel pepper plants to the Tabalu chiefs by hamlet managers of the Malasi clan, who consider themselves descendants of those women and men who came from the same place of origin as did the Tabalu. In return, the Tabalu are obligated to participate in mortuary distributions in which the hamlet managers are centrally involved.

bukumatula: bachelor house.

bulukupeula: man wealthy enough to do *pokala* for land.

buwa: areca nut or betel nut. Betel chewing occurs throughout Melanesia, as well as in parts of Africa, Madagascar, Tanzania, India, Pakistan, the southern part of Tibet and China, Ceylon, Vietnam, Formosa, the Philippines, Thailand, Micronesia, and Malaysia. In New Guinea, the areca nut (*Areca catechu* Linn.) is chewed with the betel leaf or fruit (*Piper betle* Linn.) and slaked lime manufactured from coral and sea shells. Certain nicotinelike properties of the nut give the chewer a feeling of well-being and a capacity for hard work. Betel chewing eliminates feelings of hunger, tiredness, and crossness.

bwagau: "poison" magic or sorcery or the practitioner of such magic.

dala: unnamed ancestral beings through which Trobrianders trace their descent through women. True kin (*veyola tatola*) are identified with the same set of women and are referred to as having the "same blood." *Dala* also refers to hamlet and garden lands ("same land") founded by men and women with the same *dala* identity, who came from the same origin place and claimed land in the name of their *dala*.

doba: general term for women's wealth, consisting of colorful skirts and bundles of dried banana leaves. All skirts except mourning skirts are called *doba*.

giyobubuna: those Tabalu who never made a "mistake" and did not lose the right to wear all their decorations and the right to maintain all their social taboos; specifically refers to the Tabalu of Omarakana and neighboring hamlets of Kasanai and Omulamwaluva.

giyobubusi: all Tabalu of the Trobriand Islands whose founders lost the right to wear all their decorations, as told in the origin stories.

gubwauli: gardens of taro grown by men for women.

gudukubukwabuya: bastard child.

guyapokala: continual presentations of the fruits of coconut and areca palms, pork, and betel pepper plants to the Tabalu of Omarakana by other Tabalu hamlet managers who live elsewhere in the Trobriands. The Tabalu of Omarakana in return are obliged to participate in mortuary distributions in which the other hamlet managers are centrally involved.

guyau: person of eminence and rank distinguished from other Trobrianders by special social and food taboos and a variety of body and house decorations. *Guyau* refers to those founders who, in the origin stories, came to the Trobriands with the above prerogatives and symbols of their rank. *Guyau* also refers to all people identified through birth with an ancestral spirit from a *guyau dala* and to those few men in each generation who manage their own *dala* land. Only *guyau* hamlet managers have the right (from the origin stories) to be polygamous, and *guyau dala* are ranked in terms of power and numbers and kinds of prerogatives. *Guyau* is also used as a term of address and can be used to compliment someone whose father is a *guyau.*

kabiyamila: first exchange prior to the beginning of the women's mortuary ceremony, in which all women who have received yams and taro from a man give women's wealth to his wife.

kada: mother's brother and, by reciprocity, a man's sister's son and a man's sister's daughter.

kakaveyola: person in ego's same clan who is neither blood kin (*veyola tatola*) nor origin kin (*veyola*) nor *keyawa* to ego.

kalakeyala kakau: giving valuables to the spouse of the deceased at the end of the women's mortuary ceremony.

kalakeyala kapu: giving valuables to the father of the deceased at the end of the women's mortuary ceremony.

kalala: mullet fish caught periodically off the northern shore near the village of Labai. *Kalala* are important in exchanges with the Tabalu of Omarakana, and magic spells are extensively used when the fish are being caught.

kalitonai: "true parents," as distinguished from adopted parents.

kaniku: woman's cutting tool for making skirts and bundles from banana leaves, usually a sharpened shell or the sharpened edge of an empty tin of fish.

karewaga: term indicating authority, control, ownership, and/or law.

katuposula: general term for a hamlet. Each hamlet is controlled by one or two men, who are usually descendants of the original founders.

katuvila: first yams presented by a girl's relatives to her husband's relatives after a marriage.

katuyuvisavalu: food distribution to open the way for dancing, singing, and playing games during the period of mourning.

kaula: "good food"—yams, taro, and sweet potatoes.

kaweluwa: all food (e.g., breadfruit, tapioca, beans, corn) other than "good food" (see *kaula*). Also, the name of a set of transactions during the women's mortuary distribution, when all people who brought *ka-weluwa* to the deceased's mourning kin are repaid in bundles.

kayasa: competitive harvest, organized by a hamlet manager, in which all the men of his village plant extra gardens, the produce of which will be given away to people from other villages at the harvest.

kaymata: large, principal yam garden usually cultivated by one man for another man. When a woman marries a chief, her kinsmen and her father each cultivate a *kaymata* for her.

kaymelu: important presentations during the women's mortuary distribution, when women give bundles and skirts by name to men who contributed yams and taro to all mortuary distributions.

kaymwila: small yam garden cultivated by a man for his married daughter, his married sister, or his sister's married daughter.

keyawa: called "others" by Trobrianders. Specific individuals within ego's own clan and in other clans, who through three generations of marriages maintain important reciprocal exchange obligations with ego.

kitoma: armshells and necklaces not circulating on a *kula* road and individually owned.

kosi: spirit, thought to be malevolent, which emerges following burial from the body of a person who was known to have knowledge of powerful magic spells.

kovisi: baskets of yams given to women and men by the owner of a yam house prior to the filling of the yam house at harvest time.

kubula: denotes the ownership of the yams growing in an exchange garden (*kaymata* and *kaymwila*) being cultivated by someone other than the owner of the yams.

kula: international exchange network in which armshells and necklaces circulate throughout the islands in the Massim. In Kiriwina, the verb *kula* means "you go."

kuliya: clay pots of various sizes, manufactured in the Amphlett Islands, used in the Trobriands as cooking pots, especially important for cooking taro pudding. Also used as objects of wealth when *beku* and other shell valuables are not available.

kumila: division of the Trobriand social universe into four named exogamous sections or clans. Each Trobriander is born with identity through women in one section. There is no origin myth or property associated with clans, and all members of a clan never congregate together. But individuals within and between particular clans maintain important relationships through marriage and mortuary exchanges (see *keyawa*).

kuvi: larger species of yam, *Dioscorea alata*. There are many varieties of this species in the Trobriands. The most important variety for exchange purposes is the long yam, which may grow to twelve feet in length.

kuwa: neck band made of red spondylus shells, signifying sexuality and attractiveness, usually worn by young unmarried villagers. Also neck bands traditionally woven from the deceased's hair (now woven from plant fibers or a strip of cloth), blackened and worn by the deceased's spouse, father, and other related mourners.

laduba tamala: name of one of a man's ancestors that he gives to his child a few weeks following its birth.

lapala: last day of dancing (see *usigola*), when people from all other villages are invited to see the dancers. *Lapala* is similar to *kayasa*.

libu: high bed on which a mourning spouse sits as part of the appropriate mourning ritual. Also, a mourning house in which daily crying for the deceased takes place. The crying for the deceased.

liku: particular style of yam house; also, the long, round, cylindrical poles used for the frame of the yam house. Only a yam house made with these poles can be called a *liku*. Often men have small storage houses for their yams. A *liku* can be built only when a man has another man who is making a large garden for him.

lisaladabu: literally, "shaving one's head for mourning." Also, the term used for the women's mortuary distribution, which occurs four to eight months after a death.

litutila sepwana: cutting of the long *sepwana* mourning skirt.

lula: valuables given to the relatives of a man's wife to prevent a divorce. Also, valuables given as a peace offering after a fight.

mapula: balanced reciprocity; also indicative of a relationship between giver and receiver through which future *mapula* exchanges will take place.

migileu: clean bundles of banana leaves, which have either recently been remade or are still fairly new.

mwali: shell arm bands used in *kula*; also used as objects of wealth in Kiriwina.

mwasawa: game; to play a game; to engage in any activity in which there is competition.

nakakau: mourning name for the widow of the deceased.

namakava: poor, without father or father's kin providing things for ego.

napweyaveka: wealthy woman; big-woman.

nunu: breast, nipple, mother's milk; term of endearment used after a mother's death; same *dala*. The verb means "to suck."

nununiga: bundles of banana leaves made by women and exchanged as wealth; the major medium of exchange in women's mortuary ceremonies.

okayvata: competitive recital of magic spells following a burial.

pari: presentations made at the beginning of *kula* transactions; large *kula* shells, *beku*, or pigs are given.

paya: earrings made from tiny rings of polished tortoise shell. For girls, red flat polished spondylus disks (*kaloma*) are attached to the bottom of the tortoise-shell rings.

pokala: continual exchanges between two people, most often involving exchanges of valuables for land, magic spells, and coconut and areca palms.

sagali: as a noun, *sagali* refers to a distribution of any kind of object of exchange, including food. As a verb, it means "to divide among everyone present," "to settle accounts," or "to reclaim ownership." It is also used as a general term for all mortuary distributions.

sasopa: lying or tricking someone. Usually refers to false statements or acts made in a public forum, but no one is deceived because everyone privately knows the actual situation.

sasova: cooked food, tobacco, pork, or betel given by the owner of a yam house on the day of the filling of the yam house to all who brought the owner yams.

segadula: long string of red spondylus shells worn as a hair tail. The length of the string indicates rank.

sepwana: mourning skirt made with long banana-leaf fibers. A *sepwana* skirt is woven prior to each women's mortuary ceremony, and short *sepwana* skirts are worn during the period of mourning.

sewega: the basket of a dead man which is covered with betel nuts and his personal possessions. Also, a woman's skirt which is similarly decorated at her death. The skirt and basket are usually carried by a woman from the deceased's father's *dala* from the time of death until the women's mortuary ceremony.

sigilivalaguva: distribution held after the skull of a dead person has been carried to the beach and placed on a cliff. *Sigili* means *sagali*; *valaguva* means "to climb up a hill."

sigiliyawali: first mortuary distribution following burial, to repay all those who cried and sang prior to the burial and those who carried the body and prepared the body and grave for burial. *Sigili* is another form of the word *sagali*; *yawali* refers to the night of singing.

soulava: spondylus-shell necklaces used in *kula*, also used as objects of wealth in Kiriwina.

tabu: kinship term for the following kin types: father's sister, father's sister's daughter, grandparent (father's father, father's mother, mother's father, mother's mother), and, by self-reciprocity, grandchild. Also used in reference to women and men who founded land after coming from specifically named origin places throughout the islands. Used in the first part of magic spells to refer to recently deceased past owners of the spells. Ancestors in the domain of historical time (see *baloma*).

takola: return of a valuable following a first presentation of yams, taro, coconut and areca palms, betel pepper plants, or pork. *Takola* is usually part of a series of exchanges at marriage, following *urigubu*, *taytupeta*, or *kovisi*.

talilisa: beauty magic said while passing a pearl shell over the face of the recipient of the benefits. This magic can be recited over a person's face only by her or his father's sister.

taytu: smaller species of yam, *Dioscorea esculenta*. In the Trobriands, these are the major yams (of which there are many varieties) for food and exchange purposes.

taytumwedona: refers to the produce of a yam exchange garden at the time the yams are brought to the yam house.

taytupeta: baskets of yams given by men to other men and women at any time throughout the year, except at the time of the filling of the yam house. See *kovisi*.

tilewai: taking an article of decoration from a person who is beautiful, who sings well, or who dances well; a return must be made by the performer to the person who took the article, also called *tilewai*.

tobesobeso: "rubbish" man who does not make a yam garden.

toesaesa: "rich" man who owns several *beku*.

tokai: person of lower rank whose founders did not bring any special decorations of rank or social and food taboos.

tolibaleko: man who controls garden lands, including land other than that of his own *dala*.

toliuli: owners of mortuary ceremonies, that is, usually the true *dala* members of the deceased.

toliyouwa: workers in mortuary ceremonies, that is, those from clans other than that of the deceased.

tomakapu: mourning name for the father of the deceased.

tomakava: nonclansperson.

tumila: foundation of a house.

uli: taro plants.

urigubu: presentations of the fruits of coconut and areca palms, pork, and betel pepper plants to those for whom ego makes a yam garden or to kinsmen or kinswomen as a substitute for a harvest of yams.

usigola: dancing which lasts for several months following a very large yam harvest (*kayasa*).

valova: exchanges made in order to accumulate women's wealth; to sell things for payment in bundles.

valu: village.

vayuvisa: valuable given to a man who makes a very large yam garden by the recipient of the yams.

vegilevau: newly married.

veguwa: general term for such valuables as stone ax blades, clay pots, money, shell necklaces, shell arm bands, strings of cowrie shells, and bands of flat spondylus shells. Women's skirts given at mortuary ceremonies to the spouse and father of the deceased are also called *veguwa*. In *kula*, *veguwa* refers to necklaces, shell arm bands, and waist bands.

vesali: special two-step dance performed throughout the night prior to a burial.

vewoulo: return payment of yams for a valuable given after an initial presentation of yams, taro, or coconut and areca palms. This exchange is between one giver and one receiver (see *vilakulia*).

veyola: member of ego's clan; a clansperson, but not a true kinsperson (see *veyola tatola*), whose founders came from the same origin place as ego's founders; a general term for kinsperson.

veyola mokita and **veyola tatola:** true "blood" kinsperson, tracing descent through women.

vilakulia: return payment of yams by a woman's relatives for valuables given by her husband's relatives at the time of the first marriage exchanges (see *takola* and *katuvila*). Yams are presented to each man who contributed a valuable (see *vewoulo*).

viloguyau: hamlet where a *guyau* chief lives.

vilotokai: hamlet where the hamlet manager is not a man of rank.

vituvatu sepwana: weaving of the long *sepwana* mourning skirt.

waiwaia: spirit child from a *baloma* which is thought to cause conception; fetus; infant.

wakeya: variety of banana tree whose leaves are used to make bundles and skirts.

wasesi: members of nonrank *dala* in the Malasi clan whose founders of *dala* land came from the same place of origin as the Tabalu. Hamlet managers who are *wasesi* give *bopokala* to the Tabalu of Omarakana.

winelawoulo: ritual of removing the mourning neck band from the spouse and father of a deceased.

yabwabogwa: old bundles of banana leaves, which have become flattened out and a bit faded.

yagada tatola: name given at birth from a child's matrilineal forebear.

yapagatu: dirty bundles of banana leaves, which are often taken apart and reused in making skirts.

yawovau: newly made bundles of banana leaves, which are very light in color.

Bibliography

Adams, Richard N.
1975. *Energy and structure: A theory of social power*. Austin: University of Texas Press.
Allen, Michael R.
1967. *Male cults and secret initiations in Melanesia*. Melbourne: Melbourne University Press.
1972. Rank and leadership in Nduindui, northern New Hebrides. *Mankind* 8:8, 270–282.
Austen, Leo
1934. Procreation among the Trobriand islanders. *Oceania* 5:102–113.
1939. The seasonal gardening calendar of Kiriwina, Trobriand Islands. *Oceania* 9:237–253.
1941. Applied anthropology in the Trobriand Islands. *Mankind* 3:67.
1945a. Cultural changes in Kiriwina. *Oceania* 16:15–60.
1945b. Native handicrafts in the Trobriand Islands. *Mankind* 3:193–198.
Barnes, John A.
1962. African models in the New Guinea Highlands. *Man* 62:5–9.
1973. Genetrix: genitor::nature:culture. In *The character of kinship*, ed. Jack Goody, pp. 61–74. London: Cambridge University Press.
Barth, Fredrik
1966. *Models of social organization*. Royal Anthropological Institute Occasional Paper 23. London.
Bateson, Gregory
1958. *Naven*. 2d ed. Stanford: Stanford University Press.
1972. *Steps to an ecology of mind: Collected essays in anthropology, psychiatry, evolution, and epistemology*. San Francisco: Chandler.
Beattie, John H. M.
1964. Kinship and social anthropology. *Man* 64:101–103.
Bellamy, R. L.
1913. Magisterial report, Trobriand Islands. Papua Annual Reports. Port Moresby.
Belshaw, Cyril S.
1955. *In search of wealth*. American Anthropological Association Memoir 80.
Berde, Stuart J.
1974. Melanesians as Methodists: Economy and marriage on a Papua and New Guinea island. Ph.D. dissertation, University of Pennsylvania.
Berger, Peter L., and Thomas Luckmann
1966. *A social construction of reality: A treatise in the sociology of knowledge*. New York: Doubleday.

Bradfield, Richard M.
1964. Malinowski and "the chief." *Man* 64:224–225.
1973. *A natural history of associations: A study in the meaning of community.* Vol. 1. London: Gerald Duckworth.
Brookfield, H. C., and Paula Brown
1963. *Struggle for land: Agriculture and group territories among the Chimbu of the New Guinea Highlands.* Melbourne: Oxford University Press.
Brookfield, H. C., with Doreen Hart
1971. *Melanesia: A geographical interpretation of an island world.* London: Methuen.
Brown, Paula
1962. Non-agnates among the patrilineal Chimbu. *Journal of the Polynesian Society* 71:57–69.
Bulmer, Ralph
1967. Why is the cassowary not a bird? A problem of zoological taxonomy among the Karam of the New Guinea Highlands. *Man*, n.s., 2:5–25.
Carroll, Vern, ed.
1970. *Adoption in eastern Oceania.* Association for Social Anthropology, Oceania, Monograph Series 1. Honolulu: University of Hawaii Press.
Chowning, Ann
1973. *An introduction to the peoples and cultures of Melanesia.* Addison-Wesley Module in Anthropology 38. Reading: Addison-Wesley.
Codrington, R. H.
1891. *The Melanesians: Studies in their anthropology and folklore.* Oxford: Oxford University Press.
Colson, Elizabeth
1974. *Tradition and contract: The problem of order.* Lewis Henry Morgan Lectures Series. Chicago: Aldine.
Corris, Peter
1968. "Blackbirding" in New Guinea waters, 1883–1884: An episode in the Queensland labour trade. *Journal of Pacific History* 3:85–106.
Cunnison, Ian, and Max Gluckman
1963. *Politics of the* kula *ring.* Manchester: Manchester University Press.
Damon, Fred
1975. Personal communication.
Davenport, William
1959. Nonunilinear descent groups. *American Anthropologist* 61:537–572.
Deacon, Arthur B.
1934. *Malekula: A vanishing people in the New Hebrides.* London: Routledge & Kegan Paul.

de Beauvoir, Simone
1953. *The second sex*. Trans. H. M. Parshley. New York: Knopf. Original publication in French, 1949.
de Laguna, Frederica
1972. *Under Mount Elias: The history and the culture of the Yakutat Tlingit*. Washington, D.C.: Smithsonian Institution Press.
de Lepervanche, Marie
1967–1968. Descent, residence, and leadership in the New Guinea Highlands. *Oceania* 38:134–158, 163–189.
Evans-Pritchard, E. E.
1929. The morphology and function of magic: A comparative study of Trobriand and Zande ritual and spells. *American Anthropologist* 31:618–641.
Firth, Raymond
1936. *We the Tikopia: A sociological study of kinship in primitive Polynesia*. New York: American Book Co.
1967. Themes in economic anthropology: A general comment. In *Themes in economic anthropology*, ed. Raymond Firth, pp. 1–28. Association of Social Anthropologists of the Commonwealth Monograph 6. London: Tavistock.
1975. Seligman's contributions to oceanic anthropology. *Oceania* 45: 272–282.
———, ed.
1957. *Man and culture: An evaluation of the work of Bronislaw Malinowski*. London: Routledge & Kegan Paul.
Forge, Anthony
1970. Prestige, influence, and sorcery: A New Guinea example. In *Witchcraft confessions and accusations*, ed. Mary Douglas, pp. 257–275. Association of Social Anthropologists of the Commonwealth Publications 9. London: Tavistock.
1972. The Golden Fleece. *Man*, n.s., 7:527–540.
Fortes, Meyer
1949. Time and social structure: An Ashanti case study. In *Social Structure: Studies presented to A. R. Radcliffe-Brown*, ed. Meyer Fortes, pp. 54–84. Oxford: Clarendon Press.
1953. The structure of unilineal descent groups. *American Anthropologist* 55:17–41.
1957. Malinowski and the study of kinship. In *Man and culture: An evaluation of the work of Bronislaw Malinowski*, ed. Raymond Firth, pp. 157–188. London: Routledge & Kegan Paul.
1958. "Introduction." In *The developmental cycle in domestic groups*, ed. Jack Goody, pp. 1–14. London: Cambridge University Press.
Fortune, Reo F.
1932. *Sorcerers of Dobu*. New York: E. P. Dutton.
1964. Malinowski and "the chief." *Man* 64:102–103.
Friedl, Ernestine
1975. *Women and men: An anthropologist's view*. New York: Holt, Rinehart & Winston.

Gardner, Robert
1961. *Dead Birds*. Produced by Film Study Center, Peabody Museum, Harvard University.
Geertz, Clifford
1967. Under the mosquito net. *New York Review of Books* 9:12–13.
1973. *The interpretation of cultures*. New York: Basic Books.
1975. On the nature of anthropological understanding. *American Scientist* 63:47–53.
Geertz, Hildred, and Clifford Geertz
1975. *Kinship in Bali*. Chicago: University of Chicago Press.
Gennep, Arnold van
1960. *The rites of passage*. Trans. Monika B. Vizedon and Gabrielle L. Caffee. London: Routledge & Kegan Paul.
Glasse, R. M.
1959. The Huli descent system: A preliminary account. *Oceania* 29: 171–184.
Goffman, Erving
1959. *The presentation of self in everyday life*. Garden City: Doubleday.
1967. *Interaction ritual: Essays on face-to-face behavior*. Garden City: Doubleday.
Goodale, Jane C.
1971. *Tiwi wives: A study of the women of Melville Island, North Australia*. Seattle: University of Washington Press.
————, and Ann Chowning
1971. The contaminating woman. Paper presented at the 70th Annual Meeting of the American Anthropological Association, New York City, 1971.
Goodenough, Ward H.
1955. A problem in Malayo-Polynesian social organization. *American Anthropologist* 57:71–83.
1962. Kindred and hamlet in Lakalai, New Britain. *Ethnology* 1:5–12.
1970. *Description and comparison in cultural anthropology*. Chicago: Aldine.
Goody, Jack, ed.
1958. *The developmental cycle in domestic groups*. Cambridge Papers in Social Anthropology 1. London: Cambridge University Press.
1973. Polygyny, economy, and the role of women. In *The character of kinship*, ed. Jack Goody, pp. 175–190. London: Cambridge University Press.
Groves, M.
1956. Trobriand Islands and chiefs. *Man* 56:190.
Guidieri, Remo
1973. Il *kula*, ovvero della Truffa. *Rassegna Italiana de Sociologia Anno quattordicesimo* 8 no. 4.
1975. Note sur le rapport mâle/femelle Mélanésie. *L'Homme* 15:103–119.

Haddon, A. C.
1893. Wood-carving in the Trobriands. Bound in *Anthropological Pamphlets*, pp. 107–112; reprinted from *Illustrated Archaeologist*.
Hallowell, A. Irving
1955. *Culture and experience*. Philadelphia: University of Pennsylvania Press.
Harris, Marvin
1968. *The rise of anthropological theory*. New York: Thomas Y. Crowell.
Hart, C. W. M., and A. R. Pilling
1960. *The Tiwi of North Australia*. New York: Holt, Rinehart & Winston.
Heider, Karl G.
1969. Visiting trade institutions. *American Anthropologist* 71:462–471.
1970. *The Dugum Dani: A Papuan culture in the Highlands of West New Guinea*. Chicago: Aldine.
Hoffer, Carol P.
1974. Madam Yoko: Ruler of the Kpa Mende confederacy. In *Woman, culture, and society*, ed. Michelle Zimbalist Rosaldo and Louise Lamphere, pp. 173–187. Stanford: Stanford University Press.
Hogbin, Ian
1968. Review of *A diary in the strict sense of the term*, by B. Malinowski. *American Anthropologist* 70:575.
1970. *The island of menstruating men: Religion in Wogeo, New Guinea*. San Francisco: Chandler.
Homans, George C.
1941. Anxiety and ritual: The theories of Malinowski and Radcliffe-Brown. *American Anthropologist* 43:164–172.
———, and David M. Schneider
1955. *Marriage, authority, and final causes: A study of unilateral cross cousin marriage*. Glencoe: Free Press.
Jansen, J. Victor
1961. *De Trobriand Eilanden: een door ergelijke aristocratie beheerste maatschappij*. Rotterdam: Museum voor Land-en Volkenkunde.
Julius, Charles
1960. Malinowski's Trobriand Islands. *Journal of the Public Service* 2: 1, 2.
Keesing, R. M.
1967. Statistical models and decision models of social structure: A Kwaio case. *Ethnology* 6:1–16.
Krueger, Walter
1953. *From down under to Nippon*. Washington, D.C.: Combat Forces Press.
Labov, William
1972. Rules for ritual insult. In *Language in the inner city: Studies in the black English vernacular*, by William Labov, pp. 297–353.

Conduct and Communication Series. Philadelphia: University of Pennsylvania Press.

La Fontaine, Jean

1973. Descent in New Guinea: An Africanist view. In *The character of kinship*, ed. Jack Goody, pp. 35–52. London: Cambridge University Press.

Langness, Lewis L.

1964. Some problems in the conceptualization of Highlands social structure. In *New Guinea: The Central Highlands*, ed. J. B. Watson. *American Anthropologist* Special Publication 66 (pt. 2):162–182.

1967. Sexual antagonism in the New Guinea Highlands: A Bena-Bena example. *Oceania* 37:161–177.

1969. Marriage in Bena-Bena. In *Pigs, pearlshells, and women*, ed. R. M. Glasse and M. J. Meggitt, pp. 38–55. New Jersey: Prentice-Hall.

1974. Ritual, power, and male dominance in the New Guinea Highlands. *Ethos* 2:189–212.

Lauer, Peter K.

1970a. Sailing with the Amphlett islanders. *Journal of the Polynesian Society* 79:381–398.

1970b. Amphlett Islands' pottery trade and the *kula*. *Mankind* 7:165–176.

1971. Changing patterns of pottery trade to the Trobriand Islands. *World Archaeology* 3:197–209.

1973. The technology of pottery manufacture on Goodenough Island and in the Amphlett group, S.E. Papua. In Anthropology Museum Occasional Paper 2, pp. 25–61. University of Queensland.

Leach, Edmund R.

1951. The structural implications of matrilateral cross-cousin marriage. *Journal of the Royal Anthropological Institute* 81:23–55.

1957. The epistemological background to Malinowski's empiricism. In *Man and culture: An evaluation of the work of Bronislaw Malinowski*, ed. Raymond Firth, pp. 119–138. London: Routledge & Kegan Paul.

1958. Concerning Trobriand clans and the kinship category *tabu*. In *The developmental cycle in domestic groups*, ed. Jack Goody, pp. 120–145. London: Cambridge University Press.

1961a. *Rethinking anthropology*. London School of Economics Monographs on Social Anthropology 22. New York: Humanities Press.

1961b. *Pul Eliya: A village in Ceylon*. London: Cambridge University Press.

1967. Virgin birth. *Proceedings of the Royal Anthropological Institute, 1966*, pp. 39–50.

1967. Correspondence: Virgin birth. *Man*, n.s., 3:655–656.

Leach, Jerry W.

1975a. Trobriand cricket: An ingenious response to colonialism. Produced under the sponsorship of the government of Papua New Guinea.

1975*b*. Personal communication.

Lévi-Strauss, Claude

1963. *Structural anthropology*. Trans. Claire Jacobson and Brooke Grundfest Schoepf. New York: Basic Books.

1966*a*. The future of kinship studies. *Proceedings of the Royal Anthropological Institute*, pp. 13–22.

1966*b*. Introduction à l'oeuvre de Marcel Mauss. In *Sociologie et anthropologie*, by Marcel Mauss, pp. ix–lii. Paris: Presses Universitaires de France.

1969*a*. *The elementary structures of kinship*. Trans. James Harle Bell. Ed. John Richard von Sturmer and Rodney Needham. 2d ed. Boston: Beacon Press. Original publication in French, 1949.

1969*b*. *The raw and the cooked*. Trans. John Weightman and Doreen Weightman. New York: Harper & Row. Original publication in French, 1964.

1971. *L'Homme nu*. Paris: Plon.

Lounsbury, F. G.

1964. The structural analysis of kinship semantics. In *Proceedings of the Ninth International Congress of Linguistics*, ed. H. G. Hunt. The Hague: Mouton.

1965. Another view of the Trobriand kinship categories. In *Formal semantic analysis*, ed. E. Hammel. *American Anthropologist* Special Publication 67 (pt. 2):142–185.

Malinowski, Bronislaw

1916. Baloma: The spirits of the dead in the Trobriand Islands. *Journal of the Royal Anthropological Institute* 45. Reprinted in *Magic, science, and religion and other essays*, by Bronislaw K. Malinowski, pp. 149–254. New York: Doubleday.

1918. Fishing and fishing magic in the Trobriand Islands. *Man* 53:87–92.

1920. *Kula*: The circulating exchanges of valuables in the archipelagoes of eastern New Guinea. *Man* 51:97–105.

1922. *Argonauts of the western Pacific*. New York: E. P. Dutton.

1925. Magic, science, and religion. In *Science, religion, and reality*, ed. J. A. Needham, pp. 20–84. London. Reprinted in *Magic, science, and religion and other essays*, by Bronislaw K. Malinowski, pp. 17–98. New York: Doubleday.

1926*a*. *Crime and custom in savage society*. New York and London: International Library of Psychology, Philosophy, and Scientific Method. [Paterson: Littlefield, Adams, 1962.]

1926*b*. Myth in primitive psychology. Psyche Miniatures General Series 6. London. Reprinted in *Magic, science, and religion and other essays*, by Bronislaw K. Malinowski, pp. 99–148. New York: Doubleday.

1927. *Sex and repression in savage society*. New York: Meridian Books.

1929. *The sexual life of savages in north-western Melanesia*. New York: Harvest Books.

1930. Parenthood: The basis of social structures. In *The new genera-
    tion*, ed. V. F. Calversten and Samuel D. Schalhausem, pp. 113–
    168. New York: Macauley.
1931. Culture. In *Encyclopaedia of the social sciences*, vol. 4, pp. 621–
    646. New York: Macmillan.
1935*a*. *Coral gardens and their magic: A study of the methods of tilling
    the soil and of agricultural rites in the Trobriand Islands*. Vol. 1.
    New York: American Book Co. [Bloomington: Indiana University
    Press, 1965.]
1935*b*. *Coral gardens and their magic: A study of the methods of tilling
    the soil and of agricultural rites in the Trobriand Islands*. Vol. 2.
    New York: American Book Co. [Bloomington: Indiana University
    Press, 1965.]
1954. *Magic, science, and religion and other essays*. New York: Double-
    day.
1967. *A diary in the strict sense of the term*. London: Routledge & Kegan
    Paul.

Marx, Karl
1906. *Capital: A critique of political economy*. Trans. S. Moore, E. Avel-
    ing, and E. Untermann. Chicago: Charles H. Kerr.

Matthiasson, Carolyn J., ed.
1974. *Many sisters: Women in cross-cultural perspective*. New York:
    Free Press.

Mauss, Marcel
1954. *The gift: Forms and functions of exchange in archaic societies*.
    Trans. Ian Cunnison. London: Cohen & West.

Mead, Margaret
1930. *Growing up in New Guinea*. New York: William Morrow.
1935. *Sex and temperament in three primitive societies*. New York:
    William Morrow.

Meggitt, M. J.
1964. Male-female relationships in the Highlands of New Guinea.
    American Anthropologist Special Publication 66 (pt. 2):204–224.
1965. *The lineage system of the Mae-Enga of New Guinea*. Edinburgh:
    Oliver & Boyd.

Miller, John, Jr.
1959. *Cartwheel: The reduction of Rabaul*. Washington, D.C.: Govern-
    ment Printing Office.

Mintz, Sidney W.
1964. The employment of capital by market women in Haiti. In *Capital,
    savings, and credit in peasant societies*, ed. Raymond Firth and
    B. S. Yamey, pp. 256–286. Chicago: Aldine.
1971. Men, women, and trade. *Comparative Studies in Society and His-
    tory* 13:247–264.

Montague, Susan
1971. Trobriand kinship and the virgin birth controversy. *Man*, n.s.,
    6:353–368.

1973. Correspondence: Copulation in Kaduwaga. *Man,* n.s., 8:304–305.
1974. The Trobriand society. Ph.D. dissertation, University of Chicago.
1975. Personal communication.
Munn, Nancy D.
n.d.*a*. The symbolism of perceptual qualities: A study in Trobriand ritu-
    al aesthetics. Paper presented at the 70th Annual Meeting of the
    American Anthropological Association, New York City, 1971.
n.d.*b*. Symbolic time in the Trobriands of Malinowski's era: An essay
    on the anthropology of time. Unpublished paper.
1973. *Walbiri iconography: Graphic representation and cultural sym-
    bolism in a central Australian society.* Ithaca: Cornell University
    Press.
Needham, Rodney
1962. *Structure and sentiment: A test case in social anthropology.* Chi-
    cago: University of Chicago Press.
1971. "Introduction." In *Rethinking kinship and marriage,* ed. Rodney
    Needham, pp. xiii–cxvii. London: Tavistock.
Ortner, Sherry B.
1974. Is female to male as nature is to culture? In *Woman, culture, and
    society,* ed. Michelle Zimbalist Rosaldo and Louise Lamphere, pp.
    67–87. Stanford: Stanford University Press.
Panoff, Michel
1972. *Bronislaw Malinowski.* Paris: Petite Bibliothèque Payot.
Powdermaker, Hortense
1970. Further reflections on Lesu and Malinowski's diary. *Oceania* 40:
    344–347.
Powell, H. A.
1950. *Trobriand islanders.* Produced by University College, London.
1956. An analysis of present day social structure in the Trobriand
    Islands. Ph.D. dissertation, University of London.
1960. Competitive leadership in Trobriand political organization. *Jour-
    nal of the Royal Anthropological Institute* 90:118–148.
1968. Correspondence: Virgin birth. *Man,* n.s., 3:651–652.
1969*a*. Genealogy, residence, and kinship in Kiriwina. *Man,* n.s., 4:177–
    202.
1969*b*. Territory, hierarchy, and kinship in Kiriwina. *Man,* n.s., 4:580–
    604.
Radcliffe-Brown, Alfred R.
1950. Introduction. In *African systems of kinship and marriage,* ed.
    Alfred R. Radcliffe-Brown and Daryll Forde, pp. 1–85. London:
    Oxford University Press.
1952. Taboo (1939). Reprinted in *Structure and function in primitive
    society,* by Alfred R. Radcliffe-Brown, pp. 133–152. London: Ox-
    ford University Press.
Rappaport, Roy A.
1968. *Pigs for the ancestors.* New Haven: Yale University Press.

Read, Kenneth E.
1952. Nama cult of the Central Highlands, New Guinea. *Oceania* 23:
1–25.
1965. *The high valley*. New York: Scribner's.
Reay, M. O.
1959. *The Kuma: Freedom and conformity in the New Guinea Highlands*. Melbourne: Melbourne University Press.
Rentoul, C. Alex
1931. Physiological paternity and the Trobrianders. *Man* 31:152–154.
1932. Papuans, professors, and platitudes. *Man* 32:274–276.
Richards, A. I.
1950. Some types of family structure among the central Bantu. In *African systems of kinship and marriage*, ed. Alfred R. Radcliffe-Brown and Daryll Forde, pp. 207–251. London: Oxford University Press.
Robinson, M. S.
1962. Complementary filiation and marriage in the Trobriand Islands. In *Marriage in tribal societies*, ed. Meyer Fortes, pp. 121–155. Cambridge: Cambridge University Press.
Rosaldo, Michelle Zimbalist
1974. Woman, culture, and society: A theoretical overview. In *Woman, culture, and society*, ed. Michelle Zimbalist Rosaldo and Louise Lamphere, pp. 17–42. Stanford: Stanford University Press.
———, and Louise Lamphere, eds.
1974. *Woman, culture, and society*. Stanford: Stanford University Press.
Sahlins, Marshall D.
1963. Poor man, rich man, big man, chief: Political types in Melanesia and Polynesia. *Comparative Studies in Society and History* 5: 285–303.
1965. On the ideology and composition of descent groups. *Man* 65:104–107.
1972. *Stone age economics*. Chicago: Aldine.
Salisbury, Richard F.
1956. Unilineal descent groups in the New Guinea Highlands. *Man* 56: 2–7.
1964. New Guinea Highlands models and descent theory. *Man* 64:168–171.
1965. The Siane of the eastern Highlands. In *Gods, ghosts, and men in Melanesia*, ed. P. Lawrence and M. J. Meggitt, pp. 50–77. Melbourne: Melbourne University Press.
Sanday, Peggy R.
1974. Female status in the public domain. In *Woman, culture, and society*, ed. Michelle Zimbalist Rosaldo and Louise Lamphere, pp. 189–206. Stanford: Stanford University Press.
Scheffler, Harold W.
1965. *Choiseul Island social structure*. Berkeley and Los Angeles: University of California Press.

1966. Ancestor worship in anthropology: Or, observations on descent and descent groups. *Current Anthropology* 7:541–551.

1973. Kinship, descent, and alliance. In *Handbook of social and cultural anthropology*, ed. J. J. Honigmann, pp. 747–793. Chicago: Rand-McNally.

Schneider, David M.

1964. The nature of kinship. *Man* 64:180–181.

1968a. *American kinship: A cultural account*. Englewood Cliffs: Prentice-Hall.

1968b. Correspondence: Virgin birth. *Man*, n.s., 3:126–129.

1972. What is kinship all about? In *Kinship in the Morgan centennial year*, ed. R. Reining, pp. 32–63. Washington, D.C.: Anthropological Society of Washington.

Schwimmer, Erik

1973. *Exchange in the social structure of the Orokaiva: Traditional and emergent ideologies in the northern district of Papua*. New York: St. Martin's Press.

Seligman, C. G.

1910. *The Melanesians of British New Guinea*. Cambridge: Cambridge University Press.

Sider, Karen Blu

1967. Kinship and culture: Affinity and the role of the father in the Trobriands. *Southwestern Journal of Anthropology* 23:90–109.

Silverman, Martin

1971. *Disconcerting issue: Meaning and struggle in a resettled Pacific community*. Ed. David W. Crabb. Symbolic Anthropology Series. Chicago: University of Chicago Press.

Spiro, M. E.

1968. Virgin birth, parthenogenesis, and physiological paternity: An essay in cultural interpretation. *Man*, n.s., 3:242–261.

1972. Correspondence: Reply to Montague. *Man*, n.s., 7:315.

Stack, Carol B.

1974. Sex roles and survival strategies in an urban black community. In *Woman, culture, and society*, ed. Michelle Zimbalist Rosaldo and Louise Lamphere, pp. 113–128. Stanford: Stanford University Press.

Stocking, George W., Jr.

1968. Empathy and antipathy in the heart of darkness: An essay review of Malinowski's field diaries. *Journal of the History of the Behavioral Sciences* 4:189–194.

Strathern, Andrew

1970. The female and male spirit cults in Mount Hagen. *Man*, n.s., 5: 571–585.

1971. *The rope of moka: Big-men and ceremonial exchange in Mount Hagen*. Cambridge: Cambridge University Press.

1972. *One father, one blood descent, and group structure among the*

Melpa people. Canberra: Australian National University Press.
1973. Kinship, descent, and locality: Some New Guinea examples. In *The character of kinship*, ed. Jack Goody, pp. 21–33. London: Cambridge University Press.
———, and Marilyn Strathern
1971. *Self-decoration in Mount Hagen*. London: Gerald Duckworth.
Strathern, Marilyn
1972. *Women in between: Female roles in a male world, Mount Hagen, New Guinea*. London: Seminar Press.
Tambiah, S. J.
1968. The magical power of words. *Man*, n.s., 3:175–206.
1973. Form and meaning of magical acts: A point of view. In *Modes of thought*, ed. R. Horton and R. Finnegan, pp. 199–229. London: Faber & Faber.
Tanner, Nancy
1974. Matrifocality in Indonesia and Africa and among black Americans. In *Woman, culture, and society*, ed. Michelle Zimbalist Rosaldo and Louise Lamphere, pp. 129–156. Stanford: Stanford University Press.
Turner, Victor
1964. Betwixt and between: The liminal period in *Rites de passage*. In *Symposium on new approaches to the study of religion*, Proceeding of the American Ethnological Society, ed. June Helm, pp. 4–20. Seattle: University of Washington Press.
Uberoi, J. P. Singh
1962. *Politics of the kula ring: An analysis of the findings of Bronislaw Malinowski*. Manchester: Manchester University Press.
Wagner, R.
1967. *The curse of Souw: Principles of Daribi clan definition and alliance in New Guinea*. Chicago: University of Chicago Press.
Watson, L.
1956. Trobriand island clans and chiefs. *Man* 56:164.
Wax, Murray L.
1972. Tenting with Malinowski. *American Sociological Review* 37:1–13.
Weiner, Annette B.
n.d. Trobriand magic: An epitaph to "savage anxiety." Paper presented at the 72d Annual Meeting of the American Anthropological Association, New Orleans, 1973.
1974. Women of value: The main road of exchange in Kiriwina, Trobriand Islands. Ph.D. dissertation, Bryn Mawr College.
White, Leslie
1959. *The evolution of culture*. New York: McGraw-Hill.
Williams, F. E.
1930. *Orokaiva society*. Reprinted 1969. Oxford: Clarendon Press.
Wolf, Margery
1974. Chinese women: Old skills in a new context. In *Woman, culture,*

and society, ed. Michelle Zimbalist Rosaldo and Louise Lamphere, pp. 157–172. Stanford: Stanford University Press.
Young, Michael W.
1971. *Fighting with food: Leadership, values, and social control in a Massim society.* Cambridge: Cambridge University Press.

Index

Abraham, 135
Adolescents, 34, 36, 37, 104. *See also* Beauty
  female. *See also* Father/daughter; Mother/daughter
    autonomy of, 176–177
    dress of, 36
    mourning attire of, 6
    premarital sexual activities of, 169–173
    prospective marriage of, 174–176
    reputation of, 95
    skirts worn by, 33, 92
    skirts woven by, 95
  male. *See also* Father/son; Mother/son
    attack upon, 171
    bachelor houses of, 141–146
    beautification of, 170
    beauty and productive ability of, 146
    entry of, into exchange system, 137
    premarital sexual activities of, 169–173
    prospective marriage of, 174
    reputation of, 95
Adoption, 123–124
Adultery
  attitude toward, 122, 191
  cause of land loss, 164
  cause of marital separation, 190
  signs of, 66
  symbolism of skirt in, 93
Affinal relationships, 59
Age. *See also* Life/death cycle; Old/young
  frame of reference, 21
  process, 19
  reversal of, 131–133
Ahistorical. *See also* Cosmic; Transgenerational
  time, 21, 120, 210
  time and space, 20
Allen, Michael, 45

Amphlett Islands, 179
Ancestors
  founders of land, 39
  regeneration of, 15
Ancestral
  beings, vs. founders of land, 233
  essence, 16, 22
  substance. *See also* Baloma; *Dala* substance; *Waiwaia*
    regeneration of, 21
    transmission of, 15–16
Areca
  nuts, 206, 207
  palms, 31, 140, 156
Argonauts of the Western Pacific (Malinowski), 3, 11, 25, 85, 91, 211, 227
Arm bands, shell (*mwali*)
  decoration of personal basket, 83
  exchange of, 33, 70
  kitoma, 180
  in mourning ritual, 6
Artifacts. *See also* Blood; Decorations, body; Food; Land; Magic spells; Milk; Taboos; Valuables, shell; Women's wealth
  attachment and separation of, 20–23
  control of, 183
  symbolism of, 23
Austen, Leo, xv
Australian Aborigines, 235
Autonomy
  of adolescent girls, 176–177, 178–179
  of children and adolescents, 136
  of individual, 86–90, 212, 213, 214, 219, 223, 234
  vs. control over others, 212–226 *passim*
  vs. dependence, 213, 218–219
  of women, 117, 118, 135–136, 193

Bachelor houses (*bukumatula*),

tinction
Natokamu, 110
Nature/culture paradigm, 193, 228
Naven (Bateson), 11
Neck band. *See Kuwa* neck band
Necklace, shell, 178
Net bags, 13, 15–16, 93
New Guinea Highlands, 13
  kinship and descent in, 16–17,
    118
  role of women in, 117
  societies of, 15
  trade networks in, 138
New Hebrides, 45
Nunu. See Milk
Nununiga. See Bundles of banana
  leaves
Nurturance
  basis for understanding kinship,
    16–17
  bundles as symbols of, 119
  father as source of, 123, 125
  mother as source of, 123
  recycling of, 119

Objects of exchange. *See also indi-*
  vidual objects
  control of, 221
  display of, 214
  home-grown vs. foreign, 138
  at marriage, women as, 228
  medium of communication, 87
  symbolic meaning of, 211–212,
    213
  in *valova*, 78–80
  valuables as, 179–183
Obukula, 46, 52
Obwelela, 77–78, 103, 109–116
Oiabia, 32
Old/young, 6, 71, 131–133
Omarakana, xv, xix, 3, 30, 31, 40,
    68–69, 77, 169, 171, 190, 223.
    See also Tabalu of Omarakana
Omulamwaluva, xix, 49
Origin kin. *See Veyola*
Origin stories, 38–42, 44. *See also*
    Founders; Place of origin; Ta-
    balu origin story
  importance of, 164–166
  political dogma of, 42, 233
Orokaiva, 13, 15–16, 139

Ortner, Sherry, 233
Other as opposition, 85, 86, 87, 89,
    225
Others
  control over, vs. autonomy,
    212–226 *passim*
  control over, through magic,
    217–219
  ethic of equivalence, 212
  ethic of generosity, 212. *See also*
    Giving
  influence over, 212
  opposition between self and,
    212–213
  role of, 20–23
Owners of *sagali*, 62–63, 104
  female, in *kalipewalela kabeya-*
    mila, 112
  male
    in *ligabwa*, 114
    wives of, 104
  payment by, 107
  role of, 72–74, 107–115 *passim*

Panaeati Island, 93–94
Pandanus
  mats, 66, 69, 74
  pubic covering, 34, 66, 97
  strips, 116
Papua New Guinea, xv, 33, 79
Pari, 79
Patrilineal society, 15–16
Paya, 127–129
Pearling, 33
Pearl shell, 133
Peter, 124, 133, 207, 232
Pigs, 35. *See also* Pork
  distribution of, 82, 135
  given as *vayuvisa*, 147
  objects of exchange, 135, 181
  payment for magic spells, 152
  raised by Highlands women, 15
  and stone ax blades, 180
Place of origin, 38, 40, 62. *See also*
    Founders; Origin stories
  determining kinship, 54, 69
  of Tabalu, 46, 52
Pokala, 156–167, 213
  for land, 74, 156
  need of valuables for, 181
Political. *See also* Conflict; Power;